Mastering
Project
Management

Mastering
Project
Management

Second Edition

APPLYING ADVANCED CONCEPTS TO

Systems Thinking

Control & Evaluation

Resource Allocation

James P. Lewis

McGraw-Hill

New York   Chicago   San Francisco   Lisbon   London

Madrid   Mexico City   Milan   New Delhi   San Juan

Seoul   Singapore   Sydney   Toronto

3 4 5 6 7 8 9 0   DOC/DOC 0 9 8

ISBN-13: 978-0-07-146291-4
ISBN-10:   0-07-146291-0

This publication is designed to provide accurate and authoritative information in regard to the subject matter covered. It is sold with the understanding that neither the author nor the publisher is engaged in rendering legal, accounting, or other professional service. If legal advice or other expert assistance is required, the services of a competent professional person should be sought.

> —*From a Declaration of Principles jointly adopted*
> *by a Committee of the American Bar*
> *Association and a Committee of Publishers*

McGraw-Hill books are available at special quantity discounts to use as premiums and sales promotions, or for use in corporate training programs. For more information, please write to the Director of Special Sales, Professional Publishing, McGraw-Hill, Two Penn Plaza, New York, NY 10121-2298. Or contact your local bookstore.

The Lewis Method and High-Performance Project Management are registered trademarks of The Lewis Institute, Inc. PMI, PMBOK, and PMP are registered trademarks of the Project Management Institute. Mind Map is a registered trademark of Tony Buzan. HBDI is a trademark of Herrmann International. The grid containing a thinking profile is also copyright by Herrmann International, and all such figures in this book are used by permission.

Library of Congress Cataloging-in-Publication Data
Lewis, James P.
    Mastering project management / by James P. Lewis. — 2nd ed.
      p. cm.
    ISBN-13: 978-0-07-146291-4 (hardcover : alk. paper)
    ISBN-10: 0-07-146291-0
    1. Project management.   I. Title.

    HD69.P75L489 2007
    658.4'04—dc22   2007009036

This book is printed on acid-free paper.

This book is dedicated to

Linda FitzRandolph Clark

With admiration for her mastery
of project management.

CONTENTS

PREFACE

Next year will mark the 10th anniversary of the first edition of this book. I don't know that the state-of-the art in managing projects has changed all that much, but the profession has grown from infancy to at least a moderate maturity, though I believe it will be some time for full maturity to be reached.

Nevertheless, the Project Management Institute (PMI®) has grown at an exponential rate during this time, reflecting the importance of project management as a profession (www.pmi.org). And more organizations are requiring their project managers to become certified as project management professionals (PMP®) through PMI. For that reason, developing your skills is important if you want to advance in your career as a project manager and beyond to higher levels of general management.

There will always be only a small percentage of any group that actually master the skills of that discipline. In sports, there are only a few masters in golf, basketball, soccer, or tennis. The same is true in management. How many of them do you know who are really masters at what they do?

For those who do master a discipline, the rewards are usually far greater than those available to the masses of individuals who are only adequate at the required skills. Of course, it requires dedication to self-development and a lot of hard work to master anything, and project management is no exception.

I personally do not believe anyone can master project management unless he or she is willing to engage in a program of personal or self-development of interpersonal skills, the ability to be self-aware and aware of others, and to be able to live fully in the moment. The best way I know to do this is to engage the help of a life coach who approaches coaching from a holistic perspective; that is, an approach which addresses the improvement of one's mental, physical, intuitive, and spiritual development. One such approach is practiced by James Flaherty (2005), which he calls Integral Coaching™. My own organization, The Lewis Institute, Inc., is offering such coaching following Flaherty's approach, which we call Collaborative Coaching™.

What this book offers is a broad range of topics that are needed to fully master project management. What is important to note, however, is that mastery is defined as the mastery of skills—that is, the application of knowledge, which might be called the art of project management. Skills are not mastered by reading a book. What you will have to do is read, practice, assess yourself, practice some more, and continue this until you reach your goal. It is a process of lifelong learning, and there will always be more to learn, so it is an exciting journey.

I wish you the best in your travels on this path. I would like to hear from you about your experience. You can contact me at the email address shown below.

James P. Lewis
Vinton, Virginia
jlewis@lewisinstitute.com

June 2007

ACKNOWLEDGMENTS

Much of what I know about project management I have actually learned through discussions with clients and students in my seminars. I am very grateful to them for sharing their experience with me, and for challenging me to think about project management in new ways.

I have also been impressed with the natural project management skills of my friend Linda FitzRandolph Clark, to whom this book is dedicated. She organizes a guitar recital each year for some forty-odd students and friends, and this year I witnessed the best practices in project management, which included risk management with contingency planning, resource allocation, scheduling, estimating, and so on. She usually holds her event outdoors, but a big threat to success is rain, and this actually happened this year. Her indoor backup location worked beautifully, and the event went off without a hitch.

My thanks to Lora Hansen, my assistant, who has prepared illustrations for this second edition. Lora has worked on several of my books and always does a very nice job to enhance the appearance of the publication.

In addition, Judy Brown has now typeset all of my McGraw-Hill books, and working with her is always a pleasure. She is very patient with me when I fail to practice good project management—getting behind on my copy edits and page proofs. Her work is excellent and the final product always pleases me.

My partner, Tom Boldrey, has been a source of much discussion and thinking around leadership and management, and we are attempting to integrate the two disciplines in our training. Tom has contributed a chapter to this work, and my thanks to him for challenging me to think harder about these subjects.

As is always true, I owe much of what is good in this book to others. The flaws are entirely my own.

WHAT'S IT ALL ABOUT

1

CHAPTER

So You Want to Master Project Management

It seems safe to assume that you bought this book because you want to be more than a casual project manager. Indeed, you want to master the discipline. Congratulations. You have chosen a worthy goal. Why? Because I believe project management is the key to your future career success.

Project managers are fortunate in that they often work with almost every function in an organization. That is great training for future chief executive officers. So, if you aspire to higher management levels, you will have made the right move by mastering project management.

WHAT IS MASTERY?

The dictionary definition of mastery is to have a command of, or a sure grasp on, a subject or discipline. This implies that you are so good at performing an activity that few other individuals could perform at a higher level.

**Mastery:
To have a
command of,
or a sure grasp
on, a subject
or discipline.**

ACHIEVING MASTERY

How do you achieve mastery? Practice, practice, practice! And study the subject thoroughly until you know everything that is to be known about it. Unfortunately, for some disciplines this is nearly impossible. Consider cardiology, for example. Not long ago, over 30,000 articles were written on the subject in one year. No cardiologist could hope to read even one-tenth of them. Fortunately, project management is not such a fast-moving subject. Also, it is more of a *performing art* than a cognitive discipline.

One of the best models for achieving project management mastery is to study actors and athletes. That they rehearse and practice is obvious. But two other components might be overlooked. One is observing and emulating people who are already masters. We call these people role models. By imitating the very best, one learns the key behaviors that contribute to their skill.

The second component is coaching. It is a major factor. Every great actor and athlete owes much of his or her success

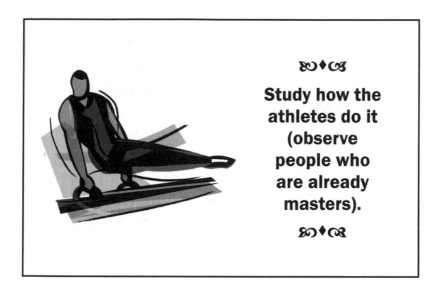

to being coached. The fascinating thing about coaching is that the coach often can't perform as well as the person being coached, but he or she can see what needs to be corrected or augmented and provide advice on how to improve.

A coach also challenges the person being coached to excel. Andrea Bocelli, the singer, is so adept at his art that he can walk into the studio and record a single "take" that will be good enough. But his coach always challenges him to do better, thus inspiring a level of performance that even Bocelli may not dream possible.

Mastermind Groups

Another approach, not used by athletes or actors particularly but used by many successful individuals to develop themselves, is to assemble a *mastermind group* of advisors that can help you deal with issues that you are uncertain how to handle. This was an idea presented by Napoleon Hill in 1937 in his book, *Think and Grow Rich*. Andrew Carnegie and Henry

More can be accomplished by a group working together than by an individual working alone.

Ford both formed mastermind groups. Among members of Ford's group were Thomas Edison and Harvey Firestone.

The fundamental principle of a mastermind group is that more can be accomplished by a group working together than by an individual working alone. Such a group comes together on a regular basis—weekly, monthly, or whatever. They share ideas, thoughts, information, and knowledge. They may be people from your own discipline, or from more diverse backgrounds. My personal belief is that more is to be gained by diversity. You acquire much better perspective with a diverse group. Another advantage of a mastermind group is that members can introduce you to people in their networks—people you will find good to know.

Whatever you want to accomplish with your group, choose people who are already where you would like to be in life, or at a level above you. One benefit to the members of your mastermind group is that they get to interact with other people on their level and, in the process, they develop themselves even further.

Remember, *you* are orchestrating the group meetings, so stay in charge of the process. This may occasionally be difficult to do because of the very nature of the group members—most will be strong, influential individuals. But if you conduct the meetings with a clear agenda, are efficient and clearly goal-driven, you should find that they will follow your lead.

The ideal size for a mastermind group is five or six. If it is smaller, you won't have enough resources. If it is larger, there won't be enough time in a meeting for everyone to participate evenly. The group will normally meet weekly or biweekly, and the meeting can be in person, over the phone, or via the Internet. With the rapid growth in technology, it is becoming very feasible to meet online with members anywhere in the world. I have personally used a program provided by the Intellor Group (www.intellor.com) to conduct training sessions and meetings with people in Canada, India, China, and Singapore. The voice-over IP quality is excellent, and you have the ability to view a whiteboard on which people can write, draw, type, project slide presentations, and run applications such as Microsoft Project®. For those of you who use Mac computers, they have an excellent video-conferencing program. A good friend of mine owns a marketing communications company based in Sweden and recently opened an office in Princeton, New Jersey. His people meet frequently online and are able to talk to and see each other throughout the meeting.

SHOULD YOU GET YOUR PMP® CERTIFICATION?

The Project Management Institute (PMI) certifies project managers as professionals, or PMPs. The certification process requires that you document 4,500 hours of work experience and pass an online exam. If you want to truly master project management, I recommend that you get your PMP certification. In addition, there are numerous certificate programs in

project management, such as the ones offered at North
Carolina State University in Raleigh and the University of
Wisconsin in Madison, which provide you with a broad spec-
trum of skills that you need to be effective. The PMP exam
only tests for content knowledge, though, while most certificate programs provide you with hands-on skills, which are
invaluable for day-to-day project management.

In addition to PMP certification, if you live near a large
city there is a good chance that there will be a local PMI
chapter monthly meeting. These meetings provide a good
way to network with other project managers and stay current
in the discipline of project management. I strongly recommend that you take advantage of such chapter meetings if
they are convenient to you. To find a chapter near you, visit
the PMI Web site: www.pmi.org.

This chapter has merely touched on mastering project management. Until you have read the entire book, you won't
have the complete "story." In particular, read the comments
at the end of Chapter 3 on integrating leadership and management for some suggestions on what mastery really means.

2 CHAPTER

The Job of Managing

In the 30-plus years of my career I have observed that there are a lot of people who want to be *managers,* but a lot of them don't want to actually *manage!* Part of the reason is that managers have status, some authority, and generally make more money than nonmanagers do. Even in technical organizations that claim to have dual career paths, the managerial path usually goes higher than the technical path, both in terms of hierarchical level and salary. In fact, I met a fellow a few years ago who had done a study for his MBA degree on organizations with

> A lot of people want to be managers, but many of them don't want to *manage.*

dual career paths, and he had found that the number of companies actually having such paths was very small, and in many cases the technical path was a dumping ground for individuals who could not make it in management.

MAKING CHOICES

When I was about 14 years old, I got interested in electronics. I became a ham radio operator, and built almost all of my equipment. I soon knew that I wanted to design radios as a career, but coming from a small town with only 90 students in the senior class, most of whom did not go to college, I had no idea how to go about becoming a radio designer. One of my friends told me that he was pretty sure you studied electrical engineering. Further, he said, he and two other of my friends were going to visit N. C. State University in Raleigh in a couple of weeks, and he suggested that maybe I should go along. Until then, going to college had never crossed my mind, because my family couldn't afford it.

But the idea had been planted, and I went with them to visit the school. I never applied anywhere else, and was lucky enough to be accepted at NCSU. I got my degree in Electrical Engineering and then spent 15 years in two companies designing radio equipment.

What I discovered was that designing radios in industry is nothing like designing them for fun. I absolutely loved the design activity itself, but that was only part of the job. You had to make drawings of everything, compile bills of material, do endless testing to certify that the product met Federal Communications Commission requirements, and if you sold it in Canada or some other country, you had to test for their requirements as well. The design part I loved. The rest I hated.

At this point in my life, I wouldn't take anything for that 15 years in industry, because it has served as the foundation for my present career, which is training and consulting. I don't think you should teach or consult in something that you've never done, because I don't think you can understand the problems your clients have. So the experience was invaluable.

However, had I known what an electrical engineer actually does, I might not have taken that route. And this is the problem that many people have. They think they would like a certain job, career, or position, but they don't really know what the person does, and therefore often find that they made a bad choice. So if you are considering being a project manager, it would be helpful to know what they actually do, so you can make an informed choice.

WHAT MANAGERS DO: MYTH AND REALITY

If you read any text on management, you will learn that managers plan, organize, direct, and control. They don't do any actual work themselves. That is done by other people. In fact, one of the most pervasive definitions of management is that they *get work done by other people*. It doesn't take much thought to realize how simplistic and unhelpful this definition is. Guards over chain gangs get work done through other people. Would you call that managing? I don't think so. Dictators, tyrants, bullies, and politicians get work done by other people, but again, they are not managing when they do it. It is pretty obvious that we need a better definition.

A proper definition should be congruent with reality, and not some platitude about what *should* be. Professor of management at McGill University in Canada, Henry Mintzberg has written that ". . . it is surprising how little study there has been of what managers actually do" (Mintzberg, 1989, p. 7). He goes on to say, "There has certainly been no shortage of material on what managers *should* do . . . Unfortunately, in the absence of any real understanding of managerial work, much of this advice has proved false and wasteful. How can anyone possibly prescribe change in a phenomenon so complex as managerial work without first having a deep comprehension of it?" (Mintzberg, 1989, p. 7).

To answer the question, Mintzberg shadowed a number of managers, meticulously recording what they do, how long they do it for, and with whom they do it. His findings are enlightening, and certainly raise questions about the wisdom of the prescriptive material written by professors of management who have never managed. What I find in Mintzberg's book is confirmation of my own experience in managing. I have been both a department manager, with 63 people in my department (three of whom were supervisors of others), and a project manager. Much of what Mintzberg found to be true of department managers is also true of project managers, in my experience. I have summarized his principle findings in Table 2.1

T A B L E 2.1

What Managers Do

The Myth	The Reality
The manager is a reflective, systematic thinker.	Managers actually work at an unrelenting pace, on activities characterized by brevity, variety, and discontinuity. They are strongly oriented to action and dislike reflective activities.
The effective manager has no regular duties to perform.	In addition to handling exceptions, managers perform regular duties, including ritual and ceremony, negotiations, and processing the soft information that links the organization with its environment.
The senior manager needs aggregated information, which a formal management information system best provides.	Managers strongly favor oral media—namely telephone calls and meetings.
Management is, or is quickly becoming, a science and a profession.	How managers do their work—to schedule time, process information, make decisions, and so on—remains locked deep inside their brains.

A DESCRIPTION OF MANAGERIAL

The manager's job can best be described as a set of roles. These are organized sets of behaviors in which they engage. Mintzberg has iden roles that fall into three categories.

> The manager's jo
> described as a set o

Interpersonal Roles

The first interpersonal role is the *figurehead* role. By virtue of his or her position as head of an organizational unit, every manager must perform some ceremonial duties. These can include having lunch with important customers, attending weddings of employees, and meeting with touring dignitaries. Some of these may seem trivial, but they are important to the smooth functioning of an organization and cannot be ignored by the manager. I would say that project managers have a certain number of these functions to carry out, so that this finding applies to project managers as well as to general managers.

The manager must also perform the *leader* role. Being in charge of an organizational unit, the manager is responsible for the work of the people in that unit. There may be both direct and indirect leadership roles to perform. Encouraging and motivating members of a project team would be a direct role in a pure project organization and an indirect role in a matrix. As we have all heard so often, project managers usually have a lot of responsibility but little formal authority, so they must use influence to get things done. Leadership itself involves a great deal of influence activity, so it is one of the most important roles for the project manager.

The third interpersonal role mentioned by Mintzberg is the *liaison* role. This is a role in which a manager makes contacts

13

WORK

b can best be
roles.

tified 10

ιo doubt that
extent. Some
se managers
nit. In fact, it
it that is crit-
ιjor functions
fect, the liai-
ɔwn external
nevertheless

ιm members
and with the network of contacts, the manager becomes the nerve center of his unit. He may not know everything, but he usually knows more than any one of his team members. Mintzberg found that managers spend nearly 40 percent of their contact time on activities devoted to the transmission of information. To a great extent, communication is the work of a manager.

As a *monitor*, the manager is always scanning the environment for information. Much of the information that the manager receives is in oral form, and consists of gossip, hearsay, and speculation. This soft information can be very important in alerting the manager to problems before they occur.

Managers must *disseminate* information, or it is of no use to the team. This is one area in which some managers fail, because they realize that information is power, and they try to keep it to themselves. The net result of this is that decisions cannot be made effectively by other members of the team, but must be made by the manager. Our favorite expression for this is that such a manager is a mushroom manager: he keeps people in the dark, feeds them a lot of nonsense, and when they grow up, he cuts them off at the knees and cans them.

The *spokesperson* role is one in which the manager passes some information to people outside their units. This includes making presentations to higher-ranking managers, military officers in defense contracting projects, and sometimes to stockholders who are concerned about a major project.

Decisional Roles

Information is the basic input to decision making. Since the manager usually has more information than any single team member, she often plays a major role in making project decisions. Mintzberg has identified four decisional roles that the manager must perform.

The *entrepreneur* role is that of trying to improve the unit. In the monitor role, the manager is constantly on the lookout for good ideas. When she finds one, she may initiate a development project—this is the entrepreneur role. Even project managers may occasionally play this role, suggesting projects to senior managers. This would be especially true of technical project managers, who think of applications for technology and suggest new product development projects. We also find some corporations doing new business development projects, so that the project manager must play the entrepreneurial role to the hilt.

Another decisional role is that of *disturbance handler*. Managers are initiators in the entrepreneurial role. In the disturbance handler role, they are reacting to pressures in which change is outside their control. For the project manager, this can be changes in scope, accidents, loss of key personnel, and conflicts with functional managers over priorities.

The *resource allocator* role might be more the privy of the functional manager than the project manager, but even project managers have responsibility for deciding who will get what in the project team. One of the most important resources that the manager allocates is his or her own time.

Access to a manager exposes the person to the team's nerve center and decision-maker.

Finally, we have the role of *negotiator*. There can be no question of the importance of this role to project managers. Together with their leader role, this is the means of getting things done when you have no authority. Managers at all levels actually spend considerable time in negotiations, but negotiation is a way of life for the project manager.

The Integrated Job

It is important to stress that the ten roles described by Mintzberg are not separable. They form a *gestalt*, an integrated whole. This does not mean that all managers give equal attention to all ten roles. The function that the manager performs will dictate that more time be given to one role than the others. However, you cannot neglect one completely in any management job.

The fact that they do form an integrated whole is one reason for the difficulties of managing teams. "Two or three people cannot share a single managerial position unless they can act as one entity. That means they cannot divide up the ten roles unless they can very carefully reintegrate them" (Mintzberg, 1989, p. 22). The biggest problem is with the informational role. Unless there is a full sharing of managerial information, team management breaks down. Since this is nearly impossible to achieve, we naturally can expect some problems with teams.

PRESCRIPTIONS BASED ON REALITY

It has often been said that to be effective we must understand ourselves. Insight into management work is a step in that direction. Success depends on how well managers understand and respond to the pressures and dilemmas of the job. Mintzberg has suggested three specific areas of concern for managers. I believe all of these apply to project managers.

1. *The project manager must find systematic ways to share his or her privileged information.* This can be done through regular debriefing sessions with key team members, by maintaining a diary of important information for limited circulation, or by a memory dump to a dictating machine. To the degree that key team members have better information, they can make many of the decisions that would otherwise have to be made by the project manager. In her book, *Leadership and the New Science,* Margaret Wheatley has written that information is self-organizing, and that teams can benefit greatly by having the same information at their disposal that the manager has.

2. *The project manager must avoid the pressures that would lead to superficiality by giving attention to issues that require it, by looking at the big picture, and by making use of analytical data.* This boils down to knowing what is a priority and what is not, so that you don't spend as much time on the trivial many as you do the vital few. Members of the team have time to deal with analysis of project status. The project manager must take full advantage of what these people have to offer and act on it appropriately.

3. *Project managers must gain control of their own time by turning obligations into an advantage and by turning those things they want to do into obligations.* There are a lot of things that managers are obligated to do that could be just a waste of time. The effective manager makes the obligation into something positive. For example, a presentation can become an

opportunity to lobby for resources for the team. A visit to a customer might be a chance to actually gain more business. If a manager initiates a project or subproject, he might obligate others to report back to him.

A WORD OF CAUTION

It would be easy to conclude that, because few managers really spend a lot of time planning, that this is appropriate for project managers. Every major study that I have seen on the correlates between what the project manager does and project success have shown planning to be vital. What may be important is that good project managers *facilitate* good

> Just because few managers do much planning does not mean that project managers should abandon planning. If you have no plan, you have no control!

project planning. They don't do it themselves. As I have written in all of my books, the first rule of planning is that the people who must do the work should do the planning. There are two principle reasons why this is true:

1. They have no commitment to someone else's plan, not because of ego, but because it is generally not correct—either in estimates, sequencing, or in being inclusive of everything.
2. Collectively, the team will think of things that no one individual (namely, the project manager) would think of.

It is a fact that project managers are supposed to be in control, in the sense of getting results from the project team.

And, since control is defined as comparing where you are to where you are supposed to be, so you can take corrective action when there is a deviation, it follows that if you have no plan, you cannot have control, since you have nothing to compare progress against. For that reason, planning in not an option—it is a requirement! Perhaps if more general managers spent time planning, we would have fewer organizations operating in crisis mode.

Nonmanagement Roles

While the Minzberg roles may describe most of a manager's official duties, there are other roles that effective managers perform that go with the territory, even though they have no "official" status. They would never appear in a job description, but the manager who does not perform them will lose an opportunity to develop loyalty and commitment from his or her followers.

Counselor

When a member of your project team has serious personal problems, you may be called on to show sympathy, concern, and to help the individual get through the crisis. Of course this isn't required and isn't part of the official job of managing, but to some degree employees expect it. I have long believed that people relate to their supervisors in ways much like they do with their parent of the same sex. That is, if you are male, the follower will relate to you as she might to her father. And we expect parents to show sympathy for us in times of trouble.

The manager who does not do this may be seen as cold and uncaring. Such managers can hardly expect that followers will be highly committed to them or their teams. In many cases followers will do the bare minimum that must be done to get by on the job, and no more.

Mentor or Coach

Functional managers have a fairly clear responsibility to develop the members of their departments. This is done through mentoring and coaching. But what about project managers? Should this be part of their job as well?

I believe it is, but not necessarily in terms of helping them do better work. Rather, it might be helping them manage better. I believe it is safe to say that project management ability requires skill in self-management, and the project manager can help followers develop that skill.

It is outside the scope of this book to explain in detail how one coaches followers, but the project manager who wants to have a high-performance team should learn this valuable set of skills.

As a part of this role, the manager may help followers develop their careers. To some it may seem insane to help a follower move out of his department, but doing so leaves a very good impression on followers and increases loyalty to the group. Furthermore, trying to hold a person in a job when he has the capacity to move into a new challenge is selfish and damaging to the organization in the long run.

3

CHAPTER

Integrating Leadership and Management

It is customary to discuss management and leadership separately, but in reality a manager must exercise both simultaneously in order to be effective. Mintzberg defined management as the exercising of 10 different roles, and he said that these must be integrated. I agree 100 percent. If you consider the degree to which each is expressed at any given time, they may not both be of "equal strength," but they must both be present.

DEFINING LEADERSHIP AND MANAGEMENT

We saw in the previous chapter how difficult it is to define management. Nevertheless, most experts agree that management involves the practice of scheduling, planning, budgeting, and other purely administrative activities that have predominantly a *task* focus. That is, management deals with the work which must be done.

Management deals with the work that must be done.

Leadership, however, is defined as the art of getting others to *want* to do what must be done. This definition can be summed up as meaning that a leader influences people to do the work that must be done. It involves dealing with individuals, and requires knowledge of what makes them "tick," in order to be effective.

In any given situation, you must interact with a person or a group to specify what work is to be done, and you must get the person or group excited about doing the work; thus, you are exercising both leadership and management at the same time. This combination of leadership and management behaviors can be thought of simply as the *style* of leadership. This is shown in Figure 3–1. Leadership embraces management—but not the other way around. Management deals almost exclusively with schedules, budgets, and plans, while leadership deals with people and may include discussions of plans and so on.

As shown in Figure 3–1, there are four general styles of leadership. These have been fully described in the literature.

In quadrant one is the *structured* or *directive* style. The primary emphasis here is on the work, so most of the leader's behavior is management behavior. This involves telling followers what to do, how to do it, by when, and so on. Because there is never a complete absence of interpersonal influence or leadership behavior, we do not consider a low level of leadership to be zero.

A leader using the directive style is not coercive or highly authoritarian. I would say that the approach is more like that of parenting a small child. You are firm but helpful. You express caring for the individual. You "show her the ropes." It is a "hand-holding" way of getting a person acclimated to a project. This style is appropriate for a person's direct supervisor.

F I G U R E 3–1

Four Styles of Leadership

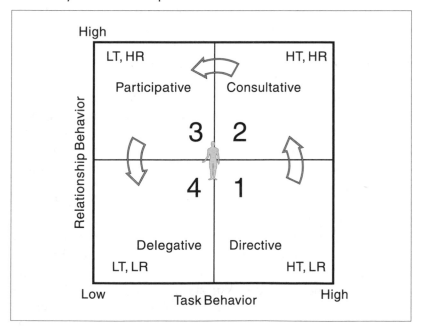

‽♦‽
**Leadership is
defined as
"getting
others to want
to do
something
that must be
done."**
‽♦‽

For a project manager, this would take a slightly different slant. Since you often do not directly supervise the work of team members, you are providing structure in the form of schedule guidelines, and you are emphasizing how one person's work interacts with that of other team members.

In quadrant two you have strong leadership behavior combined with strong management behavior. This style can be called *selling* or *persuasive*. It will be particularly useful to project managers who do not directly supervise team members.

The quadrant three style is called *participative* by most leadership specialists. The emphasis on management is lower than in quadrants one and two, but the leadership component is still high. In this approach the follower has more autonomy; you ask for his thoughts on how the work should be done, and involve him more in the planning process itself.

Finally, the quadrant four style is called *delegative*. It involves low levels of both management and leadership behaviors. It can be thought of as telling a follower to "take the job and run with it." Clearly, such a style requires that a team member have a high degree of competence to do the required work, coupled with a strong willingness to accept full responsibility for the work.

WHAT DETERMINES WHICH STYLE TO USE?

Hersey and Blanchard (1981) originally developed a model they called *situational leadership,* based on the fact that the appropriate style to use is a function of the situation itself. This means that for a given work assignment, you must ask yourself two questions:

1. Can the team member do the work?
2. Will the person take responsibility for it?

In essence, the two questions are summed up as *Can you* and *Will you*? If the answer to both questions is no, then you should use the quadrant-one style. If it is a definite yes, then you can move to quadrant four. Quadrants two and three are appropriate for mixed responses, as shown in the Table 3–1.

T A B L E 3–1

Appropriate Leadership Style Based on Answers to the Can and Will Questions

Can?	Will?	Appropriate Style
No	No	Directive
No	Yes	Persuasive or Selling
Yes	No	Participative
Yes	Yes	Delegative

LEADERSHIP BEHAVIOR

Leadership was defined earlier as "getting others to *want* to do something that must be done." The operative word in this definition is *want*. You are not leading people if you are coercing them into doing what must be done. They will comply, but they won't be committed to the work. True leadership is granted by followers—that is, they *willingly* follow a leader. In fact, it is accurate to say that you are not a leader if you have no willing followers.

If you are going to get people to want to do what must be done, then you must understand what motivates them. And there is no blanket prescription for this, since not everyone is motivated in the same way. I will cover motivation in Chapter 5, so I will not repeat that material here, but you should read that chapter and practice what is taught so that you can determine what motivates every member of your project team.

LEADERSHIP PRACTICES

In a landmark study, Kouzes and Posner (1987) studied the behavior of nearly a thousand managers and determined that leadership consists of three core components that can be broken down into five practices, each of which contains two parts. The three core components are called *vision, involvement*, and *persistence*—or VIP.

Leaders must inspire a shared vision in followers, they must involve them in achieving that vision, and they must encourage and demonstrate persistence in the face of adversity. As you will find when you read Chapter 5 on whole-brain thinking, some of us are natural visionary leaders and some must work at it, but I believe every individual can be visionary if the importance of doing so is recognized.

One thing that *does not* exemplify leadership is the solitary hero commanding the troops to charge onward and tackle difficult obstacles. True leadership *involves* people in pursuing the vision. People who are involved are committed and motivated to give their best efforts to achieve difficult objectives. You want people to be committed to the project, not just involved in it.

Finally, when situations become difficult, persistence is required, and leaders must react accordingly. As Alan Mulally, CEO of Ford Motor Company told me, a leader's job is to set the context for the team. If the leader falls down on the floor and starts screaming whenever problems occur, team members will think the project is doomed. So a leader must maintain a positive attitude in the face of difficulties.

Subpractices

Kouzes and Posner describe five subpractices, each having two components, as follows:

1. Challenging the process
   a. Search for opportunities
   b. Experiment and take risks
2. Inspiring a shared vision
   a. Envision the future
   b. Enlist others
3. Enabling others to act
   a. Foster collaboration
   b. Strengthen others
4. Modeling the way
   a. Set the example
   b. Plan small wins
5. Encouraging the heart
   a. Recognize individual contributions
   b. Celebrate accomplishments

Challenging the Process

One difference between leaders and managers is that managers are often very oriented to keep things stable. They are usually operations experts, and their job is to keep the ship on course. If it drifts off course, their job is to bring it back on track. This means that they resist change, not because they are being difficult but because it is their mindset to keep things running smoothly, and change is seen as disruptive.

Leaders, on the other hand, are always looking for new and better ways to do something. For that reason, there is often a clash between the leader and manager. However, as I said at the beginning of this chapter, if you are going to be effective you must integrate leadership and management practices, which means that you must know when to make a change and when to maintain stability. The important thing to remember is that there are two kinds of organizations—those that are getting better and those that are dying. If you are standing still, you are dying—you just don't know it yet.

This means that an organization must engage in continuous improvement, and it is the leader/manager's job to initiate

ဆာ◆ణ
You must know when to make a change and when to maintain stability.
ဆာ◆ణ

such change by constantly asking, "Isn't there a better way of doing this?" The key here is to involve the team in developing new approaches. A principle applies here: people don't resist change, but they resist *being* changed. If you can make them part of the change process, you won't encounter resistance.

As the two components of this practice indicate, you must constantly search for opportunities to improve performance. You must also experiment and take risks. This is another source of conflict for some managers, who are actually risk-averse. And it is especially true for very left-brain individuals (see Chapter 5). If this is true of you, then you will have to stretch yourself a bit to exercise this practice.

Inspiring a Shared Vision

One of the factors that is most motivating to people is the pursuit of a dream. A dream is an image of some desired future state—one that is better than the present situation. Dr. Martin Luther King, Jr. dreamed of a nation in which racial differences would not be the basis for unequal treatment. Alan Mulally dreamed of building the world's best airplane when he was chief engineer of the Boeing 777 development program, a dream which became reality.

It is not absolutely essential that the leader create the entire vision, but it *is* necessary that she facilitate development of it by the team, so that every member shares in it. As the practice states, she must enlist others in developing and pursuing that dream.

Note that vision precedes everything we do. Our mission is always to achieve our vision of some desired future state. This means that the vision comes first and the mission second. In fact, I believe that one of the difficulties managers encounter is that they declare a mission for which members of the team have no clear vision. This is a very important consideration. You should work very hard to ensure that your team has a shared vision before you proceed with the work to be done.

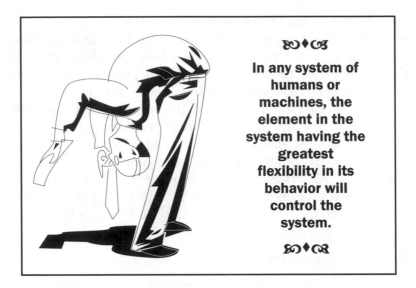

෩◆ඏ

In any system of humans or machines, the element in the system having the greatest flexibility in its behavior will control the system.

෩◆ඏ

Enabling Others to Act

This may be the one practice that is most violated in organizations in general, and American firms in particular. There are several reasons for this. One is based on the law of requisite variety, which applies to systems. This law states that in any system of humans or machines, the element in the system having the greatest flexibility in its behavior will control the system. Since a manager is supposed to control a system of humans, in the sense of ensuring that they achieve desired objectives, this law says that the manager must have more flexibility in his behavior than the variability of behavior in the system.

It is easy to see why this presents a problem. Imagine the variability of behavior presented by even a small team of three or more people. It is almost unlimited. The fact is that no manager is likely to be able to match that unlimited variability in behavior, so the inevitable conclusion is that she won't be able to control the system.

However, it is unacceptable to not control the system, so most managers seem to know intuitively that they must reduce the variability of the system to a level which they can match. Unfortunately they usually do this by prescribing rules for behavior, which limit the flexibility of team members. In doing so they gain some control, but they also stifle creativity, which needs flexible behavior to exist. I call this the negative approach to gaining control.

The positive approach to gaining control is to employ good project management practice. This can be summarized by recognizing the following guidelines:

1. Each member of the project team must have a clear understanding of her objective, with the purpose stated. That is, she must know *what* she is supposed to do and *why* she is supposed to do it.

2. Each individual must have a plan for how to do his part of the project work. The reason is that if you have no plan, you have no control, by definition. Thus, if the project is going to be in control, each member of the project team must be in control of his own work.

3. Each individual must have the skills and resources to perform her work adequately. It is a manager's job to ensure that this is true by either selecting those individuals who already have required skills or developing the skills that are lacking. Providing resources is also the manager's job.

4. The team member must receive direct feedback on performance so he knows exactly how he is doing compared to the plan. The reason lies in the definition of control: comparing where one is to where one is supposed to be, then taking corrective action when there are deviations from planned performance. Remember that without a plan, you can't have control, as you don't know where you are supposed to be at any given time. Furthermore, without progress feedback, you don't know where you actually *are*, so both ingredients are necessary in order to have self-control of your work.

5. Finally, the individual must have a clear definition of her authority to take corrective action when a deviation from plan exists, and that authority cannot be zero, or else the person can't control her work. This is another mistake made in organizations. We try to delegate responsibility without delegating authority commensurate with the level of responsibility. It simply doesn't work.

Modeling the Way

We have all heard the expression that leaders should "walk the talk." Sometimes they seem to practice the philosophy of "do as I say, not as I do," and followers are inclined to lose respect for such leaders. On the other hand, the leader who truly leads by example gains the respect of followers. We want to emulate such leaders. Often we refer to them as role models.

Good leaders also plan small wins for their followers, whereas less effective ones may set up situations that are so challenging that followers cannot succeed, thereby experiencing failure and becoming demotivated. We see this not only in leadership but in teaching.

ജ♦ൽ
The leader who truly leads by example gains the respect of followers.
ജ♦ൽ

As an example, I know a woman who has been teaching guitar for more than 20 years. She told me that all of the available guitar instruction methods start with beginners learning the chords C, F, and G7. To a music teacher this seems obvious. There are no sharps and flats in the C scale, so if you are playing by music it is easier than playing in a key that requires many sharps and flats. But if you just learn to play chords, it makes no sense at all. The reason? The F chord is one of the most difficult to make on the guitar.

So consider a young person, say 10 years old. Chances are that the parents of that child are reluctant to purchase an expensive guitar until they know if the child will apply himself to learning. The problem is that a really cheap guitar is likely to be very difficult to play. Couple this with trying to make the F chord, which requires a lot of strength and coordination, and you have set the child up to fail from the very beginning.

My friend starts with D, A7, and G, which are easier chords to form, and gives the beginner a successful experience! From that experience, they are motivated to work harder, whereas, when they struggle for a week trying to make the F chord, they often come back for the second lesson and say, "I don't think I'll ever be able to make that chord!"

Plan small wins!

Encouraging the Heart

This is an extremely important practice for leaders. Projects sometimes present difficulties that are hard to surmount. I have worked for managers who would berate employees when things were not going well. This only makes matters worse. People need to be supported when they are struggling, and true leaders do this.

They also recognize individual contributions to project outcomes. Managers sometimes have the misguided notion that, seeing as people are being paid for what they do, it is not necessary to tell them that they are doing a good job. This may be true in the absolute sense, but it is a belief that fails to take into consideration that people are very motivated to please their leaders. When leaders praise them for their work, followers find this very rewarding and usually strive even harder to do good work.

Effective leaders also celebrate the accomplishments of followers. Celebrations may sound trivial to some, but a celebration sends the message that what has been done is really significant and appreciated by the leader. When someone achieves a good result and nobody even notices it, there is a tendency to feel that it is unappreciated. I know that there are very "macho" managers who believe that this is a sign of being a wimp. However, as Dr. Phil McGraw says, "You either get it or you don't," and such managers simply don't get it. They don't understand human nature.

MANAGEMENT BEHAVIOR

Earlier in this chapter I briefly described the behavior that a leader exhibits as a function of the readiness of followers to take responsibility for work, combined with their ability to do the work. We saw that there are four general styles of leadership, which are a combination of leadership and management behaviors. Following are some comments about the management behavior that is appropriate for each of the leadership styles that have been identified.

Directive

This style is appropriate for followers who are new to a task, and are both unable to do it and unwilling to take full responsibility for it. We saw that the leader need not exercise a great deal of actual leadership in this situation. Rather, there is strong emphasis on the work itself. The leader is stressing *what* must be done, *how* it should be done, and by *when*.

This is a style that project managers often simply cannot exercise so far as the work is concerned. The members of the project team often report to functional managers, and it is up to that manager to directly supervise their work. So the project manager cannot directly supervise them unless she is a technical expert in the field.

What she can, and must, do is apply this approach to planning and structuring the project. She must lead members of the team through project planning , which includes developing a work breakdown structure, then sequencing the work using critical path scheduling methods. Each team member must know his or her level of responsibility for each task, and should participate in the planning itself. Otherwise, you may find that when *you* plan too much of the work itself, there will be errors in your estimates of task durations and consequently a lack of commitment of team members to your estimates.

Leading the Team

Bruce Tuckman has called the first stage of a team's development the *forming* stage (1965). In this stage, the questions foremost on the minds of team members are "Who is in charge, how do I fit in, and do we have the resources needed to succeed?" A team leader may lose the team if he does not provide assurance that he is in charge by providing clear direction, clarifying the vision and mission for the team, then addressing the concerns of every individual. This need not be done in an authoritarian way; rather, it can be conveyed by expressing confidence in oneself and in the direction the project is to take, and reassuring members of the team that the project will be a success.

Persuasive

As individuals become more willing to do the assigned tasks and gain more skills, the appropriate leadership style changes from directive to persuasive. A major difference between the two styles is that the leader emphasizes *why* the task should be done, rather than just saying what to do and when to do it. The fact of explaining "why" conveys greater respect for the team member. Furthermore, the leader's emphasis on the work itself is diminished from what it was in the directive mode. It is, however, of strong importance and should not be devalued.

Leading the Team

The second stage of a team's development is called the *storming* stage by Tuckman. In this stage team members begin to have conflict. They question who is in charge, whether they are on the right track, whether decisions are being made in the right way by the right person. They often challenge the leader.

As project leader, you must assure team members of the correctness of their mission, maintain control, and help the team stay focused on the work to be done. Failure to do so may well cost you the project. However, there is a tendency to try to bypass this stage. It can be very uncomfortable to those who find conflict undesirable. This is a mistake. If you skip over this stage without resolving the issues that have been raised, the team will keep coming back to those issues trying to resolve them. It is better to bite the bullet and get them resolved before moving on.

Participative

By the time team members are becoming more confident of their ability to do work and more willing to take responsibility for it, the leader can move to the participative style of leadership. There is now less emphasis on the work itself. The follower is given more say in decisions and more freedom to do things her own way. Leadership behaviors like celebrating accomplishments, recognizing individual contributions, and modeling the way are very much called for at this point.

Dealing with the Team

This stage of team development is called *norming* by Tuckman. Team members are developing norms for how they work together. They are beginning to accomplish good results and are developing a sense of team identity and belonging; camaraderie will usually be evident. The team leader needs to intervene less in providing structure. The behaviors mentioned above for dealing with individuals now will be appropriate for the team as well.

Delegative

When you are confident that followers can work on their own and that they will take responsibility for that work, you can pretty much leave them alone to do it. This means you don't emphasize the work very much, nor do you exercise much leadership. You don't abdicate, but you don't stand around looking over people's shoulders, either.

Leading the Team

Much the same thing as was said in "Dealing with the Team" above applies. The team has reached the stage that Tuckman calls the *performing* stage. They are getting good results. Celebrating accomplishments is appropriate, but very little else is needed at this point.

IN SUMMARY

As Mintzberg found, you must integrate leadership and management in order to be effective. As you will learn in Chapter 5, management is primarily a left-brain function and leadership is primarily a right-brain function. Since 56 percent of the population has a preference for functioning in only two of the four modes, most of us will have some difficulty being fully effective at both. If you have a triple-dominant or quad-dominant profile, you may be able to do at least part of the functions on both sides, but my guess is that there has to be another solution.

To me, it is unrealistic as well as disrespectful of individual differences to expect every individual to excel at those areas which are not her strength. Yet this is what most performance reviews suggest. "You're doing very well at these things, Jane, but you need to improve at these others." The net result is that Jane works hard to try to become good at her weaker skills, only to find that she is not very good at them in the end and may also lose ability at what were her strong skills.

We do not take a star quarterback and insist that he be a tackle. Or a ballerina and tell her she has to become good at Irish dance. Or a cardiac surgeon and tell her that she has to excel at brain surgery. Rather, we work with each individual to develop his or her skills to the fullest, to express their potential. Cross-training is only appropriate for jobs that require primarily manual dexterity.

So what does a project manager do? I suggest that you enlist the help of other members of your team to do those things you are not strong in. For example, I can do detailed project planning, but I am primarily a right-brain person, and planning is a left-brain activity. For that reason, it is very helpful if I can *facilitate* the planning and have someone else do it. Furthermore, even though I don't prefer to do detailed planning myself, I know the value of such plans, and I am very keen on having them.

The conclusion: if you want to master project management, work on maximizing your strengths and don't obsess about your "weaknesses." Find ways to enlist the help of others to do those things you aren't good at. You may not be the most "rounded" project manager, but I believe it is better to excel at a limited set of skills than to be mediocre at everything.

4

CHAPTER

Leading to Learn and Learning to Lead

Dr. Tom Boldrey

The major challenge facing organizations is sustaining proficiency in performing core tasks and processes. Employees must execute existing work effectively and be able to learn, individually and collectively, how to perform new tasks and processes quickly. The metrics of managing change include the length of time it takes to learn something new, and the byproducts of that knowledge. Time is not a luxury. Being first to bring a new product or service to market is a major factor of success. Reducing equipment down time, and reducing the time to provide a service or produce a product, requires constant attention.

This is especially important for project teams, which are often under intense pressure to complete projects in minimal time, often with scarce resources. Furthermore, they are often interdisciplinary, so the project manager has no direct authority over team members. The remainder of this chapter presents the findings of a study of cardiac surgery teams (clearly project teams) that provides important information on how to make such teams effective.

STUDY OF CARDIAC SURGERY TEAMS

A study of 16 cardiac surgery teams revealed some important findings about the factors influencing teams that were implementing difficult new procedures for cardiac surgery. New technology demanded significant changes in how the team performed the surgical procedure. As one surgeon said, "This is a transfer of pain from the patient to the surgeon." New technology enables surgical teams to perform minimally invasive cardiac surgery. Everyone on the team had to learn new tasks and unlearn old processes. The most successful teams had team leaders who deliberately managed the learning effort.

Time is critical in cardiac surgery. How quickly and effectively teams performed these new procedures varied. The most successful teams viewed the change and the challenge of implementing new technology as being how fast and how well they learned together.

They engaged in real-time learning as they worked. They analyzed processes as they occurred. They had open conversations. They extrapolated lessons learned as they worked. Although debriefs, after-action-reviews, and learning audits were held, some formally and some over Chinese take-out food at midnight, the best results occurred when learning was integrated with actual working. The degree to which the learned practices were formally documented is not clear.

Successful teams deliberately transformed themselves into learning teams. Teams that learn more quickly are explicitly managed for learning. This required surgeons to give up some of their dictatorial authority so they could become partners on the operating teams. This has implications for the role and skill sets of team leaders as well as how team leaders are chosen. Team leaders need a blend of technical expertise and interpersonal skills. If senior management views the team's challenge as purely technical and selects team leaders on the basis of technical expertise, the likely outcome is clear.

୫୦ ◆ ୯୫

**The successful
cardiac surgery
teams engaged in
real-time learning
by learning as
they worked. They
analyzed
processes as they
occurred**

୫୦ ◆ ୯୫

The successful team leaders framed the challenge not in terms of implementing new technology but in terms of organizational challenge. They emphasized the importance of creating new ways of working together.

Successful leaders stressed that the focus was not just learning new individual skills but developing new working relationships as well. This new way of working required the contribution and collaboration of every team member. The faster-learning teams tried out different approaches in their efforts to find ways to save time while not endangering patients. These teams created a safe environment for real-time learning wherein it was okay to propose something, try it, then accept or reject it. The words and actions of the team leaders—in this case, surgeons—were responsible for establishing norms whereby members felt comfortable making suggestions, trying out things that may not work, and openly admitting mistakes. In teams where these conditions did not exist, learning was stifled.

An environment wherein team learning flourishes can be greatly enhanced by the team leader. The norms and atmosphere of the team are determined early on by the leader's decisions and actions. Leaders play a critical role in setting expectations for team members, whether they are conscious of it or not. Team members pick up on even small cues and clues as to what is okay and not okay. People watch supervisors, just as children watch parents, for direction on how to behave.

Three factors distinguished the successful cardiac team leaders/surgeons. First, they were accessible, approachable, and open. They made it clear that they welcomed and valued the opinions of others. They were available and did not belittle anyone. They never made anyone feel stupid. Second, they specifically asked for input. They reinforced the importance of an atmosphere of openness and information sharing by requesting input from team members. For example, one surgeon said, "Let me know immediately, and let everyone know, if anything is out of place." Third, they were role models for learning. They openly admitted mistakes and errors in reasoning. "My judgment was bad. I did not take into account the time it would take to . . ." Such acknowledgments go a long way toward creating conditions for talking about missteps and asking questions without fear of negative repercussions. Leaders do need technical competence, but they must also be able to lead and manage disparate specialists to work together, adapt, and learn new skills. Leaders proficient in asking questions and fostering open communication not only encourage learning, but learn themselves.

Doing things right is only one part of the equation. Doing the right things is essential, too. The amount of work that is done in traditional and virtual teams, groups, and temporary systems remains significantly higher than most people think, and it takes place in a milieu of complex interconnections. Technology clearly requires individuals to spend some solo time interacting with a wide range of powerful and productive resources. Individual and organization both are increasingly exercising choice and functioning *independently* while, at the same time, individual performance and organization performance as a whole are more and more *interdependent*. The greater this interdependence, and the greater the stress or pressure people experience, the greater the importance of soft leadership skills and continuous learning. As organizations and the work environment experience constant transition, the effective leaders will be those who can balance soft skills—like empathy, encouragement, and respectful engagement—with bottom-line metrics.

REFERENCE

Edmondson, Amy C., Richard Bohmer, and Gary P. Pisano. "Speeding Up Team Learning." *Harvard Business Review*, 125–132 (October 2001).

5
CHAPTER

Whole Brain Project Management

You can't solve a problem with the same thinking that caused it.

—Albert Einstein

No doubt most of you have heard about left-brain/ right-brain orientations in thinking. Left-brain thinkers are more analytical, logical, and sequential than are right-brain thinkers, who are more parallel thinking, intuitive, and global thinkers.

Does this matter to project managers? If so, how do you make use of it?

To answer this question, I'll share an experience with you. I once hired an engineer who worked for a very prestigious company. He was supposed to design communications equipment. I asked him a number of questions during the interview about communications technology, which he answered flawlessly. Unfortunately, he didn't know how to translate theory into design practice. In a word, his design work was inadequate.

At the time, I had no training in psychology, so I had no idea what was wrong. However, I knew that his former position had been a manufacturing engineering job in which he helped solve problems with products that were already in manufacturing. I offered to transfer him to an equivalent job on the basis that if he had done satisfactory work in such a job previously, then he should work well for us.

He saw this transfer as a demotion and refused it. Then he worked for another project manager for a time before returning to my project. The other manager had similar problems with him.

His performance deficit finally came to a head. We gave him the option of finding another job, taking the transfer, or terminating him. He chose to find another job.

What I didn't know then, but do now, is that the design job requires different thinking than does the manufacturing support job. The design engineer must be able to think in terms of synthesis, whereas the manufacturing engineer must think more analytically. Synthesis is a right-brain mode, and analysis is a left-brain mode. So I actually hired the wrong person for the job based on his thinking preferences (and ability). Now, exactly what does this mean?

THINKING STYLES

Ned Herrmann was a training manager at General Electric's Crotonville Management Training Center. Ned was originally educated as a physicist, but was very interested in the social sciences, especially art. He was a gifted painter.

He heard about research that indicated that the two hemispheres of the brain seem to control different kinds of thinking, and wondered how those differences might affect learning, management, creativity, and other aspects of human performance. Because the field was in its infancy, Ned had to do a lot of research himself, and he found that the left/right dichotomy did not suffice to explain thinking differences. He

F I G U R E 5–1

HBDI Profile of Thinking Styles

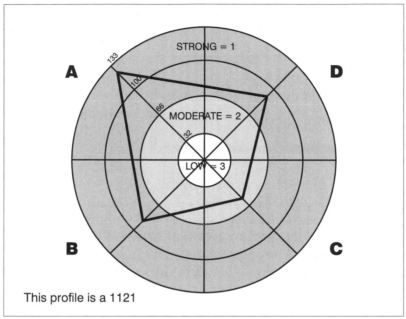

© 2007 by The Ned Herrmann Group, Inc. Used with permission from the Ned Herrmann Group, Inc., granted for this text only.

postulated another axis based on cerebral/limbic thinking (Herrmann, 1995, 1996). When this dimension is added, you have four pure styles that combine to yield a wide range of different thinking styles. Ned developed an instrument that measures these preferences, called the Herrmann Brain Dominance Instrument (HBDI™)[1]. The respondent receives a profile like the one shown in Figure 5–1.

In this profile are four concentric circles or bands, divided into about 33 points per band, so raw scores range from 0 to 133. However, to give a person a raw score implies

---

[1] HBDI™ is a trademark of the Ned Herrmann Group, Inc.

a measurement precision that simply does not exist, so Ned chose to use a ranking instead. The outer two bands have a rank of 1, meaning the person has a very strong preference for thinking in the specific mode. The next band has a rank of 2, which is weaker but still significant. Finally, the inner band yields a rank of 3, which is a very low preference. In fact, a score in this band indicates that the individual may actually reject this mode of thinking

> The HBDI measures one's preference for thinking in certain ways, not one's ability.

most of the time. There is no such thing as a 0 rank, as everyone uses all four modes to some degree. Note also that the instrument measures *preferences,* not skills or abilities.

However, there is a correlation between preference and skill. If you have a strong preference for engaging in a certain mode of thinking, you will tend to do so frequently and thus get pretty good at it. So, over time, preference probably does lead to skill.

Herrmann believed that the preference for the various thinking modes was based on brain physiology, which involves both chemistry and genetics, but whether this is true is still open to question. In the January 2005 *Scientific American* special issue on the mind, research was reported by a German team that used the MRI, rather than just the standard EKG, to observe brain activity. They found that specific areas of the brain do not cleanly correlate with certain kinds of thinking. Rather, various stimuli activated multiple parts of the brain at once. Thus, the idea of left-right hemispheres and limbic versus cerebral as determinants of certain thinking may not be accurate, but that is not important for our purposes. The fact is that four distinct modes of thinking have been identified, and the HBDI does a good job of measuring them.

At this time the Herrmann International database contains over a half-million profiles of people who have taken the HBDI. Most find that the measures represent them fairly well. Seldom does anyone say, "That's just not me!"

Profiles

As you might expect, an individual can have a preference for thinking in only one of the four modes. The HBDI profile for such a person, called *single-dominant*, looks a bit like a kite, so we sometimes refer to a profile as a kite. Only about 5 percent of the population is single-dominant. A sample profile is shown in Figure 5–2.

F I G U R E 5–2

A Single-Dominant HBDI Profile

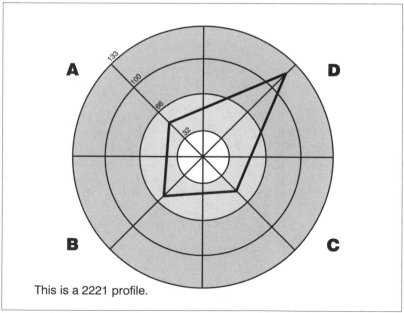

This is a 2221 profile.

When an individual likes to think in two modes, the profile is called *double-dominant*, and there are two forms that can be taken by the kite. In one, the two preferred quadrants are side by side. In the other they are diagonally opposite each other. The two possibilities are shown in Figure 5–3. Naturally, the adjacent preferences can be both left, both right, both top, and both bottom quadrants, and the diagonally opposite can be A to C and B to D. Double-dominant preferences account for about 56 percent of the population.

The *triple-dominant* profile can be any three adjacent quadrants. Approximately 36 percent of the population falls into this category. A triple-dominant profile is shown in Figure 5–4.

Finally, a mere 3 percent of the population prefers to think in all four quadrants, and of course this profile is called

F I G U R E 5–3

Double-Dominant HBDI Profiles

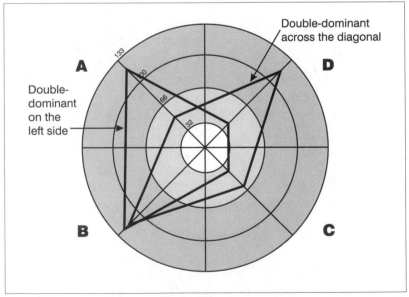

FIGURE 5-4

The Triple-Dominant HBDI Profile

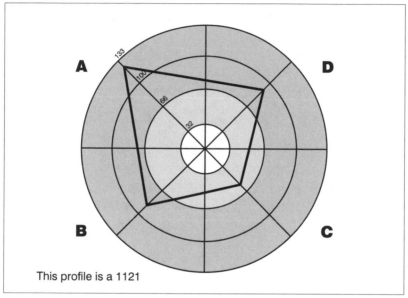

This profile is a 1121

quadruple-dominant. Such individuals are called multidominant translators, and Ned believed that they should make excellent CEOs because they can interact effectively with people from each of the quadrants. This may be hard to demonstrate, since the numbers are so small, and of those people who are quadruple dominant, only a certain percentage will ever become CEOs—so we may never know if they are good candidates. Furthermore, one's thinking preferences do not guarantee that a person will be able to deal effectively with others, so thinking is only part of the picture. A quadruple-dominant profile is shown in Figure 5–5.

What are the differences between the four modes, and how do these differences affect various work functions in a

F I G U R E 5–5

A Quadruple-Dominant HBDI Profile

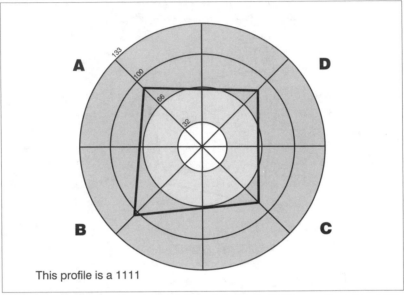

This profile is a 1111

project? Since the model is a grid containing four quadrants, each of which represents a different thought mode, we will begin in the upper left, or A quadrant, and explain each mode by progressing in a counterclockwise direction through the quadrants. Note that the progression is A-B-C-D and that, in the profile received by respondents, each quadrant is colored, in the sequence blue-green-red-yellow.

The A Quadrant

The thinking associated with the A quadrant can be described as logical, analytical, technical, mathematical, and problem solving (see Figure 5–6). Such thinking can be thought of as dealing with facts and figures. It seems reasonable that people

Quadrant A
can be
described as
logical,
analytical,
technical,
mathematical,
and
problem solving.

F I G U R E   5–6

The Herrmann Whole Brain Model—Thinking in Each Quadrant

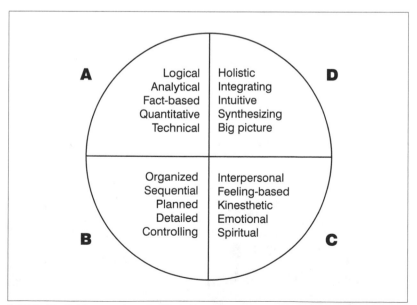

© 2007 by The Ned Herrmann Group, Inc. Used with permission from the Ned Herrmann Group, Inc., granted
for this text only.

who like dealing with facts and figures would be attracted to jobs or professions that require such thinking, and this is true. Examples of such careers include technical, legal and financial areas (including accounting and tax law), engineering, information technology, science, mathematics, and the analytical aspects of management.

A project manager with a single-dominant profile in quadrant A could be expected to be very logical, interested in technical issues affecting the project, inclined to analyze status reports carefully, and keen on problem solving. Such a project manager may be seen as cold, uncaring, and interested only in the problems presented by the project. However, since only 5 percent of the population is single-dominant, such project managers should be correspondingly rare.

The B Quadrant

The B quadrant is similar to the A quadrant, but with significant differences. Words that describe the B quadrant thinkers are organizational, administrative, conservative, controlled,

ෲ◆ඏ
Quadrant B is organizational, administrative, conservative, controlled, and planning.
ෲ◆ඏ

and planning. This is the preferred thinking of many managers, administrators, planners, bookkeepers, foremen, and manufacturers. Individuals who have single-dominant profiles in the B quadrant could be expected to be concerned with the detailed plans of a project and with keeping everything organized and controlled. Note that individuals with financial interests who are dominant in quadrant A will probably be financial managers, whereas those with dominant B quadrant profiles may be drawn to cost accounting.

If you want someone to pay close attention to details, you want someone who displays a strong preference for this quadrant. If they have a single-dominant profile, however, they may see the trees and be unaware of the forest.

The C Quadrant

People with single-dominant profiles in the A or B quadrants probably see individuals with strong C quadrant preferences as being very "touchy-feely." Words that describe this quadrant are interpersonal, emotional, musical, spiritual, and talkative.

ಐ◆ca
**Quadrant C
are often
nurses,
social workers,
musicians,
teachers,
counselors, or
ministers.**
ಐ◆ca

Individuals with single-dominant C profiles are very "feeling" and people-oriented. They are often nurses, social workers, musicians, teachers, counselors, or ministers.

A project manager with a single-dominant C profile would naturally be concerned with the interpersonal aspects of the project, perhaps to the detriment of getting the work done. Such an individual would be drawn to the coordination of project activities with people both inside and outside the team, and would be a relationship builder. This would be a good bias to have for highly political projects, as long as other members of the team are attending to the work itself.

In fact, you will remember that we have said several times that projects are people, and dealing with people is one aspect of project management that some individuals find distasteful. So you could expect that this aspect of the job will bother the person who has very low C quadrant scores on the HBDI. My counsel is that you can develop the skill if you have the desire, but given very low scores in the C quadrant naturally means this is not your "cup of tea." So you will have to work very hard at this aspect of the job if you want to manage projects.

There is an interesting finding about how we behave in terms of our least-preferred thinking styles. I have a very strong D quadrant preference, with B quadrant being my least-preferred. This means that I love developing concepts and dislike doing detail work. However, if I must do detail work in order to get one of my ideas to see the light of day, then I am very motivated to do so. This means that you can be motivated to deal with the "touchy-feely" stuff if it means achieving success in terms of your other thinking preferences.

The D Quadrant

Words that describe this quadrant are artistic, holistic, imaginative, synthesizers, and conceptualizers. Individuals who have single-dominant D quadrant profiles are often drawn

ৡ◆ల

**Quadrant D
are often
entrepreneurs,
in facilitation,
advising,
consulting,
sales leaders,
and artists.**

ৡ◆ల

to careers that involve entrepreneurial effort, facilitation, advising, consulting, or being sales leaders and artists. These are the "idea" people in a team, and they enjoy synthesizing ideas from several sources to create something new from that combination. This is the natural domain of people who are perceived to be creative. At the beginning of this chapter we discussed the need for creative thinking in projects. So you may conclude that if you are primarily a left-brain thinker having strong preferences for A or B quadrant thinking, and low preference for thinking in the D quadrant, then you are out of luck. Not so. It turns out that it is easier for left-brain thinkers to learn to do conceptual or "creative" thinking than it is for conceptual thinkers to learn analytical or detail thinking.

Project managers who have single-dominant D quadrant profiles could be expected to be "big-picture" in their thinking—they run the risk of seeing the forest without realizing that it consists of distinct trees. They are generally good at thinking strategically, so in planning a project the D-quadrant thinker will develop a gameplan but will need help from B-quadrant thinkers to make it workable.

Double-Dominant Profiles and Project Management Styles

Since only 5 percent of our population has single-dominant profiles, it would seem more reasonable to examine multidominant profiles. The simplest analysis would be for double-dominant profiles because they comprise 56 percent of the population, and this will give us insight into a host of project managers. A diagram showing the characteristics of each of the adjacent-quadrant double-dominant profiles is shown in Figure 5–7.

F I G U R E 5–7

Management Styles of Double-Dominant Managers Using the
Herrmann Model

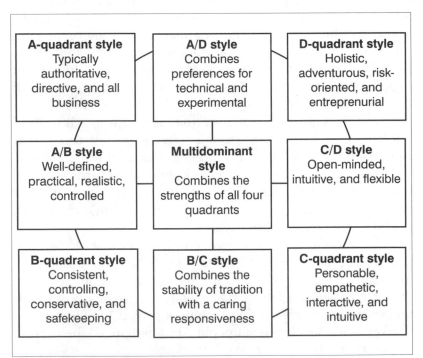

A-quadrant style	**A/D style**	**D-quadrant style**
Typically authoritative, directive, and all business	Combines preferences for technical and experimental	Holistic, adventurous, risk-oriented, and entreprenurial
A/B style	**Multidominant style**	**C/D style**
Well-defined, practical, realistic, controlled	Combines the strengths of all four quadrants	Open-minded, intuitive, and flexible
B-quadrant style	**B/C style**	**C-quadrant style**
Consistent, controlling, conservative, and safekeeping	Combines the stability of tradition with a caring responsiveness	Personable, empathetic, interactive, and intuitive

WORK MOTIVATION AND THE HBDI

One aspect of thinking preferences that you should consider is that you probably have a least-preferred thinking style (or several). Mine is the B-quadrant, which requires great attention to detail. I would find a project requiring such thinking to be drudgery. When I was an engineer, I disliked the detailed work involved in reviewing drawings or making sure a bill of materials was exactly right. It was

> People are motivated to engage in various patterns of activity, and these are derived from preferred thinking modes.

vital work, but I hated it. So knowing your most-preferred and least-preferred thinking styles should help you determine when a particular kind of project is a good match for you, or what you should do when there is a mismatch.

As a matter of fact, a person's motivation is derived from his preferred quadrants. If the preference is single-dominant, you will have a single motivation pattern. If your profile is double-dominant you will have two patterns, and so on. These patterns of activity motivate a person. As an example, a person with a strong preference for thinking in the D quadrant may be very innovative. A person whose preference is the A quadrant may be a good trouble-shooter, which requires analytical thinking.

Thus, a person's profile is a pretty good indication of the kind of activities that motivate her. If you understand the characteristics of the job, you will know whether it is likely to motivate the person or not.

Is There a Best Profile?

Ned Herrmann was always careful to say that individuals with almost any profile *can* do most jobs. The HBDI measures one's *preference* for thinking, not one's *ability*. As I pointed out

ℰ✦ℭ

**The HBDI
measures
one's
preference for
thinking, not
one's ability.**

ℰ✦ℭ

earlier there is a relationship, but presumably a person with
any profile can develop the ability to think in all four modes
and become skilled enough to be able to perform in any job.

Also, as I mentioned earlier, Ned did postulate that there
may be an ideal profile for a CEO (chief executive officer), that
being a square—a quadruple-dominant profile. The reason is
easy to understand. A CEO must deal with people who think in
all four quadrants, and if she prefers to think in all four, then
she can translate between them for all parties involved.

I met one such individual, and sure enough he was a
turnaround CEO who specialized in saving hospitals from financial disaster. Unlike some individuals who specialize in
turnarounds, this man tried to employ measures that saved
as many jobs as possible. The turnaround CEO with very low
C-quadrant thinking is often concerned only with the bottom
line, and the quickest way to improve financial performance
is to eliminate jobs regardless of the cost in human suffering.
Naturally they will justify such action by saying that sacrificing a few jobs is better for everyone in the long run.

The Herrmann group pulled a composite profile for all of the project managers that they had in their database, and that overall profile was square. They had 1,250 profiles for project managers, with the population being almost perfectly split 50-50 between men and women. These profiles are shown in Figures 5–8 and 5–9. For the overall population, there is a small "tilt" toward the A quadrant for men and a small tilt toward the C quadrant for women, and this was also true of the profiles for project managers.

This suggests that project managers come in all shapes and sizes. There has to be a fairly even distribution of profiles to get a composite square, so the distribution for project managers is not very different than for the population in general.

FIGURE 5–8

HBDI Composite Profile for Female Project Managers

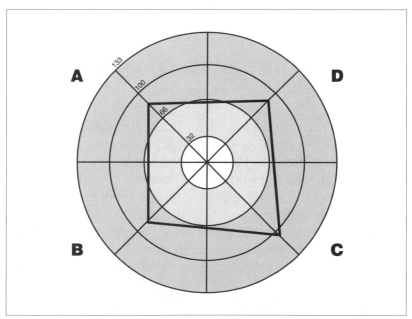

F I G U R E 5–9

HBDI Composite Profile for Male Project Managers

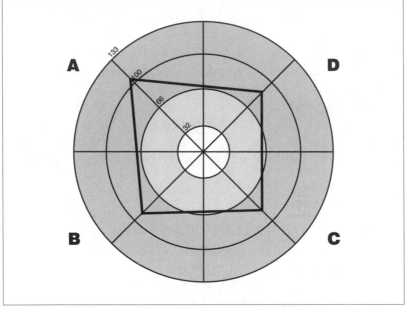

As has been stated above, an individual's thinking preference will affect his style of managing projects. One concern would be with project managers who have very little preference for C-quadrant thinking, the reason being that age-old problem of project managers: they have a lot of responsibility and very little authority, so that the only way they can get anything done is through influence, negotiation, begging, and selling. Project managers with very low preference for the C quadrant are inclined to say, "I hate dealing with people problems," and to them I suggest that they rethink whether they truly want to manage projects. This would be the one deficit that should enter into a person's decision about whether to be a project manager. If you hate dealing with people, then why subject yourself to the daily agony that you are sure to experience as a project manager?

Is there a *best* profile? Maybe.

In a recent seminar that I taught entitled "Whole Brain Project Management," I discussed the attributes of project managers having various profiles, and concluded that of the double-dominant profiles, the one that is probably most effective is the C-D profile—that is, the person who is primarily right-brained. Because project managers must use influence to get things done, they need strong C-quadrant thinking. Furthermore, project managers have a major responsibility to help a team develop a shared understanding for the vision of the project outcome, and this requires a strong D-quadrant focus.

> Your profile will affect your style of managing projects, and this could affect your success in certain environments, but any profile can be effective in project management.

I also believe that a project manager is primarily a leader and facilitator. For that reason, she need not be highly analytical, nor be a very strong planner/organizer, as long as she recognizes the need for such thinking and gets the team to do it. In fact, I believe that project managers who are strong in the A and B quadrants may be inclined to get too bogged down in technology or detail, and to possibly do too much of the planning rather than having the team do it, and this is not always good.

> I believe the project manager with a primarily right-brain preference has an advantage over other profiles in most situations.

As a matter of fact, I have now met quite a few quadruple-dominant individuals, and although they may be good

Is there a "best" profile? NO

translators between the quadrants, they seem to me to have trouble making decisions. The simple reason is that they try too hard to cover all of the quadrants, to consider all of the issues in each one, and in doing so become paralyzed. I'm not certain that this is true, and would love to hear from any of my readers who can add insight into this question. Write me at jlewis@lewisinstitute.com.

Forming Teams Using the HBDI

One application of the HBDI that is now well documented is its use in assembling teams. A team should collectively represent a "whole brain," meaning that if you overlay the profiles of all members of the team, they will form a composite profile that shows preferences in all four quadrants. Otherwise, if they have a strong aversion to one of the quadrants, you could expect that issues requiring thinking in that area may not be handled very well. However, a word of caution is in order. Ned found that whole-brain, gender-balanced teams produce better solutions and work than homogeneous or single-gender teams. However, you can also expect much more debate to take place because people approach each situation from their own perspective, and team members with multiple perspectives have a hard time reaching agreement.

> When a team lacks a "whole brain," members must learn to "walk into" the least-preferred quadrant and cover issues relevant to that quadrant.

As I've noted, many teams do not collectively represent a whole brain. For example, technical groups often have a profile like that shown in Figure 5–10. They are strong in the A, B, and D quadrants and weak in C—the one having to do with interpersonal matters.

This means that they may very well attend to technical issues, are good at details, and generate good ideas, but they neglect the "touchy-feely" attributes that may undermine their team's performance. What should they do?

The important thing is that they be aware of the profile and know how to compensate for the low preference in quadrant C. Remember, it is not that they *can't* think in this quadrant but that they simply don't have a strong preference to do so. If they can understand that failing to deal with quadrant C issues is going to cause them problems in dealing with what they really care about (namely technical matters), then they are more likely to spend time working on such issues.

Figure 5–11 offers another example. This time we have a very creative group of people; they love ideas, are interpersonal, and like doing analytical work—but they dislike detail. We can expect that they will generate good ideas but have trouble executing them—at least so far as the details are concerned. It is said that "The devil is in the details," and the devil may just get this group!

F I G U R E 5–10

HBDI Average Profile for a Technical Team

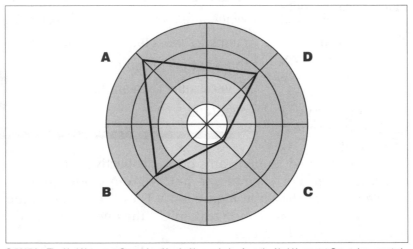

F I G U R E 5–11

HBDI Average Profile for a Creative Team

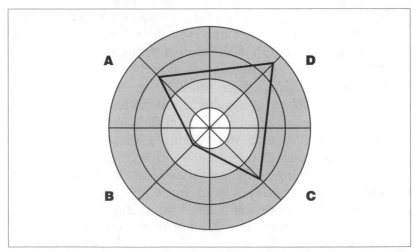

Again, however, if they are aware of the low quadrant B score for the team, they can compensate by working hard to ensure that details are not overlooked.

TEAM DYNAMICS

A project team is meeting to discuss an important project issue—a missed milestone. Everyone is a little apprehensive. They aren't sure how senior management is going to react to their failure to complete project work on schedule.

Wanda says, "I don't see how we could have done any better. We did everything humanly possible to complete the work on time. I feel really bummed out over the whole thing!"

"In looking at the numbers," Chuck says, "I believe we were set up to begin with. We were allocated to the project at a 95 percent rate, which is too high."

ೞ◆ೞ

**Team
dynamics
affect
problem
solving
significantly.**

ೞ◆ೞ

"I didn't like the concept we started with in the first place," chimes in Karen. "It was too flaky."

Don had been studying the schedule. "We should have moved these two tasks in parallel," he offers. "Then we could have finished on time."

This sets Wanda off. "You're always changing the plan, Don," she insists. "Can't you see we did everything we could to meet the deadline?"

"But the schedule is the most important part of the project plan," Don says defensively. "If we don't use the schedule properly, we can't hope to complete the work on time. It's a question of being better organized."

"It doesn't matter how well organized we are if the concept is no good to begin with," Karen interjects.

At this point, the project manager, Beth, interrupts. "Okay, let's calm down for a moment," she says. "And let's look at what's going on."

They all lean back in their chairs and wait for Beth to continue.

"Wanda, you're concerned about the effort you've put into the job, and you're feeling a little guilty that it didn't pay off," Beth says. "In terms of your HBDI profile, you're thinking in the C quadrant."

Wanda nods in agreement.

"And Karen, you're in the D quadrant, thinking conceptually, as usual," Beth says.

Karen smiles and nods. Beth has her pegged.

Beth continues around the table. "Naturally, Don is concerned about the schedule. He's a predominantly B-quadrant thinker, and Chuck is analyzing the numbers—his normal A-quadrant thinking."

Everyone laughs.

"The bad news is that each of us sees the situation from a different perspective," Beth continues. "And the good news is that each of us sees the situation from a different perspective."

She pauses to let the impact of her comment sink in.

"That's true," Karen says. "If we all saw it the same way we would probably fall into 'groupthink' and really get into trouble."

"Exactly!" Beth says. "We need every perspective to be an effective team, but our different styles make us think the other person doesn't understand what we're talking about, and we get into conflict."

They all murmur their agreement.

"Now let's see if we can use our varying points of view to get a handle on this project," Beth suggests. "How about if we come back to Karen's contention that the concept is flawed. She's right. If it is, then the detailed plan can't be any good."

From this point on, the meeting proceeds to a solution.

By understanding the fact that each member of the team sees the project in different ways, based on their individual thinking styles, Beth is able to draw on those preferences to the benefit of the project. Were she unaware of thinking preferences, she would probably see the team as dysfunctional and be tempted to disband it altogether, or perhaps ask a group facilitator to help her keep them in line.

ജ ♦ ങ

Principle: Misunderstanding sometimes occurs because of differences in thinking preferences.

ജ ♦ ങ

Of course, this scenario has been framed somewhat un-realistically. I have treated each individual team member as though he or she had a single-dominant thinking style. Most of us think in more than one quadrant, but it is true that there may be a quadrant that does dominate our thinking. When we communicate with others who are in different quadrants than our own, we have difficulties.

The opposite is also true. A couple of years ago I met a fellow with whom I seemed to have almost instant rapport. We saw eye-to-eye on so many things it was almost scary. At that time I was aware of the HBDI, but had not yet been certi-fied as a practitioner, so it didn't occur to me that this could be the source of our easy communication and understanding. I did know the Myers-Briggs, and found that we had similar temperaments. In any case, we became good friends.

After I became certified I sent a survey to my friend, and to our amazement his profile and mine are congruent to within a few points in every quadrant! No wonder we think so much alike. Naturally, we don't agree on everything, but the similarities are striking.

The danger for us, of course, is that we may too quickly agree on an issue without exercising the critical thinking that might change our opinions. As Beth told her team, we need op-posing points of view to achieve a balanced perspective on issues.

Managing Conflict

If a team is to have creative capacity, it must be able to gener-ate many ideas so that one good one will emerge. These ideas must be screened and the best one selected. During the screening process various ideas are critiqued, and it is at this point that conflict sometimes turns nasty.

There is a sense in which, if you criticize my idea, you are finding fault with me. So I respond by getting angry. Next thing you know, we are locked in an interpersonal conflict. These are often labeled as *personality conflicts*. They are in a sense. But they

"You Think Funny"

have a fundamental cause—we see things differently, and identify with our points of view and the ideas we have.

A project leader has to get people to generate ideas, and manage the critiquing of these conflicting ideas so that they don't develop into interpersonal conflicts. As this will sometimes happen, the project manager then has to resolve that interpersonal conflict, and if people understand the concept of thinking preferences this will be somewhat easier than it would be otherwise.

THE BALANCED SCORECARD

Kaplan and Norton (1996) developed the concept of using a balanced scorecard to measure the effectiveness of an organization. This concept can also be used to measure project performance. The idea is that most measures focus exclusively on financial aspects of the business and fail to consider other important factors, such as long-term strategies, developing human resources, knowledge management, and so on.

When you think about this, it is clear that the Herrmann model can be used to measure project performance. Each quadrant represents a domain of concern for project and/or organization performance. The A quadrant deals with the familiar financial measures and other numerical data. The B quadrant focuses on policies, procedures, and controls. The C quadrant provides a focus on people—training and development of employees, maintaining good relations with customers, clients, and key suppliers. The D quadrant concerns long-range planning—positioning the organization or project for the future and dealing with concepts, strategies, and the "big picture."

> Develop a whole-brain, balanced scorecard for a project so you can measure success from the perspective of each quadrant.

In planning a project it is important to decide what outcomes should be achieved in each quadrant, and what evidence will be used to show that these outcomes have been achieved. In other words, you should ask:

- ◆ What is the desired outcome?
- ◆ How will we know it has been achieved?

Once you know the desired outcomes and how you will know they have been achieved, you can develop plans to get you there. This approach will help you avoid focusing only on financials.

As an example, a project may meet all PCTS targets and still be judged negatively by a major stakeholder. This may be because he was not treated as he expected to be treated (C-quadrant). By paying attention to C-quadrant factors from the very beginning, such missteps can be avoided.

Figure 5–12 shows a general example of the factors that might be considered in a balanced scorecard for a project.

F I G U R E   5–12

A Balanced Scorecard for a Project, Based on the Herrmann Model

A   **D**

Measurable performance   Concept or model development
outcomes   Strategies and strategic thinking
Financial outcomes, ROI   Ideation, creativity, and
E-products, technical results   innovation
Research data and analysis   Global, culture issues

Administrative plans and policies   Team process and effectiveness
Process improvement   Customer or stakeholder
Operational efficiencies   relationships
Quality improvement   Training and development
                                    achievements
                                    Communication effectiveness

B   **C**

IN SUMMARY

There are many applications of the whole-brain model in managing projects, because projects involve all kinds of work. We have only scratched the surface in this chapter. I would encourage you to read Ned's book *The Whole Brain Business Book* (1996) for a more complete exposition on the many applications. And check out the Herrmann International web site, www.hbdi.com. It offers a number of resources that you may find useful.

6

CHAPTER

How to Achieve High-Performance Project Management

For as long as I can remember, the objective to which all project managers aspired was to finish a project "on time, on budget, at the required scope and performance levels." If this was accomplished, a project manager was considered to be successful. There are, however, many problems with this way of defining success. First of all, were the targets realistic to begin with, or were they based on wishful thinking? Secondly, were there factors outside the project manager's control that prevented meeting the targets? These are just two of the questions that can cast doubt on whether a project manager is effective.

This raises a basic issue: How do you determine whether a project manager is a "good" manager or not? What exactly are the criteria by which you define effective versus ineffective performance in managing projects? And how do you define high performance, as compared to low performance?

How do you
define
effective
versus
ineffective
performance
in managing
projects?

In lawsuits claiming malpractice on the part of physicians, the test is whether the physician followed accepted medical practice in a given situation. If not, then that doctor is guilty of malpractice . . . .or "bad practice."

A similar court case challenged the management of the Trans-Alaska Pipeline project many years ago. It was alleged that the project was mismanaged—and testimony supported the claim—in that no work breakdown structure was created, and only a very rudimentary critical path schedule existed for managing this very complex project.

WHAT IS MANAGEMENT?

The Project Management Institute defines project management as the ". . . application of knowledge, skills, tools and techniques to meet project objectives. This is accomplished through the processes of initiation, planning, execution, monitoring and controlling, and closeout" (PMBOK 2004, p. 8). In

1973, Peter Drucker wrote a definitive book on management, *Management: Tasks, Responsibilities, Practices*. Drucker essentially defines management as making an unsolicited contribution to an organization. Does that mean an employee who comes up with a new practice that is adopted by a company is a manager? I doubt it.

It may be that we could define management as "coordinating the efforts of a group of individuals in order to achieve a goal or result that could not be accomplished by any single person working alone." This is often simplified to "getting work done through people." This definition quickly falls apart when you realize that a guard over a prison work team is getting work done through people, too, but I don't think we would call this managing.

Ultimately it boils down to the fact that a manager engages in certain tasks and practices to ensure that a group achieves desired results. Wielding shotguns over a group is not generally included in those accepted practices, although I have known managers who essentially did just that because they used coercion as their approach to getting people to perform, so that I would question whether they were managers or prison guards.

CAN MANAGERS REALLY CONTROL ANYTHING?

Stafford Beer (1981) has pointed out that the law of requisite variety, which is a principle from systems theory, calls into question whether managers can really control anything. The law states that, "In any system of humans or machines, the element in the system with the greatest variability in its behavior will control the system." Assuming that a project manager (PM) is supposed to control the project so that desired results are achieved, this law requires that the PM must have greater flexibility in his behavior than the variability in the system in order to be in control.

When you consider that even a small group of people can exhibit great variability in their behavior, this law suggests that a manager must possess maximum flexibility in order to control the group. Or is that true? If the manager could reduce the variability of the members of the group, she might find she has enough flexibility to be in control. Indeed, this is exactly what many managers attempt to do intuitively. However, they go about it the wrong way. Many of them reduce variability in the system by imposing "thou-shalt-not" injunctions on people. That is, they impose so many rules and regulations (mostly in the form of restrictions) on their people that in the process they destroy the freedom of people to do creative work that would actually be helpful.

So, what is the answer?

My conclusion is that a manager is never in control of a group unless each member is in control of his or her own behavior. When you consider the interdependencies in a project schedule, it is easy to see why this is true. If one contributor fails to meet her targets, then the tasks dependent on her work will fall behind. In terms of a system such as an automobile, consider that if the fuel pump quits or a tire blows out, the car is out of commission. So it takes only one element in a system going out of control to wreck the entire system. (In aircraft, this is avoided by having redundant components, so that if one fails, the backup takes over.)

So the question becomes, "How do you make it possible for each individual to be in control of his or her own behavior?"

The answer is, you empower them.

ACHIEVING SELF-CONTROL

In order for any individual to have self-control, five conditions must exist:

1. She must have a clear definition of what she is supposed to do, with the purpose stated as well.

2. She must have a plan for how the work will be done (remember, by definition, if you have no plan, you have no control).

3. She must have the skills and resources needed to perform the assignment effectively.

4. She must have feedback on progress that tells her if she is on target.

5. She must have a clear definition of her authority to take corrective action when there is a deviation from plan—and that authority cannot be zero, or she cannot control.

If you examine these conditions carefully, you will note that the practice of good project management actually accomplishes this set of conditions: It enables individual contributors to control their own work.

It is also important to realize that it is a manager's responsibility to ensure that each of these conditions is met. For example, if the individual does not have the skills needed to

ଚ✦ଓ

By making an individual in control of their own behavior, *you empower them.*

ଚ✦ଓ

perform some particular task, then those skills must be developed and management must provide adequate training; this includes making sure it is budgeted.

DEFINING HIGH-PERFORMANCE MANAGEMENT

Studies have shown that the typical rework in a project ranges from 20 to 40 cents out of every dollar spent. This is in line with the findings of six-sigma studies for organizations in general. The typical organization runs at a three-sigma quality level, which means that they have scrap and rework levels of about 30 cents on the dollar of sales revenue. If an organization can improve its quality sufficiently to reach the six-sigma level, this figure drops to about 3 cents on the dollar.

It seems to me that this provides a good way to measure high performance. I suggest that a high-performance project is one that achieves a rework level of no greater than 3 cents of every project dollar spent. Another way to state this is that for every million opportunities to make an error, you only make 3.6 errors at a six-sigma level, whereas at the three-sigma level, the number of errors per million opportunities is 34,000.

This level must also be achieved while keeping the project on schedule and within scope and budget constraints. I would propose that projects that are at the three-sigma level are just typical. Those that achieve a four-sigma level are bronze-medal contenders. Those that hit a five-sigma level are silver medalists, and the six-sigma level wins a gold medal.

What Does It Take to Achieve Gold Level?

I believe that to attain the gold level, a project manager must integrate leadership and management. How this is done was covered in Chapter 3. Because leadership is primarily a set of interpersonal skills, project managers who want to achieve gold-level performance must develop these skills to a high level of competence. They must also understand the whole-brain thinking model and how to apply it to get the best possible performance from members of their project teams.

It is also important to note that excellent project management cannot be achieved in an environment that does not support it. And, while you as a project manager may not be able to control the environment in which you work, you should lobby hard to have senior managers deal with these issues. For example, I believe strongly that project management is a function, just like accounting or information technology. For that reason, a project office (or call it a project management function) is an ideal way for an organization to optimize project management.

CROSS-CULTURAL ISSUES

If you are in an environment that deals cross-culturally, you cannot consider yourself a master of your art unless you understand how to deal with other cultures. There are many situations in which projects and business deals have been wrecked simply because someone did not understand cultural differences. I think it is important to have the view that cultural differences are neither good nor bad—they just *are*. If you approach such differences with the view that they are a nuisance or a problem, you are going to have difficulty dealing with people in those cultures.

In many Asian cultures, especially Japan, people do not like to say "no" in a direct way. They will soften it. As an example, I once heard a fellow order a specific beer in a Japanese restaurant. The waitress said, "Maybe we don't have that kind. Maybe you would prefer something else." The Asian customer didn't miss a beat. He asked, "What do you have?" She named a different brand and he ordered it.

Had this been an American, I believe he would have asked her to go and check if she had his preferred choice. After all, she said *maybe* we don't have it. To an American, this suggests uncertainty. The truth is, she knew they did not carry the brand ordered by the customer, but from her cultural perspective, she could not say this directly.

Writing as an American, we find such communication mystifying. Why don't they just say it directly?, we ask. For the same reason that we don't walk naked through the streets: Our culture prohibits it. And culture is the sum total of the expectations and history of the people who embrace it.

The important point is that we are not going to change other cultures, and people from other countries are not going to change ours. Indeed, it is disrespectful for either side to attempt to do so. We must adapt to cultural differences. Actually, the differences must be *reconciled*, a subject covered in depth by Trompenaars and Hampden-Turner in their excellent works on the subject (2005, 2006). Because of the complexity of this approach, I will refer the interested reader to their work, as it would require a full book for me to cover it adequately.

7
C H A P T E R

Power and Politics for Project Managers

To many people in organizations, politics is a dirty word. When I was an engineer, my peers used to lament, "I wish we could get rid of the politics!" I agreed with them. However, I soon realized that politics is so much a part of every organization that the only option is to learn to deal with it.

No doubt you have been burned by some individual in an organization who was ruthless, an up-and-comer who ran rough-shod over you

> **Principle:** The purpose of all political behavior is to develop and keep power.

without blinking an eye. That is how we learn to hate politics. But politics doesn't have to be dirty, and I don't advocate that you play dirty.

UNDERSTANDING POWER AND POLITICS

Before you can use politics in a way that supports your projects, you have to first acknowledge its existence and its impact on project success. Since the purpose of all political behavior is to develop and keep power, we should begin by understanding just what power means.

Power: The influence or control over others that a person has.

Power is the influence or control that one person has over others. Again, I know people who say, "I don't want to control anyone else, and I don't want anyone controlling me." It's a fine sentiment, but it does not change the fact that we are always influencing others and, therefore, exercising power over them, whether we want to or not.

One premise of human interaction is that you can't avoid influencing others. When you sit beside a person on a train, bus, or airplane, and that person stares out the window and never makes eye contact with you, she is communicating very clearly that she does not want to enter into a relationship with you. "Just leave me alone" is the message. And that usually works as an influence on the behavior of all but the most interpersonally unaware individuals, who insist on trying to interact anyway.

Premise: You can't *not* influence others!

No doubt you have been in a meeting or group in which a member sat and made faces while others talked—scowls, frowns, or just a single, persistent look of disapproval. Even though he says nothing, that person has an influence on others. By the same token, you may know someone who sits smiling the entire time, nodding affirmatively once in a while. Everyone is influenced positively by that person. They think, "She's really one of us. She agrees with us."

Either way, your interpretation of the person's nonverbal behavior can be wrong. The scowling person may simply feel unwell that day and may agree with the rest of you; the smiling person may be thinking, "What a bunch of idiots!" The smile is one of condescension, not approval.

French and Raven (1959) identified five "faces" of power. These are shown in Table 7–1. Project managers who complain that they have a lot of responsibility but no authority are saying that they lack position power. They cannot tell people what to do and expect them to do it, because their position as project manager carries with it no "clout." Couillard (1995) has found that this is a big problem in high-risk projects and suggests that organizations must give more authority to project managers who run such projects (see Chapter 15).

One way that project managers can exercise greater position power is to put them on an equal footing with functional managers. If project managers are drawn from functional groups and still report to functional managers,

T A B L E 7–1

The Five Faces of Power

Expert	The ability to influence others because the person is recognized as an expert in some area.
Reward	A person exercises influence because he or she has the ability to reward others.
Legitimate	One's position in an organization or group is a source of influence over others.
Referent	A person exercises influence because he or she has the ability to identify with or attract others.
Coercion	Coercive power is the ability to force people to do something through fear of sanctions or punishment that might be inflicted on them for noncompliance.

Source: Cartwright & Zander (1968).

they have no clout. I discuss this in more detail in Chapter 10. The other aspect of this is that project managers should have input to team members' performance appraisals. While the project manager may not evaluate the person's technical performance, she should be able to evaluate such dimensions as cooperation, timeliness of work, and contributions to the team. This automatically gives the project manager some power to reward (or punish)

> One way to give project managers some position power is to put them on the same level as functional managers.

members of the team, and it is one way of developing greater commitment to projects than is often found in organizations where the project manager has no input on performance appraisals.

Managers can't use coercion power in most cases. In fact, coercive power is harder to use in organizations today than it might have been in the period from 1900 to 1960. Since the 1960s, people have been more mobile in their jobs, have a greater sense of career freedom, and have

> Coercive power is not available to project managers in most cases.

learned that they don't have to submit to coercion. This is not universally true, and you do find coercion still being used by some managers. For it to work, the person being coerced must feel that he or she has no other job options and is therefore dependent on this manager for a living.

Project managers can sometimes use expert power, but even this form is fragile in some projects. When a project is multidisciplinary—that is, cuts across a number of technical specialties—it becomes very difficult for a project manager to understand all of those specialties. This limits his expert power over members of the team. He might be seen as expert only in managing projects, dealing with the politics of the organization, and being a provider of the resources that members of the team need in order to get the job done.

> Expert power is useful to project managers, but it must be real—not assumed.

Reward power is often limited, if you consider rewards to be tangible things like pay increases. But rewards also can be intangible—such as a pat on the back or recognition for good work—and there is no limit to the "amount" of such rewards that a project manager can dispense. One word of caution, though. A pat on the back must be sincere. Attempts to "stroke" people as a behavioral reinforcement technique come across as phony, and usually create resentment and a decline in performance. If you don't mean it, don't say it!

> Project managers may not be able to dispense tangible rewards, but they can use intangible ones.

WHAT'S IN IT FOR ME?

A principle in psychology states that people don't do anything unless there is something in it for them. This is true even when a person acts benevolently, in that he gets a warm feeling for having done something good. Or he may avoid feeling guilty for not doing good. Either way, there is a payoff. If there is no payoff, he won't do it. You can take this to the bank, whether you like it or not. It doesn't mean we are cold, calculating creatures; it just explains how we behave.

The effective project manager must consider "What's in it for me?" (WIIFM) when dealing with other departments and stakeholders, for they are not likely to help and support a project unless they perceive that it is in their interests to do

> You should *always* remember WIIFM when trying to influence people to do something you want done.

so. As Pinto says, "The worst mistake project managers can make is to assume that the stakeholders will automatically appreciate and value the project as much as they themselves [meaning project managers] do" (1996, p. 37).

This proposition is supported by Baker and Menon (1995), who show how two projects failed because of politics and one succeeded for the same reason. One of the failures was the supercollider. The project leaders went around proclaiming the merits of the project to scientists (which was equivalent to preaching to the choir), but never tried to convince Congress. When the Clinton administration came into office, the supercollider was killed. As Baker and Menon say, "The story of the project needs to be told in a way that's clear not only to the technowizards but to the masses as well" (p. 20).

USING INFLUENCE TO GET THE JOB DONE

When you have little or no authority, you have to get things done through influence or negotiation. And it turns out that this is true even when you *do* have authority. I have asked a number of company presidents and CEOs this question: "You have a lot of authority. Does your authority guarantee that people do what you want them to do?" They always answer no.

"Then what *does* get people to do what you want done?" I ask.

"They have to want to do it," is the answer every time. "My job is to get them to want to do it."

They are saying that they still have to influence their people, in spite of the position power that they hold. If a company president has to do this, project managers can expect no better. So we had better hone our influence skills.

The dictionary defines influence as the capacity to "sway or affect" the behavior of others. Robert Cialdini (1993) calls influence the psychology of persuasion. As a project manager, you must use influence frequently, as I have already said, since you have no direct authority over many of the people with whom you deal.

> **Influence:** Capacity to sway or affect based on prestige, wealth, ability, or position.
> —*American Heritage Dictionary*

Besides the members of your own organization, you often have to influence outsiders—vendors, customers, and partners in certain ventures. One way of doing this is to address the WIIFM issue, as discussed in the previous section. This is such a fundamental principle that it cannot be overlooked.

There are other methods of exerting influence besides WIIFM. One is through reciprocity. This is a very powerful way to gain influence in an organization. It is based on our belief that an exchange should, over time, be fair and balanced. I do something for you, and you, in turn,

> The rule of reciprocity is a powerful influence "tool."

reciprocate. This rule is seldom discussed, but if it is violated, people become very upset. They feel cheated, and this is sometimes the cause of relationship damage. By building relationships in the organization, and by doing favors for others when it is appropriate, you build a "bank account" that you can draw on when you need something from others. This shouldn't be done in a selfish or manipulative manner, though. The plain fact is, if you never do favors for others, there will be no one for you to turn to when *you* need help.

Relationship-building is a powerful way to bolster influence. We are far more willing to do things for people we like than for those we dislike or hardly know. A study at Bell Labs found that networking was a major factor in the success of engineers (Kelley and Caplan, 1993). Those who were most successful used the informal network to their advantage. However, it was not just that they were willing to call someone and ask for help that made the difference. These engineers took time to build alliances with other members of Bell Labs *before* they needed help. Then, when they called another engineer, they got a timely response. Those engineers who had not spent time building such alliances would call, too—but their calls would often not be answered for days. The finding of this study was considered so important that Bell Labs developed a program to train their engineers to use the informal network to build relationships.

> We are much more willing to do favors for people we know than those we don't know. Take time to *build relationships!*

> Good influencers are socially sensitive, articulate, and flexible.

Good influencers are socially sensitive, articulate, and flexible (Pinto, 1996, p. 38). They can often read body language and can tell how another person is reacting to their proposals, so that they can "shift gears" if they detect that a particular approach isn't working. They know when to use face-to-face methods and when a simple phone call will do. It is usually harder for people to refuse a face-to-face request than one made by phone, so if you anticipate difficulty in getting something done, talk to your colleagues directly.

DEALING WITH RESISTANCE

It is also important to know how to deal with resistance to your proposals. There are four approaches to dealing with resistance:

1. Ignore
2. Overcome
3. Neutralize
4. Go around

Ignoring resistance might be acceptable in some cases—when it is very weak or is being presented by people who can't do you much damage. However, be very careful not to underestimate that resistance. It might be stronger than you think. We sometimes think that low-status members of our organizations can't do us much damage. But such people can sometimes incite others to resist. This is itself a political action and can build to a very strong force. Strikes sometimes develop in this way.

The next strategy, to overcome resistance, is the one most frequently tried. You try to convince a person or group through the force of argument that your proposal is good for them, but they aren't convinced. If you pursue this tactic, you might notice that the more pressure you exert to get the resisting party to ac-

> If you push too hard, the person just pushes back and becomes entrenched in his resistance.

quiesce, the more resistant that party becomes. (To explain this in terms of systems thinking, the interaction becomes a system that tries to balance itself. The stronger the force on one side becomes, the stronger the resisting force grows.) When

ಹಿ◆ಲಿ
**Ignoring
resistance might
be acceptable in
some cases. Be
very careful not
to underestimate
that resistance.
It might be
stronger than
you think.**

ಹಿ◆ಲಿ

this happens, it is a good idea to back off, because continuing to push will get the person or group so entrenched in resistance that they can't change their position without losing face.

Try to neutralize the resistance instead. This does not mean blasting people into oblivion, much as you might want to. It means finding a way to dispel the resistance.

Neutralize: To find a way to make resistance go away.

The best approach that I know of is to proceed as follows:

"I understand that you have some concerns about my proposal," you say. "What would I have to do to convince you that it is a good proposal?"

The person can make two responses. One is that you will never convince him. When a person tells me that, I say, "Really? There's *nothing* I can do to convince you?" I place great emphasis on the word "nothing." If the person is willing to meet me partway, he will usually soften a bit and give me the second possible response. If he is unwilling to even meet me partway, then I might have to resort to another approach. And, sometimes, I might have to drop my proposal. You can't win every battle.

The second response you can get is for the person to say, "If you did xyz, that would convince me." If it is a reasonable suggestion and you can do it, you now know what to do. If it is something you can't do, you can now negotiate, which is discussed in the next section of this chapter.

The fourth approach to dealing with resistance is to go around a team member and ask her functional manager to make her cooperate. It is always the least-preferred approach, in my opinion, because of the downside that it carries. Using this approach, you may win the battle but lose the war. However, it may be necessary when the stakes are extremely high—for example, if a safety issue is involved.

There is another go-around method that sometimes works: turn to the person's peers, convince all of them of your position, and let *them* put pressure on the resisting person. It all depends on how easily the person is influenced by his peer group.

NEGOTIATING SKILLS

No matter how much position power you have, a fact of life in organizations is that you have to influence and negotiate to achieve your objectives. Some people think of negotiation as being synonymous with compromise, but that is not correct. When possible, a negotiation should always take a win-win approach. In win-win, you try to see that both par-

> All project managers have to influence and negotiate to get the job done.

ties to the negotiation achieve their objectives to the greatest degree possible. Yes, there may be some give-and-take. The problem with serious compromise, where each side gives up strongly desired objectives, is that both sides feel cheated at the end. Win-win solutions lessen such feelings.

Win-lose, of course, is an attempt to run roughshod over the other person to get what you want. This approach always creates enemies and over the long run tends to become lose-lose. This is what happened in the fight between the machinists' union and management at Eastern Airlines. The union was determined not to let CEO Frank Lorenzo break their union, as he had done at Continental. They succeeded, but in the process Eastern went under. When it was all over, they said, "We won." It was a hollow victory, in my opinion. They won the battle and lost the war!

Since a negotiation is always a conflict between the aims of two parties, conflict resolution and negotiation are nearly the same. If you are good at negotiating, you will usually be good at dealing with conflicts. Following are guidelines on how to approach either a conflict or a negotiation.

- ◆ Choose a neutral setting in which to discuss the problem. Your office is not the best place, since it automatically puts the other person at a disadvantage.

- ◆ State your sincere desire to resolve the conflict or difference to the satisfaction of the other person and yourself. If you feel an impulse to trash the other person, wait until you have cooled off before you begin. (Keep in mind that if you truly want to stomp someone, it will come out sooner or later—you can't fake it.)

- ◆ Do not assume that you know the other person's motives, intentions, thoughts, or feelings. To do so infers you are a mind-reader, and that only makes the conflict worse.

- ◆ Deal with the issues, not the character of the person.

◆ Where values differences have caused the conflict, deal with the *tangible effects* of the difference, not the values themselves. You generally cannot change the other person's values. You can, however, ask that they take certain actions, consider certain consequences, and so on.

◆ Practice *active listening*. Don't just glibly say, "I understand." *Demonstrate* your understanding by rephrasing what the other person has said. Note also that, when the person feels you understand her, the problem is half solved in many cases. One frequent cause of conflict is the feeling that the one party does not understand or appreciate the concerns of the other.

◆ State what you want as a request, not as a demand. Ask what the other person wants of you. If you cannot or will not comply with the other party's request, make a counterproposal. Try for win-win. Compromise only as a last resort.

◆ Keep in mind that the other person is not bad, mad, or crazy just because you have a difference. If you judge people, it is hard to remain objective and deal only with issues.

◆ When several issues exist, work on one at a time. Begin with the one on which you are most likely to reach agreement.

◆ Don't rush the process. Conflicts resolved in haste may come back to haunt you later.

◆ Once an agreement has been reached, ask the other party if there is anything that could prevent their complying with the agreement. Ask the same question of yourself. If there are any potential obstacles, try to find contingencies. This is called doing an "ecology check" at the end of the negotiation. Failure to do this can result in failed conflict resolution.

- Don't make promises you can't keep. It is disastrous for a manager to promise something to an employee and then have his boss overrule him. If you need to check with your boss before making an agreement, say so, and reconvene the meeting after you have seen your boss.

- *Always* give the other person a chance to save face. Never belittle his position. Remember, all behavior makes sense from the perspective of the actor, but not necessarily from the perspective of the observer. If you fail to observe this rule, you may "win" the negotiation but make an enemy for life. And in the corporate world, that person may be your boss one day, or may at least wait for an opportunity to stab you in the back to retaliate for the humiliation.

> All behavior makes sense to the person doing the behaving.

8

CHAPTER

Dealing with Cultural Differences

With the advent of the global economy comes an increased interaction between people of different countries, and an increase in the need to deal with cultural differences. In addition, there is greater migration of people within the United States, and this, too, brings a greater mix of the cultures that exist within this country. One

> **Culture:** The totality of socially transmitted behavior patterns, arts, beliefs, institutions, and all other products of human work and thought.
>
> —*American Heritage Dictionary*

definition of culture is shown in the box. Another is that culture is the sum total of the attitudes, beliefs, values, behaviors, and traditions that a person has internalized.

Every organization has a culture unique to itself, and this is true of divisions within large corporations. The important thing to understand about culture is that in most cases there is nothing *absolutely* right or wrong about cultures—they just *are!* It is only in a relative sense that you can say something is wrong in another culture. (I am excluding such glaring cultural differences as human rights abuses.) Naturally, not everyone agrees with my position. There are examples all around of people insisting that individuals from different cultures change to conform to the culture in which they are immersed at the moment. Some even go to another country and insist that the native people change their culture. One reason that some people in Europe dislike Americans is that we go there and insist that they do things *our* way!

This happened when missionaries went to the South Sea Islands and found that the women went around with their breasts uncovered. In the culture from which the missionaries came, this was shameful. To the islanders, it was a normal thing and there was no shame in it. The missionaries prevailed, however, and soon the women had their tops covered exactly as the women from Europe and America.

SOME EXAMPLES

During my first trip to Thailand, I met a fellow from Norway who had been sent there by his company to manage a plant. He was single at the time, so he started dating a Thai woman. One evening he went to her home to take her out and asked where she would like to go. To his bewilderment, she exploded.

> When you violate a person's cultural expectations, you offend him or her.

"Why do you always ask what I want to do?" she shouted. "Why don't you make a decision like a man!"

The poor fellow stammered, "I was just trying to be polite."

"Well, don't be!" she said.

"But what if I want to go somewhere that you don't like?" he protested.

"It doesn't matter," she insisted. "We'll go there!"

Because he was violating her cultural expectations of a man, she got angry at him. If his Thai colleagues at work had known of his behavior, no doubt they also would have lost respect for him. As the old saying goes, "When in Rome, do as the Romans do."

This injunction has its own problems. I have a friend who lived in Hong Kong for about 10 years. He had only been there for a short time when there was a torrential rain storm, and he was trying to catch a taxi to his office. Naturally, so was everyone else. To his chagrin, every time a taxi would pull up to the curb, someone would jump in front of him and take the taxi. After this happened several times, he realized that this was the system—whoever grabbed the taxi first was entitled to it. So the next taxi that pulled up, he dived for and got inside. In the process, he just about trampled an elderly lady. He said that he was so embarrassed at violating his own cultural norm that for a long time afterwards, he couldn't jump in front of anyone to catch a cab.

In the early days of oil exploration in Arab countries, Americans found that the people they were dealing with would move up very close to them when talking. The American would instinctively back up, and the Arab would move closer. In the Arabic culture body space is much closer than for Americans. I have been told that they like to stand close enough to literally smell each other's breath. We Americans prefer a larger distance so that we *can't* smell the other person's breath (we have a fear of this, which is why breath mints sell so well). In this interaction, *both* parties are feeling offended because the other person is violating their cultural expectation.

On one of my trips to eastern Asia, I picked up a book on how Asian managers differ from Americans, and the book highlighted a number of cultural differences that sometimes cause conflict between Americans and Asians. One of these is the difference in perception of someone who is fat.

I had taught for Petronas, the oil company in Malaysia, and after the class I had to catch a flight back to Singapore. The company had a driver take me to the airport, and he was driving a Volkswagen van. The customary thing to do is to get into the back seat, so I started to do so. The driver looked back at me and said, "You're kind of fat. Maybe you'd be more comfortable up here in the front."

Having just read about this, I was about to burst out laughing. I could just imagine this fellow coming to the U.S. and getting a job driving for a limousine service. One day he tells someone, "You're kind of fat. Would you like to sit up here?" The person is very offended, and the poor fellow is fired. His response: "What happened? I was just trying to be helpful."

> In east Asia, being fat is a sign of affluence.

And he was.

In eastern Asia, being fat is not a terrible thing, as it is in our "Twiggy" society. We think that if you are a few pounds overweight, you should lose it immediately. You're a bad person! To the Asian, however, being fat is a sign of affluence. The reason is that for a long period in their history, only the wealthy could afford enough food to get fat (not to mention the fact that they generally eat a better diet than Americans, with less fat content).

I told this story in a seminar and, during a break, a lady related a similar experience to me. She had gone to India to visit some friends, and she was a large woman. She had only been there a short time and was amazed to have people come

up to her and ask, "How much do you weigh?" It was several days before someone explained the connection for her.
They were trying to find out if she was a very affluent
woman. In effect, they were asking, "Are you wealthy?"
Even that question would be unacceptable in American society, but it is not in India.

PROJECT EXAMPLES

A company hired an engineer from India to work on a project. One day the project manager came by his desk and
asked how things were going. "Everything is fine," said the
engineer, "except for my lab work. It's at a standstill."

"What's the problem?" asked the project manager.

"I don't have a technician to do the work," said the engineer.

"Oh, yes, we don't have enough technicians for every
engineer to have one," explained the project manager. "I'm
afraid you'll have to do your own lab work."

The engineer became indignant. "I don't do lab work,"
he said.

"Well, in this lab, all engineers have to do a certain
amount of bench work," the project manager persisted. "I
think you better get in there and do the work, so you can stay
on schedule."

The engineer did as he was instructed, but he was really
angry. What the project manager didn't understand was that
this was demeaning to the engineer. In India, an engineer
would never do bench work—it is considered beneath his
status. Had the project manager understood this, he could
have said, "If you're going to live in the U.S., you either have
to find a company that has the luxury of a technician for every engineer or you have to adapt to our way of doing
things." As it was, he thought the engineer was just being
egotistical.

Another example: A project manager was doing work on a job that was a joint venture with a Japanese firm. He was discussing an issue with a Japanese engineer and asked if the fellow agreed with him on the issue. The engineer assured him that he did. Later on, he learned that the Japanese engineer had not really agreed about the issue but was merely being polite.

By way of understanding this, let me give some examples. When we hosted our first exchange student, who was from Japan, I asked her how to say *yes* and *no* in Japanese. "Well, yes is *hai*," she said, "and no is *eea*, but we don't like to say it." I didn't fully appreciate what she meant until a few years later. In Japanese society, saying no can be considered very rude, so when dealing with Japanese businesspeople, be careful to determine if yes really means agreement or just politeness.

In his book, *Dave Barry Does Japan*, Dave tells of an experience of trying to communicate in Japan. He called a travel agent to book a flight. He told her where he wanted to go, and after a minute or so, she said, "You want to fly from x to y?"

"Yes."

"Perhaps you would prefer to take a train," she said.

"No, I want to fly," Dave insisted.

There was another pause. Then she said, "From x to y?"

"Yes."

"Perhaps you would prefer to take a train."

Dave said it took several iterations before he finally realized what she was telling him: "There are no flights from x to y. If you want to go, you will have to take a train."

Another project example: A fellow in Thailand on a job went to lunch one day with some of the facility managers, and when they came back, the factory workers were nowhere to be seen. When they found them, they were at the small temple that every factory has, and they were praying. It turned out that there was a problem in the plant and they were praying for its successful resolution. They had, however, told no one in management about the problem. Managers are expected to know these things.

An American project manager was working on a job in Mexico, to install some equipment in a plant. He finished the job and went away for the evening. When he came in the next morning, the local people had called in a priest, who was sprinkling holy water on the machine and blessing it.

These things seem strange to us because they are not part of our culture. But they are real to the countries involved, and we must respect them.

BECOMING CULTURALLY AWARE

If you are going to run an international project, I strongly suggest that you try to learn as much as you can about the culture of the country with which you will be working. To find a source of information, you can call their embassy, check with some of the exchange student agencies that bring students from that country to stay in the U.S., or read a book on the subject. There are some protocol schools in areas like Washington, D. C. that teach Americans how to handle such issues.

For that matter, even if you don't run an international project, you may be faced with some of these issues. A fellow in Chicago told me that they had 21 different countries represented in his company. He needs a lot of cultural awareness to avoid problems.

9 CHAPTER

Defining Success and Failure

It probably goes without saying that no one sets out to fail in managing a project. We all want our projects to be successful. However, it is not at all clear what is meant by success or failure. What is needed is an operational definition of these terms. An operational definition

> When you fail to meet a target that was just pulled out of the air, should that be called a failure?

is one that has criteria that all parties involved can agree to use to define the outcome. How to develop operational definitions is covered in greater detail in Chapter 27, but for now, we need to agree on how to define success and failure in managing projects.

The most frequently used definition is that a project is a failure when it does not meet its cost, performance, time, or scope (C, P, T, S) targets. However, there are a couple of things wrong with this definition. First, where did the targets

ൈ❖ൽ

**No one sets
out to fail in
managing a
project.**

ൈ❖ൽ

come from? When they are just "pulled out of the air,"
should failing to meet unrealistic targets be considered a failure? Second, even if you meet all of these targets, does the
project solve the problem it was intended to solve? Does the
customer use it? If not, was it really a success? As you can
see, these are nontrivial questions.

Schutz, Sleven, and Pinto (1987) have identified four errors that can be made in solving problems, and as we have
said, project management is problem solving on a large scale,
so their concept applies equally well in this area. These are:

1. Type I error: Not taking an action when one should
    be taken.
2. Type II error: Taking an action when none should be
    taken.
3. Type III error: Taking the wrong action (solving the
    wrong problem).
4. Type IV error: Addressing the right problem, but the
    solution is not used.

Based on their terms, we can say that a project that meets its *C, P, T,* and *S* targets but is not used is either a Type III or Type IV error. In some cases, it is the fact that a Type III error has been made that ultimately causes the project to be a Type IV error. That is, we have solved the wrong problem, so no one uses the project. This happens on internal software projects sometimes when we talk to department managers about their requirements and implement the system based on their comments, but their people won't use the system because it does not really meet their needs.

OTHER PERSPECTIVES

In their book *Learning from Failure: The Systems Approach,* Fortune and Peters (1995) say, "A simple definition of failure is something that has gone wrong, or not lived up to expectations. Moving a little way beyond this simple statement, various types or categories of failure can be identified" (p. 21).

> A simple definition of failure is that something has gone wrong or has not lived up to expectations.

They go on to establish four types of failures, much like Schutz, et al. These are shown in Table 9–1. Type 1 failures

T A B L E   9–1

Types of Failures

Type 1	Objectives not met
Type 2	Undesirable side effects
Type 3	Designed failures
Type 4	Inappropriate objectives

are those that we encounter every day. Examples are software that never worked properly or a new product that won't sell.

For Type 2 failures, the original objectives are met, but there are undesirable consequences or side effects that result. Most of today's environmental problems are the consequences of solutions to problems we had yesterday. Fortune and Peters cite the drug thalidomide as an example of a product that seemed beneficial but caused numerous birth defects. We also have the example of leaking breast implants that nearly destroyed Dow-Corning. So we are surrounded by many Type 2 errors.

The next category of failure is one that is intentional and, therefore, is not considered bad. A fuse that is designed to blow (fail) when a certain current level is exceeded by an appliance is an example. Sprinkler systems fail to hold water in pipes when a fire breaks out. These are called Type 3 failures.

> It is extremely important that criteria be developed that are mutually agreed upon as definitions of success by major stakeholders before projects are started.

The fourth category of failure is similar to Schutz, et al., Type III, solving the wrong problem. Examples include installing a conveyor to reduce breakage of manufactured goods that does not solve the breakage problem, but moves goods around the factory just fine; products that work fine but don't meet the needs of the market; and the Apple III computer, which was probably technically superior to the IBM-PC at the time but was not accepted in the marketplace because of IBM's superior name and because no software was available to run business applications. We might say the same about Beta format in video players. The format was technically superior to VHS, but because Sony tried to keep it proprietary, VHS was adopted by most manufacturers and Beta eventually died in the home entertainment market. (Most studio-quality recorders still use Beta format.)

As Fortune and Peters go on to say, almost all judgments about failure are subjective; they are colored by personal perception, circumstances, and expectations. I have a client company in which people lament that the actual person with whom they work in a customer organization will regard their work as successful, while that person's boss will call it a failure. No doubt this is often true where multiple stakeholders are involved, and it illustrates how important it is that criteria be developed that are mutually agreed upon as definitions of success before such projects are started.

RESEARCH FINDINGS

In 1974, Murphy, Baker, and Fisher reported the results of a study of over 650 projects to determine the factors that affect project success. This study is summarized in Cleland and King's *Project Management Handbook*. They asked the questions, "Why are some projects perceived as failures when they met the *P, C, T,* and *S* targets?" and "Why are others considered successes even when they are late and over budget?" Based on their study, they decided that success must be defined as follows:

> If the project meets the technical performance specifications and/or mission to be performed, and if there is a high level of satisfaction concerning the project outcome among key people in the parent organization, key people in the client organization, key people on the project team, and key users or clientele of the project effort, the project is considered an overall success (Baker, et al., 1974, p. 903).

Note that this is all a matter of *perceptions*. If the right people perceive that the project was a success, then it was, for

all practical purposes. The definition does not include schedule and cost performance as criteria for success. The authors
go on to say that one reason for this is that the research was
conducted on com-
pleted projects. No
doubt those not yet
finished are under
pressure to meet
cost and schedule
targets, but once a

> If the right people consider a project a success, it is, for all practical purposes.

job is complete, if it satisfies a lot of key people in terms of
satisfying their needs, the missed cost and schedule targets
become less important.

The study identified a number of variables that are important for perceived project success and a number that contribute to perceived project failure. An important finding was
that for a project to be perceived as successful, many, if not
most, of the variables associated with success must be present. Similarly, most, if not all, of the variables associated with
failure must be absent.

They also confirmed something that contradicts what
many managers seem to believe about project management:
It is not just scheduling! PERT/CPM do contribute to project
success, but the importance of scheduling is far outweighed
by other factors, including the use of tools known as system
management concepts. These include work breakdown structures, life-cycle planning, systems engineering, configuration
management, and status reports. In fact, the overuse of
PERT/CPM was found to hamper success! The reason is that
the project manager spends so much time updating the
schedule that day-to-day managing suffers.

Baker et al. report that seven broad factors contribute to
project success. This is based on a regression analysis of the
data. Taken together, these seven factors explain 91 percent
of the variance in perceived project success, which is strongly
compelling. These are listed in Table 9–2. They are all statisti-

T A B L E   9–2

Factors That Contribute to Project Success

Determining Factor	Regression Coefficient	Cumulative R^2
Coordination and relations	+.347	.773
Adequacy of project structure and control	+.187	.830
Project uniqueness, importance, public exposure	+.145	.877
Success criteria salience and consensus	+.254	.886
Competitive and budgetary pressure	−.153	.897
Initial overoptimism, conceptual difficulty	−.215	.905
Internal capabilities buildup	+.084	.911

cally significant to a probability of less than 0.001. The table shows the standardized regression coefficient, together with the cumulative R^2 for each variable.

Note that a negative regression coefficient means that the direction of the effect is reversed. In other words, while increased coordination causes an increase in project success, an increase in competitive pressure will cause a *decrease* in project success.

Because coordination and relations alone account

> Project managers can achieve high levels of perceived success, even under adverse circumstances.

for 77 percent of the variance in perceived project success, it is instructive to take a closer look at just what this means. Box

B O X 9–1

COORDINATION AND RELATIONS FACTOR

Unity between project manager and functional
   managers
Project team spirit, sense of mission, goal commitment,
   and capability
Unity between project manager and public officials,
   client contact, and his superior
Project manager's human and administrative skills
Realistic progress reports
Supportive informal relations of team members
Authority of project manager
Adequacy of change procedures
Job security of project team
Project team participation in decision making and
   major problem solving
Parent enthusiasm
Availability of back-up strategies

9–1 contains a summary listing of the factors that make up
the overall variable.

Since there are a number of factors that cause people to
perceive a project as a failure, and since these must be
avoided, I have listed them in Box 9–2. Note again that you
must *perform* those things that cause perceived project success and *avoid* doing those that cause perceived failure.

One final note about the study: Project managers are
sometimes inclined to complain about their situation and say
that they cannot succeed because of its adverse nature. The
authors concluded that project managers actually can achieve
high levels of perceived project success, even under adverse
circumstances, if they properly attend to the factors listed in
the boxes.

B O X   9–2

CHARACTERISTICS THAT AFFECT PERCEIVED PROJECT FAILURE

Insufficient use of progress/status reports
Use of superficial status reports
Inadequate project manager administrative, human, and
    technical skills
Insufficient project manager influence and authority
Poor coordination with client
Lack of rapport with client and parent organization
Client disinterest in budget criteria
Lack of project team participation in decision making
    and problem solving
Excessive structuring within the project team
Job insecurity within the project team
Lack of team spirit and sense of mission within the
    project team
Parent organization stable, nondynamic, lacking
    strategic change
Poor coordination with parent organization
New "type" of project
Project more complex than parent has handled
    previously
Initial underfunding
Inability to freeze design early
Inability to close out the effort
Unrealistic project schedules
Inadequate change procedures

TARGETS AND VARIATION

I mentioned at the beginning of this chapter that failure is often defined as not meeting the C, P, T, or S targets, but I question whether it is failure to meet targets that have been set

based upon wishful thinking. Unless targets are realistic to begin with, everyone associated with a project is getting set up. If I, as a project manager, agree to meet targets that I am pretty sure are unrealistic, because my manager puts pressure on me to do so, then we are both being set up. Eventually, when I can't meet the unrealistic target, my manager is going to be in trouble as well. So I have an obligation to insist on committing only to targets that are realistic.

How do you know if a target is realistic? You only know if it is based on some history. Until you make estimates at a level in a work breakdown structure where tasks are somewhat repeatable and you have some history on similar tasks, you are guessing. And even then, there are tolerances on all estimates. We should understand that working times for *all* activities are probabilistic, not deterministic. Yet we assign durations to activities based on best guesses, then link them together, do deterministic calculations to find critical paths, float, and so on.

> We should understand that working times for *all* activities are probabilistic, not deterministic.

A colleague of mine, Tom Conlon, has informally studied a number of networks to see how sensitive the deadline is to variations in various task durations and has been very surprised at some of the results. The critical path itself is often trivial in determining the end date for a project. It may well be some path that has a great deal of float that "sinks the ship," because it has a great deal of uncertainty (translate that into variability) associated with the work.

If you think about it, there is reason to wonder how any project is ever successful, as defined by coming in on schedule. I believe the only way this ever happens is that we vary the effort applied to meet the times. However, if you track both schedule performance and actual hours worked against

B O X   9–3

SOME SOURCES OF VARIATION IN PROJECT WORK

Estimate of task duration is based on a small sample (it has only been done a few times before).

The person for whom the original estimate was made is not available to do the work when the time comes.

Sharing resources on multiple projects causes increased setup time, with corresponding decrease in work efficiency.

Unexpected technical problems cause tasks to take longer than expected.

People are stolen from the project to put out fires on other projects.

Long stretches of overtime cause fatigue, which causes errors, which leads to more overtime, which leads to . . .

Work has to be done over because mistakes are made. May be due to poor planning, communication errors, etc.

Illness, serious personal problems, child care, jury duty, etc.

original estimated hours, I think you will find that the price paid is in large variances of actual compared to estimated working hours. Consider the many causes of variation shown in Box 9–3.

Here, too, there are unrealistic expectations about what magnitude of variance is likely in project work. Many managers who have experience with department budgeting think that project budgets should be held to the same tight tolerances that are possible with departments. But projects aren't budgeted the same way as departments. In a department, you budget for next year by looking at forecasted headcount. You tally up the salary increases you plan to give, add in the cost of rubber bands, paper clips, computers, and other supplies, and away you go. Such budgets can often be held to a few percent.

A project, on the other hand, is based on how much work has to be done, and that exact quantity is not well

F I G U R E 9–1

Ultimate Certainty of Project Costs

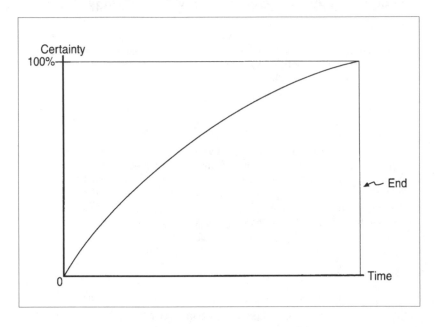

known at the outset, so labor costs cannot be accurately determined. There is a saying that the ultimate certainty of project cost increases the closer you get to the end. This is shown in Figure 9-1.

The one thing that we must all do is accept variability. It is a part of any process. You can reduce it over time, but you can never eliminate it. There is an injunction that is sometimes heard in organizations: You cannot go over budget—but neither can you come in under budget. Such an injunction is asking that people violate a law of nature. If they do it—that is, come in right on target—it is always through fancy footwork or pure accident. It is not because they were able to actually control work to achieve the result.

10

Organizing for Project Management

Strictly speaking, the form of organization used to manage projects is usually not controlled by project managers, but by senior managers. However, it is important for project managers to understand the implications of various forms of organization and even to recommend to senior managers the structure that is best for their particular environment. In this chapter, we will examine some of the more common organizational forms and consider under what conditions they are appropriate.

PROJECT ORGANIZATION

There are currently three general forms of organization structure used in projects. One is called *pure-project* form by most people. Another is the infamous *matrix*. The third is the so-called *virtual* organization. There are also a number of variations on these. Whatever form is used, the choice of structure is intended to make it possible for the project manager to control resources, communication, and coordination within the project team.

Pure-Project Structure

In pure-project form, all members of the project team are assigned on a full-time basis. Their entire loyalty, then, is to the
project. They report directly (or perhaps indirectly) to the
project manager. In some cases they are scattered throughout
the building. In others, they are all housed physically under
one roof.

When projects are multidisciplinary, that is, involve
team members from a number of different professions,
trades, or specialties, pure-project organization is often used
to ensure that everyone has complete dedication to the project. The most extreme form of pure-project organization is to
have all members of the team co-located. This way, no one
can reassign a team member to other work without going
through the project manager. In addition, by having them
close together, they can communicate with each other more
effectively than if they are scattered all over the building.
Studies have shown that people separated by more than 30
feet rarely communicate with each other. While this may no
longer be true with the widespread use of e-mail, I still believe
that there are significant differences between face-to-face communication and that done through e-mail.

There are a number of problems with pure-project format. For one thing, if the team is multidisciplinary, the project manager is going to have difficulty understanding the
problems that some team members may have. It is impossible
to be conversant in all disciplines. Further, when it comes
time to do performance appraisals, since the project manager
does not understand the work, she will have a hard time doing a valid appraisal. This is a disadvantage for the employee
as well as the manager.

Another problem is that it can be nearly impossible to
keep everyone level-loaded in a multidisciplinary, pure-project
team. You may only have enough work for one specialist to
keep him occupied 25 percent of the time. What does he do
the rest of the time? Chances are, he will spin his wheels do-

ing nothing.
project costs
When
pure-projec
are norma
where the
individua
peers to
is going
she gets
Pu
Couill
cal risk, _
project success. He io_
jects, presumably because tecnии__
easily drawn from a matrix structure than from _
ject structure. (See also Chapter 15 on managing risk for moi_
details of Couillard's study.)

Virtual Organizations

In today's global economy, a number of organizations are running projects in which team members are scattered all over the U.S. and even the world. One example of this is in software development. It turns out that India has some excellent programmers, and their pay in India is considerably less than that of programmers in the U.S. A large number of these people are located in Bangalore, which is often referred to as the software capital of India. The beauty of such work is that the people can work independently. In addition, what they produce can be transported electronically, so a lot of the code that they write is sent by satellite broadcast.

When people are scattered all over the world, we call the resulting format a *virtual organization*. Some of the stories I have heard about this working arrangement lead me to believe that it should be called a virtual *dis*-organization, but regardless of my opinion, it is used frequently. One form is that

...ere really is no difference between ...having members of your team scat-...uge building or in several buildings that ...rge plot or possibly throughout town. Ei-...e are in no position to conveniently talk ...they must resort to e-mail or telephone.

...re enough companies that have experience with ...ganization that some consultants are emerging who ...ze in helping organizations solve the special problems ...esult from this format. There are a few guidelines that ...n universal. One is that frequent communications are ab-...lutely essential, especially for members on the critical path in the project schedule. One company found that people on that path should be *virtually co-located*. This is another euphemism, but what it means is that these individuals must talk with each other daily in order to maintain coordination and communication at the required level.

Another guideline is that the entire group should be brought together near the beginning of the project for one face-to-face meeting. Otherwise, it is very hard for all the players to ever get to know each other. Ideally, this meeting would be the kick-off meeting for the project.

Matrix Organization

I earlier called matrix "infamous." The reason is that this has traditionally been the most difficult to manage. It is the form in which project managers truly have a lot of responsibility but no authority. The reason for the term *matrix* is shown in Figure 10–1. In this arrangement, the company is organized by functions. That is, we have people grouped together to perform the various functions needed by the organization. As examples, we have marketing, engineering, production, accounting, and human resources grouped together. Within each of these groups (or departments, as we usually call them), there may be specialties. In human resources, for ex-

F I G U R E   10–1

Matrix Organization

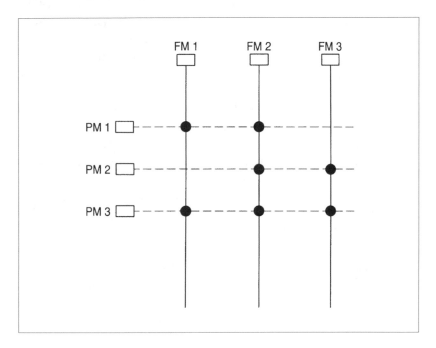

ample, there may be a person who deals with benefits, another who handles recruitment, and someone else who handles grievances.

When project teams are formed, members are recruited from the functional departments. In pure matrix form, they do not leave their departments. Rather, they stay physically where they are and still report directly to their functional manager and indirectly to the project manager. This creates the one-person, two-boss system that almost everyone will advise you to avoid.

Why, then, do we use it?

Because it solves a lot of problems for project managers. In any multidisciplinary team, there will be team members performing work that the project manager knows nothing about. When you know nothing about the work of someone on your team, you have two problems. First, you cannot be certain that the person is performing either the right quantity or quality of work. This means that you cannot tell if the time estimates given to you by the team member are valid, nor whether the person is staying on schedule once the work starts. Furthermore, you cannot give the person a valid performance appraisal, since you know nothing about the technical aspects of his job. By having team members stay in their functional departments, the functional manager can review their performance and give them guidance on their work, besides being the project manager's go-between to judge whether the quantity of work being done by the person is sufficient.

Another advantage of matrix is that many projects do not need full-time effort from all team members. By leaving them in their functional groups, the functional manager can keep the individual properly loaded. Otherwise, if the person were assigned to the team full-time, the project manager would have to pay for dead time when the person had nothing to do.

Finally, one benefit of leaving people in their functional departments is that they can draw on each other for help when they need it. If you physically remove them from their departments, they may have no one to turn to for help when they are stumped on a technical issue. True, they can still call someone on the phone, but oftentimes, if the person has been away from the functional group for very long, he loses the connections that make it easy for him to ask his peers for help.

PROBLEMS WITH MATRIX

As I said earlier, a number of authors have strongly advised against the use of matrix because of all the problems it presents. However, a recent study suggests that matrix should not be condemned out-of-hand. El-Najdawi and Liberatore (1997) presented the results of their survey of 29 project managers in corporations that are primary or secondary contractors to the U.S. government and who use the matrix format. They found that goal conflict is the primary disadvantage of the matrix organization. This means conflicting goals between project managers and functional managers. The project manager naturally has only his or her own project goals to worry about, while the functional manager is trying to meet the goals of the functional department along with the goals of all projects that he or she is supporting. The conflict of goals leads to slow reaction time in making resource allocation decisions.

The authors also found that communicating long-range project objectives to functional managers is a significant concern. They therefore conclude that this indicates a need for project managers in matrix organizations to be very skilled at interfacing and communicating with functional managers in order to ease conflicts and clarify goals (p. 30). Their finding confirms what many of us have known for a long time: The relationship with functional managers is a key to success in this organizational structure.

El-Najdawi and Liberatore conclude that "the failure of matrix management is often a result of goal conflict between program and functional managers rather than a fundamental problem with the matrix structure itself" (p. 31).

MAKING PROJECTS KING

Perhaps one of the reasons for problems with matrix is that, in most companies, the functional department is king and projects just present a nuisance to functional managers who must try to staff them. This might be acceptable when a company has only a very few projects going at any time. However, for those companies that live and die by projects, it seems to me that a simple change in perspective would be useful. That perspective is that the functional departments exist *primarily* to ensure that projects are successful. By making projects top priority, functional managers would have to think seriously before they shuffle resources from one team to another or pull them off project teams to get functional department work done. In addition, the organization would elevate the project manager's role to a status comparable to that of functional managers. I believe this thinking is needed in a lot of companies. El-Najdawi and Liberatore make the same case a little less strongly, saying ". . . the balance of power in matrix organizations in the military and aerospace industries must shift in favor of the program managers" (p. 31).

TOOLS AND TECHNIQUES

11

CHAPTER

A Review of the Standard Tools

Because this book is intended to go beyond the standard tools of project management, a firm foundation in those tools is essential. Of course, to cover them in depth would be to write a book within a book on the subject, so this chapter will be a very brief review of how to plan, schedule, and control projects using work breakdown structures (WBS), critical path or PERT scheduling, and earned value analysis (EVA). If you need more in-depth treatment of any of these than is provided in this text, you should consult my introductory book, entitled *Project Planning, Scheduling, and Control,* Fourth Edition, also published by McGraw-Hill.

Before getting into the *how* of managing projects, it might be helpful to first consider what we mean by project management. I define project management as the planning, scheduling, and controlling of activities to meet project objectives. These objectives will include cost, performance, time, and scope. The cost objective is normally called the project budget. Performance has to do with the quality of the work that is done. Time is the schedule, and most projects in today's world are deadline-driven. Scope is the magnitude of the work to be done. These are related as follows:

$$C = f(P, T, S)$$

This expression reads: Cost is a *function* of **Performance, Time,** and **Scope.** Ideally, we could write a true algebraic equation for these, but practically we cannot. We are always estimating the values of the variables. However, we do know that if this were an equation, we could assign values to any three of the variables, and the fourth one would be whatever the equation says it would be. To understand this better, consider Figure 11–1.

Note that if we assign values to the sides of the triangle, the area (scope) of the project is defined. In other words, you could say, "Here's what you will get for this cost, over this

F I G U R E   11–1

Relationship between Cost, Performance, Time, and Scope

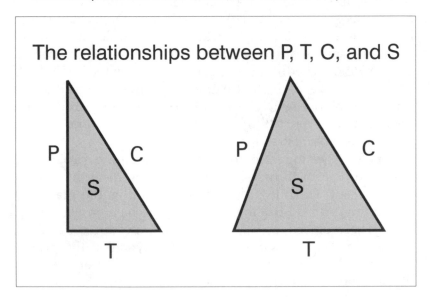

The relationships between P, T, C, and S

time, at this performance level. If you want more scope than is going to be achieved with this combination, you have to change one of the sides, usually cost."

I consider this relationship to be the most important thing that a project manager should know, because you are always making tradeoffs among them. A project manager should be prepared to show senior managers that they can pick three of the variables, but he or she (the project manager) gets to pick the remaining one.

A MODEL FOR MANAGING PROJECTS

If you are going to manage projects successfully, you need to follow some standard approach. This is sometimes called a project management *methodology* or simply a project management system. There are consulting firms that charge upwards of $100,000 for a methodology. I'm going to give you one in this book for a whole lot less. (If you want to send me a check for $100,000, I'll be glad to accept it.)

> A project is a job that is done one time. Cooking a meal is a project. Brain surgery is a project. Sending someone to the moon is also.

Before presenting my methodology, let me say that there *can* be a standard approach to running *any* kind of project, whether it be product development, construction, research, information systems, or whatever. Project management is a *disciplined thought process,* not to be confused with the content of what is being done. Two plus two equals four, no matter whether you apply it to finance, engineering, or foods. Furthermore, the same thought process can be applied to small, medium, or large projects. What differs between them is the amount of documentation required for various size projects. Small projects only require a few pages, whereas large ones require considerably more.

In Figure 11–2 is my methodology for managing projects, shown as a flowchart. If you follow this process, it will enhance your chances of being successful with your projects. If you aren't used to reading flowcharts, just follow the arrows and be aware that diamonds are decision points, where questions get answered. The questions are framed to be answered "yes" or "no."

> **Problem:** A problem is a gap between where you are and where you want to be that is confronted by some obstacle(s). If there are no obstacles, there is no problem—only a desired goal.

The first step is called the concept step. All projects begin as a concept. Someone has an idea for a project. The thing is that too often that concept is accepted as the final definition of what is to be done without ever questioning the validity of the idea. For that reason, step 2 involves defining the problem that will be solved by the project, determining the mission, and formulating a vision for the end result.

Step 2 calls for a problem statement. That is because all projects are done to solve some problem for the organization. Note, however, that we do not mean problem in a negative sense necessarily. Developing a new product is a project, by this definition, but a very positive one. So is

> Projects don't fail at the end, they fail at the beginning—usually at step 2 in my model.

reengineering an organization to improve a process. The point, however, is to define the problem correctly so that you don't make the mistake of developing the right solution for the *wrong problem*.

F I G U R E   11–2

A General Model of Project Management

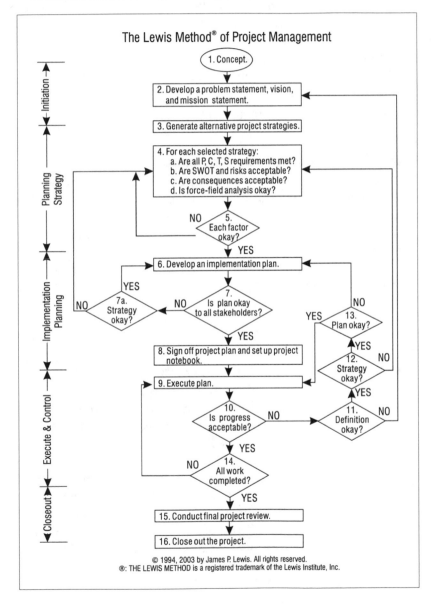

The Lewis Method® of Project Management

In fact, it is in step 2 that many projects go wrong. I often say that projects don't fail at the end, they fail at the beginning—right here in step 2. The reason is that we take for granted that we all understand the problem perfectly, when this is not the case at all.

Once the problem is correctly understood, you should try to visualize the problem as being solved. In other words, what would the world look like if the problem were solved? This image is called the vision

> **Vision:** What the final result will look like.

for the project. If you were developing a new product, the vision would be what the new product is going to look like, how it will function, and so on. If you were reengineering a process, you would visualize the new process as being more efficient, perhaps less wasteful, and so on.

Now that these two steps have been taken, writing the mission statement is simple—it is to solve the problem by achieving the vision. The formal statement should answer two questions: (1) What are

> **Mission:** What we are going to do and for whom.

we going to do? and (2) For whom are we doing it?

In step 3, you develop strategies for the project. There are two strategies that must be considered for most projects. One is the project strategy itself. The second is the technical strategy that will be employed. Let's use "feeding your family" as an example of the two strategies. First, you can feed them by cooking from scratch, ordering home delivery, cooking frozen or canned foods, or going out to a restaurant (to name a few). These are all project strategies. If you choose to cook from scratch, technical strategy might be whether you cook on a conventional stove or microwave the food. You can also bake, broil, grill, or use convection cooking.

Ideally, you would brainstorm a list of possible project and technical strategies in step 3 and then select the best combination in step 4. This selection is made through some analysis. First, can you meet your cost, performance, time, and scope targets? At this point in the planning process, this question cannot be answered very

> **Strategy:** The approach to be employed in doing the project. Two strategies may be involved: *project* and *technical.*

accurately. What can sometimes be done, however, is to reject certain approaches. This is done by realizing that you are fairly certain that you can't meet the targets with a particular strategy.

Next, you do a SWOT and risk analysis. What are our *s*trengths, *w*eaknesses, *o*pportunities, and *t*hreats for this project, what risks are there, and can we deal with them? Risk management is covered in this book in Chapter 15.

The next issue is consequences. Are there unintended consequences of adopting this particular strategy for the project? For example, I know of a company that wanted to optimize the use of capital investment, so they decided to get rid of the machines that were used to make certain parts. They sold the machinery to a local shop with the understanding that they would buy their parts from the shop in the future. This worked fine until the machine shop ran out of raw materials and had to reorder. Then the shock hit!

When the company owned the machines, they bought raw materials through corporate purchasing. These were purchased in boxcar loads, then distributed to the divisions at substantial discounts. The small machine shop, however, was ordering a few hundred feet of stock at a time, and the price was considerably higher than that of a boxcar load. So, naturally, the price increase was passed along to the company. This was an unintended consequence of a strategy to limit capital investment.

Finally, we are asked to do a force-field analysis to determine if the strategy being considered will be acceptable to all stakeholders. An example of this comes from Avondale shipyards. During World War II, they were under pressure to produce ships as fast as possible. In looking at their process, they identified two problems in the way they had always built ships. When you build ships out of wood, you build them right-side up. When you make them out of steel, however, welding in the keel area requires that you literally stand on your head. Not only is this difficult, but it is hard to do good quality work. Furthermore, when you try to weld the sides, which are formed from heavy steel plate, the shape of the ship causes that plate to deform outwards, so that you again have quality problems with the welds.

Someone suggested that it would be easier to build steel boats upside down.

Can you imagine the response from some old-timer who has been building ships for a long time? "I've been building ships for nearly 40 years," he protests, "and we never built them upside down. Dumbest thing I ever heard of."

If this person is in a position of power in the company, he is a force to reckon with. Failing to consider that force and how to deal with it could easily cause the strategy to be jeopardized.

In step 5 we ask if the strategy is okay. If the answer is yes, we can proceed to implementation planning. If not, we cycle back to step 4 and select another combination of strategies to analyze until we finally find one that will work.

In step 6 we have to decide exactly how the project will be done. We answer the following basic questions:

1. What must be done?
2. Who will do each task?
3. How long will each activity take?
4. What will it cost?
5. In what order must things be done?

And so on. Answering these questions is the essence of implementation planning. That doesn't make answering them easy, of course. In some cases, you can only answer some of these questions by reference to a crystal ball. Nevertheless, they must be answered.

In step 7 we ask if the plan is okay to all stakeholders. If it is, we can get the plan signed off (step 8) and set up in a project notebook. If not, we may have to change the strategy (step 7a) or just revise the implementation plan. The best way to get an approval of a plan is for the major stakeholders to have participated in putting the plan together.

> **Stakeholder:** Anyone who has a vested interest in the project. This includes customers, financial managers, contributors, contractors, and so on.

In step 9 we can begin working on the project. As we do the work, we review progress periodically and ask if we are on target (step 10). Note that this question is asked for all four targets—cost, performance, time, and scope. If the answer is yes, we continue. The next question is whether the work is complete (step 15). As long as the answer is no, we just cycle back to step 9 and keep going until the answer finally is yes. Then we should do a final project review (step 16) before we consider the project to be absolutely complete.

Consider now the case in step 10 where the answer to the question is no. That is, progress is not acceptable. Now we are in the control mode. The first question we ask is whether the definition of the problem is okay. That is, are we on the right track, or have we defined the problem being solved incorrectly? If we have, we must return to step 2 and redefine the problem. This is a disaster. We have to start all over on the job. This won't happen too often, but it has to be in the model as a possibility.

If the definition is okay, we go to step 12 and ask if the strategy is okay. Remember, we have to ask this about both project and technical strategies, because either one can be a problem. For example, you might have farmed out some of the work to a contractor and you find that the contractor is doing poor-quality work. You have to take steps to correct the problem, either by getting the contractor to improve his performance or by shifting the work to another contractor.

It might also be your technical strategy that is the problem, particularly if you are trying to employ some cutting-edge technology. You get into the execution stage and can't make it work. This is a pretty serious problem in some projects, because you have to start over on that part of the work and this can snowball throughout the project. I suggest that if you have questions about whether you can make a technology work, you should do a feasibility study before you launch a development project using that unproven technology. Whether the outcome of a feasibility study is yes or no, it is a success. On the other hand, when you launch a development project with unproven technology and get this far and can't make it work, that project will probably be deemed a failure.

If the strategy is okay, the next question (step 13) is whether the implementation plan is okay. If the answer is no, you are directed to change the plan, which then takes you back through the sign-off process. This is for everyone's protection. The reasons that the plan is not okay can be numerous. Some of the more common ones are: (1) the scope changes; (2) the work has fallen behind and the schedule cannot be recovered; or (3) people have been pulled off the team to cover a changing priority somewhere else.

If the implementation plan *is* okay, notice that you are directed back to step 9. The implication here is that if the plan is okay but you are not on target, then you must not be following the plan, so you are told to get back in there and do it! The problem is, most of the time this situation happens because resources have been stolen from your project. In that case, the plan really is not okay unless the people can be made available. The way to bring this issue to a head is to do a "what-if" analysis with your scheduling software, present the results to senior management, and ask that they decide what to do.

USING THE WORK BREAKDOWN STRUCTURE FOR PLANNING

When you get to step 6 of my methodology, you develop an implementation plan. This is where you dot all your i's and cross all your t's. The first question that might be asked is, "What must be done?" This is where the work breakdown structure comes in. As shown in Figure 11–3, the WBS breaks the project down into smaller and smaller units until you arrive at a level where decent estimates of time, resources, and costs can be made.

Again, if you are not familiar with how to construct the WBS, refer to my earlier book. Do note that the WBS should be constructed before scheduling and resource assignment is done.

SCHEDULING THE WORK

The tool of choice for scheduling projects is critical path method (CPM). The critical path diagram makes use of arrows to show the order in which work is performed. The method also allows the determination of which path through the project is the longest one, and thereby we can tell the earliest finish for the entire job. This is shown in Figure 11–4.

The critical path diagram is absolutely necessary in order to find the longest path in a very large schedule. Trying to do this with a bar chart can be very misleading, because you might show things being done in parallel that simply can't be done that way. However, a CPM diagram is a terrible working tool. It should always be converted to a bar chart (also called a Gantt chart, after Henry Gantt, who formalized the notation for it). This is a nonissue, since all scheduling software automatically does this.

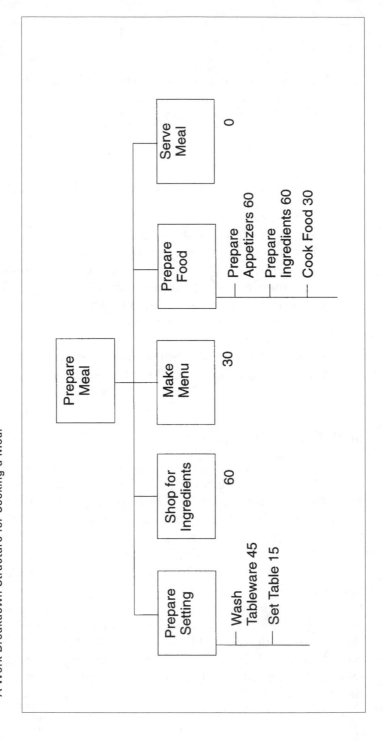

F I G U R E 11-3

A Work Breakdown Structure for Cooking a Meal

Critical Path Diagram for a Project

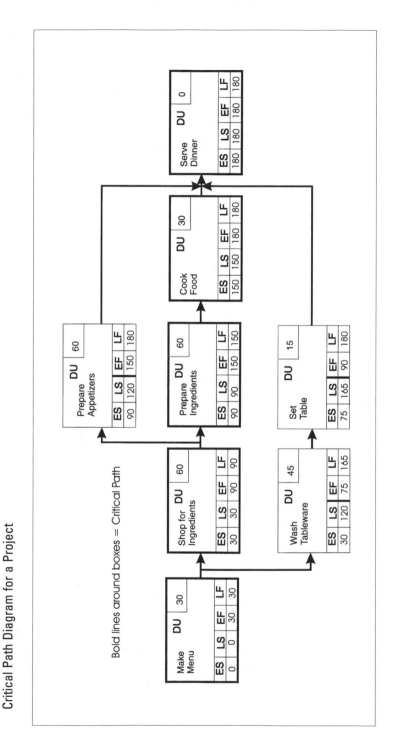

Bold lines around boxes = Critical Path

Make Menu	DU	30					
ES	LS	EF	LF
0	0	30	30

Shop for Ingredients	DU	60
ES	LS	EF	LF
30	30	90	90

Prepare Appetizers	DU	60
ES	LS	EF	LF
90	120	150	180

Prepare Ingredients	DU	60
ES	LS	EF	LF
90	90	150	150

Cook Food	DU	30
ES	LS	EF	LF
150	150	180	180

Serve Dinner	DU	0
ES	LS	EF	LF
180	180	180	180

Wash Tableware	DU	45
ES	LS	EF	LF
30	120	75	165

Set Table	DU	15
ES	LS	EF	LF
75	165	90	180

I would like to make one point about scheduling software. People seem to think that project management is primarily scheduling and, in line with that belief, that if you have a good scheduling package, you will be successful in managing projects. Nothing could be farther from the truth, as we have proven in the past 10 years. The software is just a tool, and without a proper understanding of project management methodology, all it will do is help you document your failures! Furthermore, I don't believe that one size fits all (in clothing *or* in software), and too many organizations get trapped into standardizing on a single package that won't meet everyone's needs. It has been the experience of every company that I have worked with that when they do this, people simply refuse to use the software, and they have just wasted a lot of money.

> Without a proper understanding of project management methodology, all software will do is help you document your failures—with great precision, of course.

In addition, since the software is a tool, you cannot make a valid selection until you know what you are going to do with it in the first place! In other words, we have the cart before the horse. We first need to train people in how to manage projects, then let them select software that will be best for them.

Well, that's the end of that sermon.

TRACKING PROGRESS

As far as I am concerned, the tool of choice for tracking progress in projects is earned value analysis. The method has its detractors, and it is not nearly as simple as just tracking the schedule, but it is much more robust.

Consider the progress report shown in Figure 11-5. Note that the dotted line drawn at January 20 is where we are

FIGURE 11-5

Schedule Showing Progress

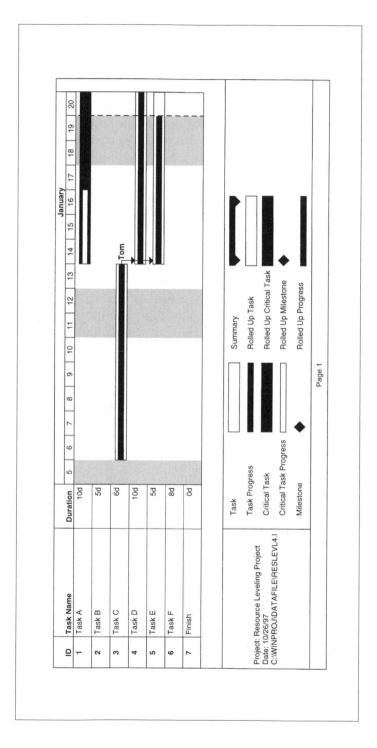

supposed to be as of today. The shaded areas represent weekends, when we are not working. The critical path is shown as a solid black bar, while those tasks that have float are shown with hollow bars. Progress is shown by the small bar that runs inside the task bars. According to this schedule, task A is one day behind schedule. This is serious, since this task is on the critical path. Unless this time can be recovered, we know that the project will slip one day.

Task C is complete. Task D is one day ahead of schedule, and task E is right on target. That is, *if* all the work has really been done correctly. What is missing from this kind of report is whether cost, performance, and scope are really where they should be. We are forced to take on faith that they are correct, but this is not always the case.

There are some organizations that don't track project costs. They either assume that costs are correct or that they don't matter. These are both dangerous assumptions. If people were exactly 100 percent efficient all the time, then you could say that one hour invested yields one hour of productive work, but we know that this is seldom true. So we don't really know what we are getting for our investment unless we track actual work performed.

When you get only $8 worth of snacks for $100, your spending efficiency is extremely low. At this rate, you will go broke very efficiently!

Does it matter?

Well, assume that you send your teenage daughter to the grocery store with $100 and a grocery list, and she returns with four big bags of snacks (worth about $8) and she has spent the $100. Would you be happy? I doubt it. You would say that what you *got* for your $100 was not enough. Your *spending efficiency* would be very low (only 8 percent). In fact, unless we know what we are getting for our money, we are going to get into serious trouble, whether the organization is a for-profit or not-for-profit one.

The other issue, of course, is quality of work (performance). This is incredibly hard to measure in many cases—especially for knowledge work—but some attempt must be made to assess quality or else the end result will be unacceptable. One indirect measure of quality is rework. It is likely that from 5 to 40 percent of design work (including software design) is rework. At 33 percent, which is often the case, this is equivalent to having one of every three designers on the job just to redo what the other two did wrong. Any improvement in quality (reducing rework) is a direct improvement in performance (call it productivity). In a later chapter, we will discuss how concepts from quality can be applied in project management.

> Rework is a direct measure of poor quality. At 33 percent, that is like having one of every three people on the job to just redo what the other two did wrong!

What we would like, rather than the simple reporting of schedule progress, is an accounting of *what we got, how much effort was required,* and *how much effort was originally scheduled.* This is best accomplished by translating everything into a dollar equivalent. For those familiar with earned value analysis, the terms used to measure progress are BCWS (budgeted cost of work scheduled), BCWP (budgeted cost of work performed), and ACWP (actual cost of work performed). These numbers give us the capability to tell where we are with regard to both work efficiency and spending efficiency and enable us to make some predictions about where the project is headed.

For example, studies have found that, by the time a project is 15 percent of the way along the horizontal time line, if it is seriously in trouble, it is very likely to stay in trouble.

You ask, "Why can't I get it back on track?" The answer is simple. The original targets were *forecasts*. If you cannot forecast accurately only 15 percent ahead, then you are not likely to be any better further out. It is like the weather forecast. Tomorrow's forecast might be fairly accurate, but the one for a week from now is likely to be completely off. To confirm that this is true, 800 defense contracts that were in trouble 15 percent of the way along were analyzed, and not one ever got back on target!

> If you can't forecast the near term with any accuracy, you certainly can't forecast the far term with any better accuracy.

Earned value analysis is covered in detail in my book cited previously. In a later chapter of this book, we will go into more depth on how EVA can be used to measure project status and forecast the future.

12 CHAPTER

The Need for Systems Thinking in Project Management

Unless you are very young or in some way exceptional, you almost undoubtedly learned to think in linear-causal terms. I say this because a few schools are beginning to teach systems thinking, some at the urging of Dr. Jay Forrester, one of the pioneers of the discipline.

For most of us, however, the proposition that cause-effect relationships can be described as "A causes B" seems reasonable, and perhaps irrefutable. This has been so often our experience of the world that we seldom stop to think that things do not always operate in this manner. When

> In human interaction, *A* causes *B* causes *A*.

an accident happens, we ask, "What caused it?" If two children get into a fight, we ask, "Who started it?" Interestingly, if the children are asked, they may both point at each other, adamantly claiming, "He did!"

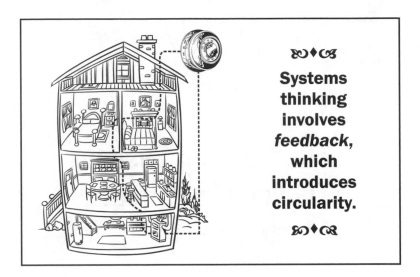

ఴ✦ಌ

**Systems
thinking
involves
feedback,
which
introduces
circularity.**

ఴ✦ಌ

Adults tend to get frustrated at that response. When I was a child and my sister and I would have an altercation, my father would ask, "Who started it?" We would both accuse the other. He would get annoyed at this response and threaten to punish both of us if the *guilty party* didn't confess. In his mind, A causes B. It could not be possible that A causes B causes A, but that is exactly how it works in systems terms.

You might say that at the microsecond level, one party made the first move. However, there is communication at both the verbal and nonverbal levels, and the nonverbal channel is operating continuously in both directions. Since some, if not most, of the influence between humans is a function of the nonverbal channel, that influence is operating simultaneously, so again, it does not operate linearly, but circularly.

In systems thinking, you must abandon linear causality and talk in terms of circular causal effects. This is because systems involve *feedback*, which introduces circularity. This is shown in Figure 12–1. When you are heating your home in the winter, the thermostat senses the room temperature and tells the furnace to turn on when the temperature drops be-

Heating System

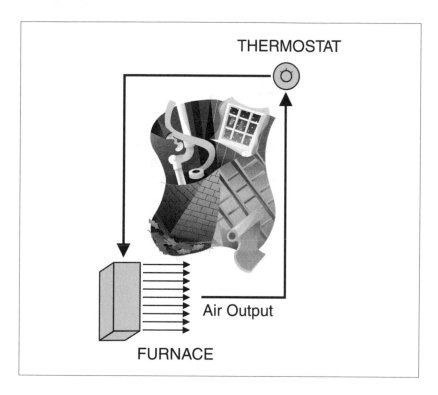

low the level at which the thermostat is set. As the heat causes the room to warm up, the thermostat sends another signal to the furnace, telling it to shut down.

We can say, then, that as the temperature drops, the furnace comes on and causes the temperature to rise, which causes the furnace to stop, and that causes the temperature to drop and so on, in a limitless number of cycles. Notice how convoluted our language becomes when we try to describe circularity. Our language itself is inherently linear. Notice:

Johnny hit the ball.

Johnny is the subject. The action is that he *hit*, and the object is the ball. Johnny is "A" in the equation A causes B, and the ball is "B." The causal link is *hit*. Notice that the verb hit can be replaced with all kinds of action descriptors: stole, dropped, held, threw, saw, accepted, liked, and so on.

It would be just as accurate to say that the ball hit Johnny's bat, as the bat swung through an arc, and rebounded at almost the same velocity at which it hit the bat. It would be just as accurate. But it would take forever to say anything.

Consider this sentence: Johnny cried until his mother gave him some cake, and then he smiled. It is a linear flow, but it does involve a reciprocal action. The action goes from A to B and back to A. Johnny's crying causes his mother to give him some cake, which causes him to smile. A causes B causes A.

THE LANGUAGE OF MANAGING

This same linear-causal thinking carries over into managing. Managers are supposed to "make things happen." One common definition of managing is that "a manager gets work done through other people." This suggests that she is a causal agent and that she does no work herself. A causes B.

Now suppose the employee does not do what the manager has directed should be done. Then the manager will respond. She may give the directive again, probably in more forceful terms. If there is still no response, she may take disciplinary action. How do we understand this exchange in systems terms? The manager is A and the employee is B. A causes B causes A causes B causes A. The employee's response to the first directive causes the manager to give another directive, which elicits another response from the employee, which causes another directive (or discipline) from the manager, and so on.

Causality in human relations, then, is circular and must be drawn as shown in Figure 12–2.

There are times when the action of one person causes the other person to do more of what he was doing and other times when the action causes him to do less. For example, behavioral reinforcement theory suggests that rewarding a person for performing well on the job will usually make him try to perform even better in the future. Thus, positive reinforcement (sometimes called positive "strokes") increases desired performance. This is shown as a graph in Figure 12–3.

Conversely, negative reinforcement should cause a behavior to diminish. If the behavior being displayed is undesired, then negative reinforcement should extinguish it. Unfortunately, there are times when desired behavior is also extinguished because it is negatively reinforced. See Figure 12–4.

F I G U R E   12–2

Circularity in Human Relations

Positive Reinforcement Increases Desired Behavior

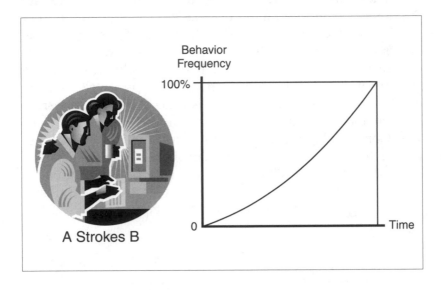

A Strokes B

Negative Reinforcement Extinguishes Behavior

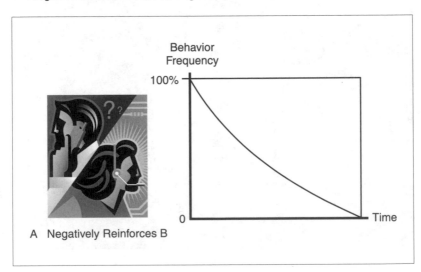

A   Negatively Reinforces B

It is interesting to consider the interaction between a manager and employee in terms of behavioral reinforcement. If a manager strokes an employee for good performance and the employee performs even better in the future, what effect does this have on the manager? She is rewarded for stroking the employee. What does she do? She strokes him even more. His performance improves. She is rewarded. She strokes the employee again, and so on. (Who is controlling whom?) This is called a *positive feedback loop,* in which each action is followed by a reaction of increasing strength. Can this go on forever? No.

Eventually the employee becomes satiated with strokes or the manager becomes fatigued from so much stroking. There are always limits to growth in any system. Note that as a person becomes satiated with strokes, each additional stroke loses some value. Thus, there is nonlinearity in the system. This is shown in Figure 12–5.

F I G U R E 12–5

The Value of Strokes Diminishes as the Quantity Increases

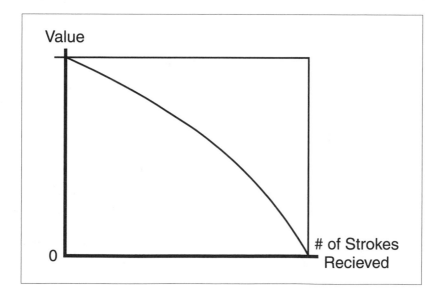

The opposite effect is also possible. An employee suffering from "stroke deficit disorder," a term I have borrowed from organization development specialist Lee Kleese (1996), values strokes much more highly than someone who is in "stroke overload." People tend to suffer from stroke deficit disorder at the left side of the curve in Figure 12–5 and to suffer stroke overload on the right side of the curve.

CONTROL IN RELATIONSHIPS

In all human relations there is a constant struggle to define the relationship. There are basically two kinds of relationships, as defined by status. These are either symmetrical, meaning equal-status, or they are complementary, which is unequal-status. Every communication between two individuals carries a proposed definition of the relationship, as defined by status. Note that the communication can be verbal or nonverbal. If you have forgotten, nonverbal aspects of a communication include body gestures and/or posture, tone of voice, inflections, phrasing, and so on. Verbal communication is strictly the words themselves.

Consider the following question:

Can you *solve* the problem?

By stressing the word *solve,* the meaning is something like, "Is it possible for the problem to be solved at all, or is it likely that it will come back again?"

Now suppose the stress is changed:

Can *you* solve the problem?

The meaning is very different. There seems to be doubt that this particular individual can solve the problem. Perhaps someone else can, but not this person. The meaning of the words has changed just by changing the stress on one word in the sentence.

Now suppose a supervisor says to an employee:

Have your report to me by 3 o'clock tomorrow.

This communication suggests that the supervisor sees the relation with this employee as very complementary (unequal status). Compare this to:

Would you please get your report to me by
3 o'clock tomorrow?

In both cases, the message is the same: The supervisor wants the report by 3 o'clock tomorrow. However, in the second case the relationship definition offered by the supervisor is more equal-status or symmetrical.

Does it matter?

Sometimes it does. In American culture, we recognize that there are status differentials between supervisors and employees, but we do not like them to be emphasized too strongly. If the employee feels that the supervisor is "coming on too strong," then he may get angry. This can result in a conflict in which the two try to define the relationship in mutually acceptable terms.

It is bad enough for us to have to interpret relationship definitions from the nonverbal component of a communication. It is even worse when a person offers a definition opposite the one he really wants.

LET'S GO OUT FOR DINNER

Lee Kleese, whom I cited previously, has a wonderful example of this. You come home from work dead tired. Your significant other says, "Dear, I've had a really hard day and obviously you have too, so why don't we go out for dinner."

"That's a great idea," you say. "Where would you like to go?"

"I don't care. Where would you like to go?"

Now you say, "I don't care," but inside you're thinking, "If you loved me as much as I love you, you'd say steak."

"Well, if it really doesn't matter, I'd like to try that new Chinese restaurant. Everyone says it's really good."

There may be a momentary flash of disappointment on your face, but this quickly changes to a forced smile and you say, "Okay. Let's go."

Inside you're thinking, "Chinese! That doesn't have *anything* to do with steak. I'll go, but you owe me one."

Some time goes by. You come home from work again, dead tired, and your significant other says, "Dear, I'm really tired and you seem to be also. Why don't we go out to dinner."

"Great idea," you say. "Where would you like to go?"

"I don't care."

"Me either." But the little voice inside is saying, "If you loved me as much as I love you, you'd say *steak*."

"Well, if you really don't care, I'd like to try that Italian place on Vine Avenue. Margie says it's really good."

"Italian!" the little voice screams. "That doesn't have anything to do with steak."

This time, the little voice wins. "I don't want to eat Italian," you say. "I want to eat steak."

"Well, why didn't you say so?" says your significant other politely. "Let's go."

So you go eat steak.

Do you think you're going to enjoy it?

Not a chance!

Now the problem is that you have offered a definition of your relationship with your significant other that is symmetrical. What you really would like to do, of course, is call the shots and choose steak. When your significant other chooses something else, you get upset. It would be much clearer if you had said, "Well, I'd like to have a steak. Maybe we can have steak this time and Chinese the next [or vice versa]." When you agree that one person chooses this time and the other chooses the next, that says the relationship is symmetrical over the long run but complementary for the specific choice. When both parties agree to this, there is no problem.

You notice that, in systems terms, the system is trying to adjust itself for stability. It turns out, though, that the most unstable system is one that is symmetrical. A tiny shift causes it to become complementary. A system that is inherently complementary, however, can experience shifts in either direction and will remain stable. This is why people who are highly concerned that they be treated as equal-status with everyone else are always being frustrated. They are constantly seeing signs that the relationship is unequal, and they attempt to restore balance. That attempt may be met with a counter-response aimed at keeping the system unbalanced, and thus a conflict develops.

This is not to suggest that all relationships would be better if they were unequal-status. It is important that we recognize that no relationship can ever be totally equal all the time for every situation. The only thing we can achieve is equal status on the average.

CONFLICT IN MANAGEMENT

Inevitably, there are conflicts in human relations. Conflict occurs when one person frustrates the concerns of another person. Those concerns include goals, values, self-interests, status, and control. This is one area in which systems thinking is essential if we are to understand and deal with such situations.

Remember the example of two children having an altercation? When asked who started it, each blamed the other. This is because *each sees his own behavior as a response to the behavior of the other child!* The way this works is shown in Figure 12–6.

Person A behaves. This is the arrow 1-2. Person B responds, as sequence 2-3. Person A responds to that behavior

F I G U R E 12–6

F I G U R E 12–6

Punctuation in Human Relationships

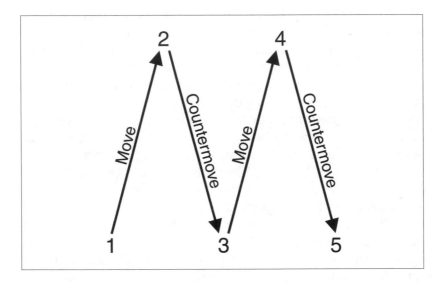

as 3-4. This goes on as a long series of interactions that we can call *move-countermove, move-countermove.* Now, as I have said previously, if you ask each person why she behaved as she did, she will tell you that she was only responding to the other person's behavior. Person A sees the exchange as sequence 2-3-4, while person B sees it as 1-2-3. This is called *punctuation* in communication (Watzlawick, Beavin, and Jackson, 1967).

In some cases, once such an interaction begins, it becomes almost impossible to stop. Each side sees his behavior as a response to that of the other. Such a sequence is called a *game without end,* and naturally, we don't mean game in the fun sense. An example of a game without end is the Middle East conflict. There have been many attempts to resolve the conflict, and they have been only temporarily successful. The conflict breaks out all over again when one side makes a move that is seen by the other as similar to previous moves.

There is only one way to resolve a game without end, and that is to break the pattern. This was done by President Gorbachev in the nuclear arms race. In this game, the United States increased its weapon stockpiles and the Soviet Union countered by doing the same. Over time, each country stock-piled massive quantities of weapons—by most estimates, enough to destroy all life on earth several times over. The cost to each country was enormous, and the money spent on weapons could not be used for improving the lives of the citizens of either country.

Finally Gorbachev realized that the Soviet Union could not continue this game indefinitely. They had limited resources (as did the U.S.). So he told President Reagan, "I am going to deprive you of an enemy." He did this by beginning to disarm the Soviet Union, without waiting for the U.S. to follow suit. This broke the move-countermove pattern. His countermove was exactly the opposite of what it had always been: Instead of increasing armaments, he decreased them, thus breaking the pattern.

In systems terminology, the exchange had been a rein-forcing loop. Each move on one side caused a corresponding and more aggressive move on the other. Gorbachev's action changed the system to a balancing loop initially. Later on, it became a reinforcing loop again, but this time in the opposite direction. As Gorbachev decreased Soviet arms, we did the same. Of course, neither side was willing to decrease their stockpiles to zero, since each faced the threat of being attacked by another foe.

This is an important lesson for project managers. When conflicts break out in teams, it is often unproductive to try to get at causes. Each party will just blame the other. When this happens, it is more productive to find some way to break the pattern. This means you have to get at least one party to the conflict to abandon the normal behavioral response and do the opposite of what he has been doing. Here I am suggesting what you would do if you were mediating a conflict between two members of your team. If it is conflict between yourself as project manager and someone else and you want to resolve it, then you will have to break the pattern by behaving differently than you have been doing.

THINKING IN SYSTEMS TERMS

The previous examples show that we must abandon linear thinking if we are to understand the dynamics of much of what happens in human affairs. This is especially true in project teams. In the next chapter, we will expand our understanding of systems thinking and introduce some tools that will help us understand how certain actions on our part can make our projects better and how some can actually make them worse.

13

Understanding Systems Thinking

For several hundred years, scientists have tried to understand the world through reductionist thinking. They initially believed that you could understand a thing by taking it apart and studying the components individually. After all, they reasoned, a machine is the sum of its parts, and

> A house is not the same as a pile of building materials.

Newtonian physics had led them to believe that the universe is a big clockwork mechanism.

At first glance, this sounds okay, until you begin to realize that a house is not the same as a pile of building materials. Furthermore, you cannot understand the qualities of a house by analyzing a single brick or an individual board that goes into the house. This is even more true of more complex aggregates of parts, such as biological organisms and complex machines.

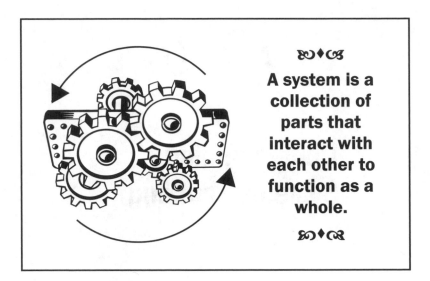

**A system is a
collection of
parts that
interact with
each other to
function as a
whole.**

WHAT IS A SYSTEM?

Even after you put all of the parts together, you still don't
have a system. There is no active quality to a house. It just
sits there. It may be cozy, comfortable, and great to live in,
but it doesn't do anything! A system, on the other hand, is active. It does do something. In fact, a system is defined as follows:

> A system is a collection of parts that interact
> with each other to function as a whole.

The parts of a system, taken separately, are often use-
less. To be of value, they must be present and arranged correctly. If the arrangement and interaction of parts does not
matter, then we are not dealing with a system, but with a
"heap." Moreover, the definition of a system leads to an interesting conclusion: A system is actually *greater* than the
sum of its parts. This has been called synergy and is one of
the things that differentiates systems from nonsystems.

The human body is a large system, and it in turn contains a number of subsystems. The nervous system is a subsystem of the body. So is the circulatory system. When a system is part of a larger system, it is called a subsystem. Likewise, the earth is a part of the solar system, which is a part of a galaxy, and our galaxy is part of the collection of galaxies known as the universe.

Returning to human beings for a moment, note that a person is a complex system in her own right. Put her with a number of other individuals and have them work together to achieve a certain result, and you have a larger system called a team. It is true that you can study each member of the team individually, and you can describe their personalities, motivations, neuroses, and other characteristics. However, this understanding will not tell you a great deal about how the individual will function in the team, nor will it tell you a lot about the team as a system. Notice that I am not saying you will know nothing about the team; I am just saying that understanding will be limited.

The reason is in part because we are different persons in different settings. The attributes of a gear might not change when you assemble it into a clock. The attributes of human beings, however, are not so stable. I am a different person when teaching a seminar than when I am interacting with my family. Naturally, some characteristics are constant, but the differences make it hard to predict group behavior by observing individual behavior. I am also not the same in all teams. It is a very context-sensitive phenomenon.

The importance of this for a project manager is that you have to be careful making predictions about what kind of project team you will have by looking only at an individual team member's qualities. As a simple example, you like Jane. You have worked with her before and found her to be reliable, hard-working, intelligent, cheerful, and resilient. You also like working with Bob. He is also very intelligent, extremely knowledgeable about a certain technology that you intend to employ, and has very desirable work habits. You are certain that if you put these two on your team, you will have a dynamite combination!

The only thing is, Jane and Bob develop an immediate disliking for each other. There is an intense jealousy that manifests as sniping, competitiveness, and other acts of sabotage. Individually, they may be great. They may even be great for *you* to work with. It is just that the two of them can't work together.

Again, the key to understanding systems is in that word *interact*. Jane and Bob interact with each other in a dysfunctional way. Naturally, for a team to be a good team, the members must interact in a harmonious, cooperative manner. So, Jane and Bob together turn out to be a bad combination for your team.

> The key to understanding systems is in the word *interact*.

Now consider a simple interaction that most of us experience every day. You are driving a car. This forms a simple human-machine system. As you drive along, you approach a hill that you must climb. The car begins to slow down, so you press down on the accelerator and the car speeds up. When you have regained your original speed, you ease up on the accelerator a bit and the car resumes a constant speed. When it reaches the top of the hill, you have to back off on the accelerator even more, or else the car will begin to speed up. This interaction between you and the car is a process called negative feedback. It is called negative because the feedback negates the change in system behavior.

As the car slows down, your pressing the accelerator negates the change in speed. As the car speeds up, your letting up on the pedal negates the change in speed again. This is diagramed in Figure 13–1.

Note that negative feedback does not have the colloquial meaning in this case. It is customary for people in organiza-

F I G U R E 13–1

Simple Feedback System for Driving a Car

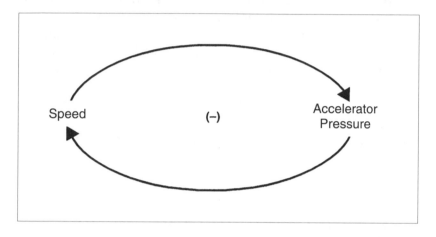

tions to talk about giving each other positive and negative feedback. By this they mean that they are either giving each other compliments (positive feedback) or criticism (negative feedback).

Returning to our example of driving a car, some people are able to maintain very good speed control going up and down hills. Others seem not to notice the feedback that tells them their speed is varying, so they speed up and slow down (even on level ground). When there is a lot of variation in a system, we say it is a *loose* system. Note that a self-stabilizing system does not prevent change; it just responds to change to try to minimize its effect on the system. The thermostat that turns your furnace on and off does this. It too has a certain amount of looseness—room temperature may vary several degrees. The typical home thermostat costs only a few dollars. A system that would maintain temperature to a single degree would cost many times more and probably wouldn't be worth it to most people. It is important to know the limits of a system.

Another characteristic of systems is reaction time. This is the amount of time it takes a signal to go around the loop. If it is too slow, the system can be damaged. An example: if you touch a hot surface and don't feel it instantly, you can be seriously burned. This is, in fact, the problem with sunburn. It takes so long for you to realize that you are being burned that, by that time, it is too late. The damage is done. This is analogous to placing a frog in a pot of water and slowly heating it up. The frog doesn't react. It just feels warmer, until the temperature is too hot. It lets itself be boiled. If you were to drop the frog into very hot water, however, it would jump out.

ANTICIPATION

What if you can't afford the delay of even a fast-response system? For example, it is better not to get burned in the first place than to react to being burned. Systems cope with this problem by reacting to *warnings.* Avoiding a growling dog is

ଚ୨◆ଓଷ
When systems only respond to problems, rather than anticipating them, it may be too late.
ଚ୨◆ଓଷ

better than taking a chance that he might bite. Countries that wait until they are attacked to arm themselves may never get the chance. It is more prudent to pay attention to intelligence reports that indicate imminent danger and arm in advance. Figure 13–2 shows the difference between avoiding danger and simply responding to it.

When systems only respond to problems, rather than anticipating them, it may be too late to deal with the problems, and the system is destroyed. The lesson for managers is that we should try to anticipate problems and deal with them ahead of time, rather than simply reacting to them. This is the difference between reactive and proactive management. This is also called risk management and is covered in Chapter 15.

F I G U R E   13–2

Avoiding Danger versus Simply Responding to It

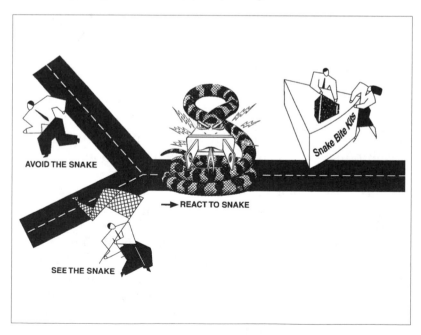

POSITIVE FEEDBACK

So far we have discussed systems that contain negative feedback loops. Negative feedback loops keep systems stable.
They *resist* change. We often encounter such feedback systems when we try to change organizations. The French have
a saying about such systems, which, roughly translated, is,
"The more things change, the more they stay the same"
(Watzlawick, Weakland, and Fisch, 1974). In fact, it seems
that most systems employ negative feedback to protect themselves from being affected by outside influences.

How then, do systems change, develop, or grow?

The answer is, they contain some kind of positive feedback loop. Again, we are not referring to the colloquial use of
the term, meaning to give someone positive strokes or compliments. Here, we mean that a small perturbation introduced
into the system leads to a large system effect. Some examples
include the growth of compound interest, rabbit populations,
knowledge, personal power, and audio systems that howl at
you. The audio system is diagrammed in Figure 13–3.

When you speak into the microphone, the sound of your
voice is amplified and fed to the speakers. The microphone
picks up the sound from the speakers and amplifies it, and so
a positive loop is created. You might ask why the system
does not get louder and louder. There are always limits to
growth. In the case of an electronic system, the amplifier can
only produce so much power, so when the sound reaches
that level, it can go no higher.

Likewise, rabbit populations can grow only so far. They
reach a point at which there is not enough food to feed them
all. They either have to move to new areas or begin to starve.

Even compound interest might reach a limit. The bank can
only pay interest on your deposits if they can lend the money to
someone, so if they reach a point at which no one wants to bor-
row the money you have deposited, they would no longer be
able to pay you interest on it. Of course, you would have to be a
very large depositor indeed for this to happen.

F I G U R E 13–3

F I G U R E 13–3

An Audio System That Howls

BUILDING COMPLEX SYSTEMS

Every complex system that you will ever encounter is built from the two basic elements—positive and negative feedback loops. Therefore, when you see two systems that have the same loop structure, you can expect them to behave in very similar ways. The beauty of this is that we can learn how a system behaves in one area and transfer that knowledge to systems of the same structure in other areas.

As I explained in the previous section, positive loops would grow indefinitely if something didn't limit them. In the case of rabbits, it is the food supply. Consider a similar system composed of bacteria. These single-cell organisms multiply by dividing. In the right environment, a cell will divide in about half an hour. The two cells will divide in another half hour; by then, you have four cells. This progression continues—8, 16, 32, 64, 128, and so on. As incredible as it might seem, after only 10 hours, there are more than a million cells!

This assumes that no cells die, of course. However, all living organisms do die, so to calculate how many bacteria you would have after a certain period, you must factor in the death rate. The overall system is shown in Figure 13–4.

F I G U R E   13–4

System for Bacteria Population Growth

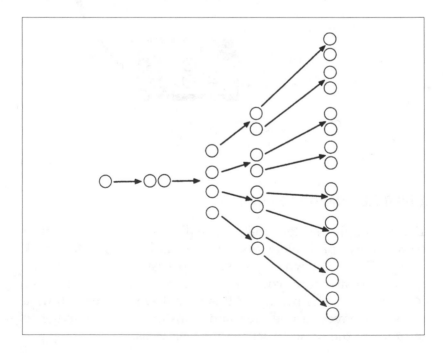

As you can see, the two loops work against each other. If 10 bacteria are "born" and 6 die, the net increase in population is 4. However, if 12 die for every 10 that are born, the population will gradually decline. The overall system behavior is determined by which loop is stronger or dominant.

This basic model can be applied to other populations. A city grows or declines in the same way that bacteria do. However, in addition to being born and dying, people also move into and away from cities, so the situation is more complicated. In this case, you might have four loops, as shown in Figure 13–5.

We might also ask what controls the rate at which loops operate. For example, in the case of population growth, we would ask what affects the birth and death rates. If the population in question consisted of animals, death would be affected by the food supply, predators, and disease. For simplicity, we can begin by adding the effect of food alone, to get the diagram in Figure 13–6.

In the same way, we can add the effects of predators and disease to arrive at the system shown in Figure 13–7.

F I G U R E   13–5

Growth of a City

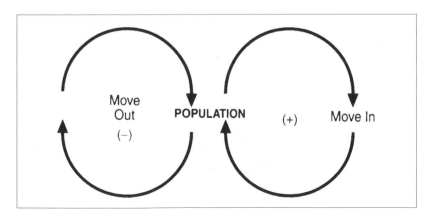

F I G U R E   13–6

Effect of Food Supply on Death Rates

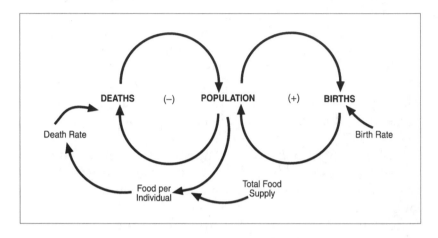

F I G U R E   13–7

Effects of Food, Predators, and Disease on Death Rates

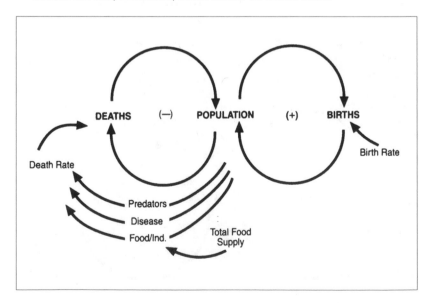

Is this everything? Not really. For animal populations, overcrowding introduces a significant factor (The same may be true of human populations, too). For example, when rabbits get too crowded, they may go into shock and die at the slightest stimulus—a loud noise, the sight of an enemy, or even another rabbit. They literally die of fright or excitement. This means that if the other negative loops fail to control the population, the overcrowding loop takes over.

In addition, some animals use the amount of food or space to control population by moderating the actual birth rate. Considering all of these factors together, we can construct a diagram like the one in Figure 13–8.

F I G U R E 13–8

Major Factors Affecting Animal Populations

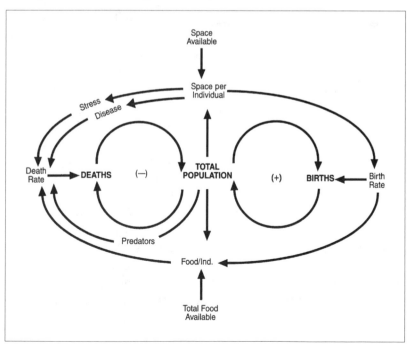

In this system, the loop that will eventually stop population growth depends on the particular situation. In some cases the loops all work together to control the positive loop. Sometimes a few do the major job and others are kept in reserve in case these fail.

One problem we have is that people sometimes intervene in a system to eliminate a negative feedback loop that they don't like. The next thing they know, a worse one takes its place. For example, if disease is reduced by medicine, and nothing is done to limit the birth rate, the population might grow to the point where not enough food is available and famine occurs, which kills even more people. Even if the food supply is not a problem, we can already see the effects of people living longer because of improved health care. They now wind up in nursing homes or suffer Alzheimer's, which would not have occurred had they died younger.

> Any change that affects the relationship between the positive and negative loops is going to alter the long-term behavior of the system.

Most systems will balance themselves if left alone and will return to the balance point if disturbed. It is important to look for the balance point in complex systems. By understanding the nature of the positive and negative feedback loops, you can also differentiate between factors that are going to affect the system temporarily and those that will have a lasting effect. Any change, no matter how big, that does not change the important positive or negative loops of a system will be temporary only. Conversely, any change—no matter how small—that does affect the relationship between the positive and negative loops is going to alter the long-term behavior of the system.

From a practical point of view, this means that if we want to change a complex system, we must find a way to change the relationship between the loops that keep the system balanced. Otherwise, every change we try to make will end up being "resisted" by the system, which will just return to the status quo state.

That is a brief introduction to systems thinking. In the next chapter, we will look at ways to apply these ideas to projects.

14

CHAPTER

How to Apply Systems Thinking in Managing Projects

In the previous chapters, I showed how systems thinking can help us understand the dynamics of human interactions. Since project work is generally performed by people, it should be possible to apply systems concepts to the understanding and management of projects.

FIXES THAT FAIL

Let's begin by considering a fairly common problem in projects: The work is falling behind schedule. It seems that the only thing to do is ask the person doing the work to increase his working hours each day; that is, to work a few hours of overtime to get back on track. He agrees. The first week, he works 12 hours a day and is making progress. The amount of work being done is definitely greater than what was previously accomplished. However, after a couple of weeks, you discover that he is making a lot of mistakes, and these must be corrected. Furthermore, his output is down from what it was the first week. In fact, you find that the amount of work he is turning out is just about equal to what he was doing in a normal 40-hour week before! You are actually losing productivity, because he now has to spend time correcting the errors he has made, and this drops his output even more.

Something must be done.

You decide that if overtime is not the answer, then extra resources must be obtained. You convince your boss to assign a new person to help. To your amazement, the work accomplished by both of them is barely the same as for one person working alone, and there are considerably more errors being made. What is going on?

You talk to your original team member, and he says, "It's very simple. The guy you gave me knows nothing about what I'm doing, so I spent most of Monday getting him on board. Then I found that he's making a lot of mistakes, so I had to help correct those, and I'm still having to work overtime to take care of training him and to correct all the errors. I would be better off with no help at all!"

This is an example of "fixes that fail." Having the person on overtime initially worked until the long-term effect of fatigue kicked in. Then the person started making more errors, which had to be corrected, which caused him to fall further behind, which required him to work harder, which caused more fatigue, and more errors, and on and on it goes. Then a helper was assigned to the project. The original worker had to train the helper, which dropped his productivity, which caused him to work harder, which made him more fatigued, and the helper made errors, which had to be corrected, which made him even more tired, and so on.

Another example. I know of a company, we'll call it Acme Electronics, that makes components that go into products manufactured by other companies. Occasionally, their customer has a problem with one of the components, and the design engineers are sent to the field to see if they can correct the problem. Since they are currently working on designing new components, that work comes to a standstill. They manage to correct the problem for the customer and return to work.

Unfortunately, the deadline for completing the current component design has not changed, and they have fallen behind. The only solution is to work hard to try to catch up. The result is the same as described previously in this chapter—they do poor-quality work, which is not caught. The new component is released. The customer again has problems with the new part. The engineers are sent to the field to correct the problem. Current work comes to a standstill. They work hard to catch up, turn out another bad design, and the cycle begins all over again.

The common expression that describes this situation is fire-fighting. The engineers are doing a reasonable job of fire-fighting, but nothing is being done to prevent future fires.

LEVELS OF UNDERSTANDING

There are numerous levels from which we can understand the world around us. Systems thinkers are concerned with four of these, as shown in Figure 14–1. At the level of *events* are things that occur on a day-to-day basis. Accidents happen, we go to work, eat lunch, perform a work task, or write a memo. In the case of the engineers, they correct a problem with a component—they put out a fire. This level is called *reactive,* because we are always reacting to the event rather than trying to control its occurrence.

At the next level are *patterns of events.* In the case of our engineers, we begin to notice that the same pattern keeps happening. Note that patterns can only be seen over a period of time. When we see patterns developing, we might be able to be *adaptive* in our response. We give the engineers training in fire-fighting, so that when they encounter a fire, they can extinguish it quickly. This still does nothing to prevent fires.

We are often reacting to an event rather than trying to control its occurrence.

At the *systemic structure* level we begin to ask what causes the patterns of events to occur. This level is called *creative*, because we might be able to prevent fires if we can understand the patterns. This level is future-oriented. By preventing fires, we create a different future than the one that would have occurred normally. At this level, we might decide to set up a fire-fighting group, separate from the design engineers. This would free the engineers from any fire-fighting so that they could concentrate on doing new designs really well, which over the long run should reduce the number of fires that break out.

The next tier is called the *shared vision* level. This level generates the structures that form patterns. This level is called *generative* and it too is future-oriented. At this level, we ask questions like, "What is the real role of design engineers? How should fire-fighting be handled? What trade-offs are we willing to make between resources devoted to design and those dedicated to fire-fighting?"

F I G U R E   14–1

Levels of Understanding

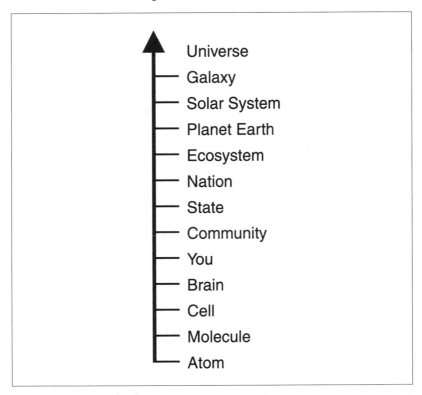

THE TRAGEDY OF THE COMMONS

Complex systems have many strengths, but they also are like everything else—you don't get anything for free. Complex systems create their own set of problems.

One of these is called the tragedy of the commons. In medieval England there were commons, or common pasture areas. This idea was brought to the United States by the colonists. All members of a community were entitled to graze their livestock in the commons.

Say an individual livestock owner soon begins to think, "The more cows I have, the better off I'll be, and since the grazing is free, I will increase my herd as fast as I can." This creates a positive feedback loop.

It also creates a situation that each individual is powerless to avoid. Each person tends to think the same way, so herds start growing. Soon they reach a point where the cows eat the grass faster than it can grow. Faced with nothing to eat, the animals crop the grass down to the roots, killing it, so that there is nothing at all to eat. The cows are now starving and the entire village is faced with disaster.

Notice that it does no good for a single villager to voluntarily keep down the size of his herd. That just leaves more pasture for the others, who then have more incentive to add more cattle. Thus, the unselfish action will not prevent the disaster, and the person will just be poorer in the meantime, while his neighbors are prospering. The significant thing about this situation is that if every person makes the best decision from his own point of view, everyone winds up worse off!

Peter Block has pointed out that *enlightened* self-interest would mean that every villager would do what is best for the village—not himself individually (Block, 1987). In doing so, he knows that he will benefit himself over the long run. Of course, it is very hard to get people to do this. People tend to look out for number 1, never realizing that their actions may eventually destroy them. We see this with many of the environmental problems that are being created today.

But what does this have to do with project management? One significant aspect of project management is that managers are always competing for scarce resources to get our jobs done. If we realized that our real self-interest lies in cooperation rather than competition, our project teams would function better. Instead, we sometimes get locked into win-lose conflicts over resources. Each project manager wants to optimize his "herd" with no regard for the impact to other teams. From a systems point of view, anything that I do to help my organization in one area tends to help the entire system, and conversely, anything I do to hurt it hurts everyone.

I showed in Chapter 12 how we sometimes get locked into games without end because we set up a move-countermove interaction. Now that you understand negative feedback loops, you can see that such a system tends to balance itself and resists being changed. As I said at the end of Chapter 13, systems tend to return to the balance point if disturbed, so if you try to reduce the conflict, it just comes back after awhile. Unless you can interrupt the pattern—that is, disturb the negative feedback loop—the interaction will continue, unabated, forever! (Or until both parties get tired of it.)

LIMITS TO GROWTH

In his book *The Fifth Discipline* (1990), Peter Senge presents a number of systems archetypes that appear over and over again in organizations, groups, and even in individual performance. One of these is the limits-to-growth model. This archetype is almost always found in situations where "growth bumps up against limits" (Senge, 1990, p. 96). Organizations grow for awhile, then stop growing. Teams get better for awhile, and then stop getting better. The same happens to individuals. Attempts to improve organizations through reengineering might succeed for awhile and then reach a limit.

This would certainly apply to project teams. In Chapter 27, I deal with improving processes in project teams. However, you might find that there are limits to the improvements you can achieve. We try to solve deadline problems by working longer hours, but as I showed at the beginning of this chapter, the stress and fatigue begin to slow our work speed and reduce quality, thus reducing the benefit of the longer hours.

A limits-to-growth system has a structure like the one shown in Figure 14–2.

F I G U R E 14–2

Limits-to-Growth System Structure

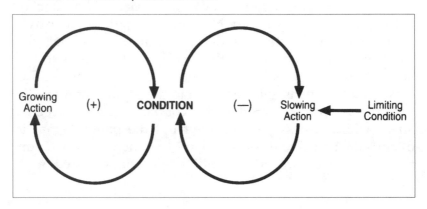

SHIFTING THE BURDEN

This archetype is prevalent throughout government and corporate organizations. There is a problem that causes symptoms that demand attention, but the underlying problem is difficult for people to address, either because it is obscure or costly to confront. So people shift the burden of the problem to other solutions. These are well-intentioned, easy fixes that seem efficient. However, the fixes just deal with the symptoms and leave the underlying problem unchanged.

One example of this, at the personal level, is when an individual is overworked, possibly because the department is understaffed. She tries to juggle work, family, and her ongoing education, always running from one thing to another. When her workload increases beyond her capacity, her only solution is to limit the workload. That might mean declining a promotion, or prioritizing and making choices. Instead, she decides to juggle faster and tries to relieve her stress with alcohol or meditation, but neither provides a real solution. The problem persists, and so does the need for drinking.

We also see this in our attempts to deal with difficult team members. Rather than dealing directly with the person, the manager tries to develop his human relations skills. Perhaps the HR department tries to intervene. They talk to the person, coach, counsel, and maybe "write him up." However, he persists in his problematic behavior. The real solution would be to remove him from the group (and probably the company), but no one wants to take that *hard medicine*.

A system model for shifting the burden is shown in Figure 14–3.

F I G U R E 14–3

Shifting-the-Burden System Structure

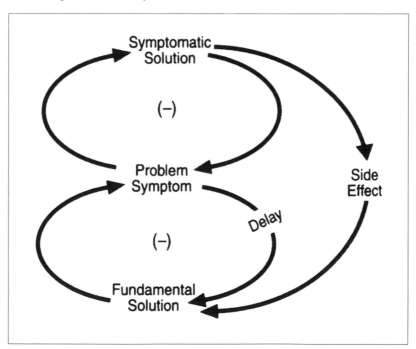

I hope these examples show how systems thinking could be useful to project managers. For in-depth treatment of systems in organizations, I know of no better source than Senge's *The Fifth Discipline* and a companion book, *The Fifth Discipline Fieldbook* (Senge et al., 1994). You might also want to subscribe to *The Systems Thinker Newsletter*.

15

CHAPTER

Managing Project Risks

Perhaps the most famous "law" of all is Murphy's Law, which is usually stated as, "Whatever can go wrong *will!*" Given that this seems to be true in the experience of most people, it seems reasonable to ask how one should deal with Murphy's Law. It seems clear that when something goes wrong, we have *the possibility of suffering harm or loss*, which is defined as *risk*. I therefore define risk as anything that can go wrong in a project, and since things that go wrong can cause me to suffer harm or loss, I then need to ask how we can manage risks in projects.

> **Principle:** We are all inclined to overestimate our ability and underestimate difficulties. As someone has said, "Even Murphy was an optimist!"

In my experience, this is a neglected area in managing projects. Of course, it is fair to ask if it really matters. My response is that it does matter, because when things go wrong

ᔓ◆ᔕ
When things go wrong, they can seriously throw the project off balance.
ᔓ◆ᔕ

unexpectedly, they throw you off balance and often cause major crises for your projects.

As an example, I have seen design engineers put all of their effort into a design that they couldn't make work. They never even *considered* the possibility! It may be that to consider that they might not be able to make the design work would be to admit their fallibility, and that might be too much for

"It is an unhappy fact of life that there are usually more things that can go wrong with a project than can unexpectedly go right."

—John R. Schuyler (1995)

some perfectionist types to do. Whatever the reason, those engineers who encounter design problems are often thrown into the panic mode and may have to start over, since they have put "all of their eggs into one basket." Naturally, such a setback can have a serious impact on the project.

If you refer to my project methodology (the flowchart), presented in Chapter 11, you will see that there are two places in which risk management needs to be done. The first is in planning project strategy. The second is in implementation planning.

In planning strategy, you are trying to develop an approach for managing the project that may involve the choice of technology as well as an execution method. I have called these *project strategy* and *technical strategy* in Chapter 11.

Both strategies have risks in most cases. When proven technology is being employed, the risks of failure are usually low. However, if cutting-edge technology is being applied, then the risks are much higher. Further, some project strategies have higher risks than others. For example, a "farm-out" project strategy might be more risky than one in which all work is done internally.

Either way, the first step in risk analysis is to identify what might go wrong. (This is true at both step 4 and step 6 of the flowchart.) When I do this with a team, I have them brainstorm a list of potential pitfalls and record them on a flip chart, with no ensuing discussion or evaluation. To help them identify risks, I simply ask, "What could go wrong that could impact schedule, cost, performance, or scope in the project?"

THREATS VERSUS RISKS

You will notice in step 4 of the flowchart that you are supposed to test a strategy against risks and SWOT analysis. SWOT stands for *s*trengths, *w*eaknesses, *o*pportunities, and *t*hreats. Unless you can manage risks, offset weaknesses, and contend with threats, your project strategy is likely to fail. The question is: What is the difference between threats and risks?

If you adopt a purist definition, risks are things that can happen without having any deliberate intention to cause harm behind them. Examples of risks might be accidents; acts of nature such as earthquakes, weather, and so on; losing key members of the team; fires; escalating labor rates or inflation; changes in the exchange rate for international projects; political instability, and so on. A threat is something that is done by a competitor or adversary to interfere with your success. For example, when an airline tries to capture a route by offering a very low fare, it is usually unsuccessful because the competition just matches its fare, and nobody gains market share. While threats and risks are technically different, for the purposes of managing projects, they can be lumped together in the same analysis.

> "It seems reasonable to say that it is always better to avoid risk than it is to manage it."
>
> —Harvey Levine

IT IS BEST TO AVOID RISK

It seems reasonable to say that it is always better to avoid risk than it is to manage it (Levine, 1995, p. 30). This should be done through better planning, not by avoiding a good opportunity. As I said above, you begin by identifying what can go wrong that might affect time, cost, performance, or scope in your project. Then you ask what might be done to avoid these effects. If it is not possible to avoid the effect, can you reduce the impact?

As an example, weather can hold up projects and cannot be avoided. The solution is to examine the weather history for the area and time of year and to build into the schedule a reasonable amount of delay. If the weather is better than usual, you will get ahead of schedule, and conversely.

On the other hand, I would rather avoid the risk of putting an inexperienced project manager on a highly important project than to try to manage the risk once I have done so. Prevention is always less expensive than failure, as is discussed in Chapter 26 on quality.

QUANTIFYING RISKS AND THREATS

It is helpful to have some measure of the impact a risk or threat might have on a project. Naturally, for the most part, this cannot be quantified in any really objective way, but we can use a subjective method that seems to work fairly well. The approach was first devised by engineers to identify where product designs might fail and is therefore called failure mode effects analysis, or FMEA. For those of you who are math-challenged, this is a foreboding term, but don't be intimidated by it. The approach is really very simple and requires nothing more difficult than multiplication.

I am going to call the approach project risk analysis and management, because I want to emphasize that it is not enough to simply *identify* risks—you have to manage them as well. Furthermore, I am lumping risks and threats together, so I don't have to keep saying "risks and threats" every time. From now on, you will understand that "risks" refers to both.

ASSESSING PROBABILITY

Once we have brainstormed a list of risks, we have to estimate the probability that they might occur. To do so, we use the information shown in Table 15–1. In the FMEA terminology, something that goes wrong is referred to as a failure. I have changed that word to "occurrence," since the word "failure" does not always apply. For example, political unrest that might affect an international project is not a failure but an occurrence or event. You will note that the probability scale is a logarithmic scale, whereas the remaining scales are linear.

Next, we need to consider how severe the effect of the event or occurrence is on the project. An event that has a high probability of happening but a low impact on the project is of little concern, whereas an event that is low probability but se-

T A B L E 15–1

Probability of Occurrence

Probability of Occurrence	Possible Occurrence Rates	Rank
Very High: Occurrence is almost certain	≥ 1 in 2	10
	1 in 3	9
High: Repeated occurrences possible	1 in 8	8
	1 in 20	7
Moderate: Occasional occurrences	1 in 80	6
	1 in 400	5
	1 in 2,000	4
Low: Relatively few occurrences	1 in 15,000	3
	1 in 150,000	2
Remote: Occurrence is unlikely	≤ 1 in 1,500,000	1

vere impact is of great concern. In this table, you will note the word "customer" is used several times. For this analysis, *customer* can mean an actual customer for the project or your company management, whichever is appropriate. See Table 15–2.

The next thing we want to look at is how easy it is to detect that the event is going to happen before it actually takes place. For example, if the oil runs out of your car while you are driving it, the effect will be severe. If you have an oil gauge, you should be able to see that the oil pressure is getting

T A B L E 15–2

Severity of the Effect

Effect	Criteria: Severity of Effect	Rank
Hazardous-without warning	Project severely impacted, possible cancellation, with no warning.	10
Hazardous-with warning	Project severely impacted, possible cancellation, with warning.	9
Very High	Major impact on project schedule, budget, or performance; may cause severe delays, overruns, or degradation of performance.	8
High	Project schedule, budget, or performance impacted significantly; job can be completed, but customer will be very dissatisfied.	7
Moderate	Project schedule, budget, or performance impacted some; customer will be dissatisfied.	6
Low	Project schedule, budget, or performance impacted slightly; customer will be mildly dissatisfied.	5
Very Low	Some impact to project; customer will be aware of impact.	4
Minor	Small impact to project; average customer will be aware of impact.	3
Very Minor	Impact so small that it would be noticed only by a very discriminating customer.	2
None	No effect.	1

T A B L E 15–3

Detection Capability

Detection	Rank
Absolute Uncertainty	10
Very Remote	9
Remote	8
Very Low	7
Low	6
Moderate	5
Moderately High	4
High	3
Very High	2
Almost Certain	1

low and take action before the situation becomes serious. If you have a broken oil gauge or an indicator light that comes on at some threshold level, it is not as easy to detect the problem beforehand.

In projects, things like bad weather can be predicted with some accuracy, and steps can be taken to compensate. Accidents, however, tend to happen without warning, so they are harder to deal with. Table 15–3 is used to measure the detection capability of a risk in a project. Note that this scale is reversed; that is, the more certain it is that you can detect a hazard, the lower the number.

THE RISK PROBABILITY NUMBER

For each risk that you have identified, you now have three measures—a probability level, severity measure, and detection capability index. These three numbers are multiplied to obtain a risk probability number (RPN). The higher that

F I G U R E   15–1

Risk Analysis for a Project

Identified Risk	P	S	D	RPN
Bad weather	3	2	4	24
Loss of key team member	2	8	8	128
Technology won't work	6	10	8	480

number, the more serious the risk. To show how this works, consider the three risks shown in Figure 15–1.

The general approach to dealing with high RPNs is to ask whether any of the three individual components can be reduced. That is, can risk or severity be lowered and/or can detection be increased (which will lower its number). As an example, we can reduce the probability of a weather delay in a project by doing it during a calendar period that historically has good weather. We can reduce severity of weather delays by padding the schedule, and we can increase our ability to detect forthcoming bad weather by paying close attention to weather forecasts.

For the examples in our table, the RPN for bad weather is so small that it can be ignored. However, the other two risks have significant RPNs, and we should consider what to do. First, let's examine loss of a key team member. While it has a probability of only 2, it has a high severity and high detection. As a general rule, whenever severity is high, regardless of the RPN, special attention should be given to this particular risk.

An example of this is the *Challenger* disaster. It was believed by some members of the team that the probability of O-ring failure at the low launch temperature was quite low. However, the severity of failure was a 10, because the astronauts on board would be killed. Because of this fact alone, greater caution should have been exercised. It has been my experience that when people think the probability of something is low, they throw caution to the wind. An example is that some people think the probability that they will have an automobile accident is very low, so they take chances with their driving—and often get killed or seriously injured.

The severity of losing a key team member can be reduced if we have someone available to cover for her. This is what live theatrical productions do. They have an understudy who can play the part of a regular performer in the event of illness or accident. We might not be able to reduce detection in this case, but reducing severity alone might be enough.

The third risk in the table is that technology won't work. There are a couple of possibilities in this case. First, the probability of failure is shown as six points, which is moderate. This might not give us too much cause for concern. However, if probability of technology failure were higher, say around eight or nine points, then I would suggest that a feasibility study be conducted before any application of that technology be attempted. A basic premise is that, if you are to have control over project schedules, discovery and development should be separated.

Even if we have low probability, the severity of a technology failure can be very high. One way to deal with this is to be ready with an alternative. In some very high-risk projects, where it was not possible to do feasibility studies, I have known some companies to launch parallel development paths. The first technology that worked was the one they continued with. This obviously costs a lot of money and would only be done where time is more important than cost, which is the case in some projects.

Finally, can we detect failure of technology with any ease? Perhaps not. However, it might be prudent to establish some decision criteria about how many failures will be tolerated before an approach is abandoned in favor of one that is more certain. This can be a blow to the ego of a professional, but in business, we must do what is prudent rather than what is self-serving. An exception might be an attempt to develop a vaccine for a disease such as AIDS. However, even here we must ask if repeated failures of a particular approach might not dictate adopting an alternative strategy.

DEVELOPING CONTINGENCY PLANS

As I stated earlier, it is not enough to identify and quantify risks. The idea is to manage them. This might be done in three ways:

1. Risk avoidance.
2. Mitigation (reduction, such as using air bags).
3. Transfer (such as in loss prevention through insurance).

Risk Avoidance

In the case of risk aversion or avoidance, we want to avoid the risk altogether. In the case of the *Challenger,* the decision to delay the launch until the temperature warmed up would be an example of risk avoidance.

Japanese manufacturing has for many years employed "foolproofing" as a risk-avoidance strategy. The idea is to set up the assembly process so that it cannot be done incorrectly. One example was that workers occasionally would start to install a gas tank in a car only to find that one of the four mounting brackets had not been welded onto the tank. The solution was to set up a fixture to hold the tank while the brackets were being welded onto it. Feelers were attached to detect the presence of the brackets. If all four brackets were not in place, the welding machine would not weld any of them.

In engineering design, I mentioned using parallel design strategies to avoid the possibility that the deadline might be missed because one strategy proves difficult to implement. In any project, risk aversion or avoidance might be the most preferable strategy to follow.

Mitigation or Risk Reduction

If we can think of contingencies in the event that a risk occurs, we can mitigate its effect. Placing air bags in cars is an attempt to reduce the severity of an accident, should one occur. Stafford Beer (1981) has argued that seat belts and air bags in cars actually give drivers a false sense of security. We have defined the problem as protecting the driver from being harmed if he is in an accident. Beer argues that it would perhaps be better to redefine the problem as how to keep a driver from having an accident in the first place (risk avoidance). He suggests that if we lined the dashboard of the car with spikes, making it very clear that an accident has serious consequences, we might give drivers incentive to be more careful. His suggestion is not without merit.

In projects that involve procurement, sole-sourcing is a risk to consider. The alternative is to second-source all procured parts or equipment. That way, if a supplier can't deliver on time or at the specified price, the second supplier might be able to do so. This can be thought of as either risk avoidance or mitigation.

Temporary workers are used as backups for critical personnel who become ill or are injured. Overtime is used as a contingency when tasks take longer than estimated. This is one reason why overtime should not be planned into a project to meet original targets, if possible. Rather, it should be kept in reserve as a contingency.

Another contingency is to reduce scope to permit the team to meet the original target date, then come back later and incorporate deferred work to finish the job.

Having a fire evacuation plan in a building can be thought of as a contingency and also a loss-prevention plan.

Loss Prevention

Insurance is one way of protecting against loss in the event that a risk manifests. Having alternative sites available into which a group can move in the event of a disaster is a loss-prevention strategy. Backup personnel can also be thought of as loss avoidance. If someone else can do the work when a key person is ill, there will be no loss to the project. Of course, this is difficult to do with highly skilled personnel.

Cost Contingency

Cost contingency is also called management reserve. Unfortunately, it is misunderstood. Too often it is believed that management reserve is there to cover poor performance. This is incorrect. Management reserve is a fund that is part of a project budget to cover the cost of unidentified work. All projects should have a work budget to cover the cost of identified work and a management reserve to cover work not yet identified. In addition, on projects that are paid for by a customer, there will be a component of the total job cost called *margin*. This is the intended profit for the job. Poor performance eats into margin, not management reserve.

The management reserve account is not touched unless we identify new work to be done. This is a change in scope, of course. At that point, money is transferred from the management reserve account into the work budget, and performance is subsequently tracked against the revised budget. A log should be maintained of all scope changes and their effect on the work budget, management reserve, and margin (if the change has such an effect). In customer-funded projects, the customer may be required to pay for scope changes so that there is no impact to the management reserve account.

B O X 15–1

WAYS OF MITIGATING OR AVOIDING RISKS

Portfolio Risks

Share risks with partners

Spread risks over time

Participate in many ventures

Group complementary risks into portfolios

Seek lower-risk ventures

Specialize and concentrate in a single, well-known area

Increase the company's capitalization

Commodity Prices

Hedge or fix in the futures markets

Use long- or short-term sales (price and volume) contracts

Tailor contracts for risk sharing

Interest Rate and Exchange Rate

Use swaps, floors, ceilings, collars, and other hedging instruments

Restructure the balance sheet

Denominate or index certain transactions in a foreign currency

Environmental Hazards

Buy insurance

Increase safety margins

Develop and test an incident response program

Operational Risks

Hire contractors under turnkey contracts

Tailor risk-sharing contract clauses

Use safety margins; overbuild and overspecify designs

Have backup and redundant equipment

Increase training

Operate with redirect and bail-out options

Conduct tests, pilot programs, and trials

Analysis Risks (Reducing Evaluation Error)

Use better techniques (i.e., decision analysis)

Seek additional information

Monitor key and indicator variables

Validate models

Include evaluation practices along with project post-reviews

Develop redundant models with alternative approaches and people

Schuyler (1995) has developed a list of possible ways to mitigate or avoid risks. These are shown in Box 15–1.

PROJECT MANAGEMENT APPROACH AS A FUNCTION OF RISK

As Jean Couillard (1995) has written, much of the literature on managing projects proposes a uniform set of tools and methods to manage all kinds of projects. A study by Couillard confirms a suggestion by McFarlan (1981) that the nature of the project should dictate the proper tools and methods. Risk, in particular, is a characteristic that should determine the best management approach.

Couillard found that if project risk is not considered, standard PERT/CPM techniques, project monitoring, and control do not have a significant influence on project success. However, in high-risk projects, these techniques *do* have a significant influence on success. In high-risk projects, using PERT/CPM, which increases the frequency of project monitoring and control, does improve the likelihood of project success. He concludes that high-risk projects should be more closely planned, monitored, and controlled than low-risk projects.

The study also showed that when technical risk is high, pure-project organization structure (see Chapter 10) has a significant *negative influence* on project success. It turns out that matrix structure is better for such projects, presumably because technical expertise can be more easily drawn from a matrix structure than the pure-project (or stand-alone) structure.

To measure success, Couillard employed the factors shown in Table 15–4. Based on the findings of Baker et al. (1974) (reported in Chapter 9), his measures seem to be appropriate, as

> When technical risk is high, matrix is better than pure-project organization.

the point is that project success should be called *perceived* success, since the quantitative measures alone (cost, performance, time, scope) do not always correlate with whether a

T A B L E 15–4

Project Success Measures

Tech 1	The subjective measurement of technical success relative to the initial requirement
Tech 2	The subjective measure of technical success compared to other projects in DND
Cost	The subjective measure of budget over/underrun
Time	The subjective measure of schedule over/underrun
Process	The level of satisfaction with the process by which the project was managed; a successful project is one that requires minimal conflict and crisis management (Might and Fisher, 1985)
Overall	The subjective measure of overall project success

Source: Adapted from Jean Couillard, "The Role of Project Risk in Determining Project Management Approach," *Project Management Journal*, December 1995, pp. 3–15. (Used with permission.)

project is judged successful or not. As you can see, Couillard is explicit in calling the measures *subjective*.

Altogether, Couillard used 17 factors to indicate aspects of project management. These are shown in Table 15–5.

Using regression analysis, Couillard concluded that communication patterns and project goal understanding significantly influence all six measures of project success (Table 15–4). This supports the frequent suggestion in the literature that you must have a clear, shared understanding of the project mission in order to be successful. Good communication within the team is also essential.

The authority given to the project manager to make decisions at the project level was also a factor, as were support received from the project team and problem handling by the team. This offers some credence to the complaint by project managers that they have a lot of responsibility but no authority. Based on this finding, senior managers should be sure to give the project manager the needed authority to deal with project issues directly.

T A B L E   15–5

Management Factors

Project Manager Experience	Project Management Method	Project Management Tools and Techniques
Number of projects managed	Project goals understanding	WBS utilization
Responsibility index	Level of PM authority and responsibility	PERT/CPM utilization
	Level of PD authority and responsibility	C/SCSC utilization
	Organizational structure	Periodic technical reports
	Senior management involvement	Periodic cost reports
	Communication patterns	Periodic schedule reports
	Problem handling	Frequency of project monitoring
	Project team support	

Source: Adapted from Jean Couillard, "The Role of Project Risk in Determining Project Management Approach," *Project Management Journal,* December 1995, pp. 3–15. (Used with permission.)

Project managers in the study were also asked to assess project risk with regard to three objectives: technical performance, schedule, and cost. Couillard used a three-point scale in which risk was rated as low, medium, and high. It was found that more-experienced project managers are generally assigned to the high-risk projects. Also, PERT/CPM, C/SCSC, and periodic technical reports are more frequently used in high-risk projects.

Technical Risk

When technical risk is high, project success is influenced by project manager authority, communication, team support, and problem handling. As previously mentioned, pure-project structure is also negatively correlated with success when technical risk is high.

Cost Risk

When cost risk is high, project success is influenced by understanding of project goals by the team, project manager authority, team support, and communication.

Schedule Risk

If schedule risk is high, two factors are important: the project manager's experience and the frequency of monitoring progress.

CONCLUSION

Many success factors in projects center around human relationships, which means that project managers must master these skills no matter the project risk. High-risk projects need more careful planning, monitoring, and controlling than do low-risk projects. In general, if you have any one or a combination of technical, cost, or schedule risks, it seems prudent to follow these guidelines:

1. Emphasize team support.
2. Give the project manager appropriate authority.
3. Improve problem handling and communication.
4. Avoid the pure-project structure.
5. Increase the frequency of project monitoring.
6. Use WBS, PERT/CPM, and C/SCSC.
7. Establish clear project goals for the team.
8. Select an experienced project manager.

16

Improving Decisions in Projects

Like all managers, project managers must make many decisions every day. For example, in planning the project, step 4 of the model requires that a project strategy be selected from a list made in step 3. There are four criteria that should be considered when

> "Decision makers should be judged on the quality of the decision-making approach that they follow."
> —Marvin Patterson

making this choice. These include whether the choice will meet cost, performance, time, and scope targets; whether risks are acceptable; whether consequences are acceptable; and whether the force-field analysis can pass muster (See Chapter 11).

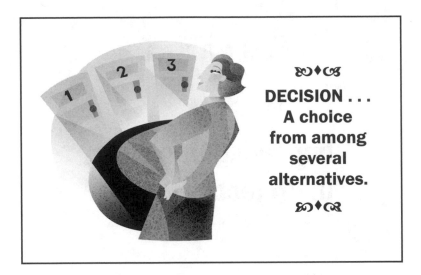

♠♦♣
**DECISION . . .
A choice
from among
several
alternatives.**
♠♦♣

THE STEPS TO EFFECTIVE DECISIONS

Marvin Patterson (1993) has written that decision makers should be judged on the quality of the decision-making *approach* that they follow, not on the quality of the decision outcomes themselves. The reason is that all decision making is done under uncertainty, and the decision maker is always trying to estimate the probability of an outcome. If decision making were deterministic, rather than probabilistic, then it would be a trivial exercise.

As an example of the problem facing any decision maker, we need to understand expected value. The expected value of a choice made under uncertainty is given by multiplying the probability of the outcome by its payoff or cost. Thus, we have:

$$EV = P \times \$$$

where:

EV = the expected value of the outcome
P = the probability of the outcome
$\$$ = the payoff or cost if the outcome occurs

Now let's assume that a manager is trying to decide which of two projects to invest in. One project has a 50-50 likelihood of success but will net the company $400,000 if it is successful. The other has a 90 percent chance of success, with a payoff of $150,000. Both projects will require an investment of about $50,000. If either one fails, of course, the company will lose the investment, not to mention the opportunity represented by the loss, which could have been applied somewhere else. Which project should she take? If we label the projects 1 and 2, the expected value for each is shown as follows:

$$EV_1 = 0.5 \times \$400,000 = \$200,000$$

$$EV_2 = 0.9 \times \$150,000 = \$135,000$$

Based on expected value of the outcome, the first project would be the better risk, with an EV of $200,000. But which choice do you think most decision makers would make? Probably the second one, because it has a higher probability of success.

The difficulty is that corporate America is largely risk-averse. If the manager chooses project 1 and it bombs, she is likely to be fired or at least severely reprimanded. However, over her career, if she made "project 1" choices, she would be more successful than the manager who always makes "project 2" choices, which are safer. Expected value computations give the decision maker a tool with which to judge choices quantitatively.

We will return to this method later in the chapter. First, however, we should examine the general approach that should be followed in making decisions. In their book, *Decision Making*, Janis and Mann (1977) outlined a series of steps that a person should follow to improve the quality of his or her decisions. These are presented as follows:

The decision maker, to the best of his or her ability, and within his/her information-processing capabilities:

1. Thoroughly canvasses a wide range of alternative courses of action.
2. Surveys the full range of objectives to be fulfilled and the values implicated by the choice.
3. Carefully weighs whatever he/she knows about the costs and risks of negative consequences, as well as the positive consequences, that would flow from each alternative.
4. Intensively searches for new information relevant to further evaluation of the alternatives.
5. Correctly assimilates and takes account of any new information or expert judgment to which she or he is exposed, even when the information or judgment does not support the course of action which she or he initially prefers.
6. Reexamines the positive and negative consequences of all known alternatives, including those originally regarded as unacceptable, before making a decision.
7. Makes detailed provisions for implementing or executing the chosen course of action, with special attention to contingency plans that might be required if various known risks were to materialize.

TOOLS FOR DECISION MAKING

All too often decisions are made based on intuition alone. If they could be evaluated—both quantitatively *and* qualitatively—a project manager would be more certain that the right choice has been made and would feel more confident about the ultimate outcome for the project. In fact, such an approach does exist, and a software package has been developed that makes the process very easy to apply. Furthermore, it can be applied individually or with a project team. It is called the "analytical hierarchy," and Dr. Thomas L. Saaty (1995) of the University of Pittsburgh is its author.

PAIRED COMPARISONS

The basis for the approach is called "paired-comparisons." When we are trying to make a choice from among a number of alternatives, what we are doing in essence is trying to rank the choices from best to worst so that we can pick the best one. To rank a list of choices requires that some criteria be used as the basis of ranking. Some examples of criteria might be: cost, quality, speed, performance, durability, appearance, flexibility, acceptability, and ease-of-use. If only one criterion is applied to do the ranking, then making a choice is fairly simple. However, few choices ever involve a single criterion, so what we might find is that one alternative is best for cost but has the worst performance, or one has the best appearance but poorest quality, and so on. For that reason, working with multiple criteria is very difficult, and software that handles such complex problems is very helpful.

We will address the multiple-criteria case later, but for now, let's focus on single criteria. Let's say that we want to rank a group of employees by using their cooperativeness as a criterion. If we could accurately measure cooperativeness, then the ranking would be easy. However, like many criteria, it is difficult to measure such a variable. It *is* fairly easy, though, to compare each employee to every other employee in the group and simply ask, "Which one is more cooperative?" This is best done using a matrix, as shown in Figure 16–1, wherein I have ranked six employees.

The matrix is set up so that the columns correspond to the rows. That is, column 1 represents Jane; column 2 represents Bill, and so on. Comparisons are made across rows. Naturally, comparing a person to himself does not make sense, so the letter x is placed down the diagonal. Once this is done, begin on row 1 by asking whether Jane is more cooperative than Bill. She is, so we put a 1 in column 2. Is she more cooperative than Shawna? Yes, so we place a 1 in column 3. The next three columns show zeros, meaning that Jane is *not* more cooperative than these three team members.

F I G U R E   16–1

Ranking of Team Members Using Cooperativeness as a Criterion

Person	1	2	3	4	5	6	Total	Rank
1. Jane	x	1	1	0	0	0	2	4
2. Bill	0	x	0	1	1	1	3	2
3. Shawna	0	1	x	1	1	1	4	1
4. Andrew	1	0	0	x	0	0	1	6
5. Melissa	1	0	0	1	x	0	2	5
6. Trent	1	0	0	1	1	x	3	3

When we get to row 2 we immediately see that we are asking if Bill is more cooperative than Jane, which was asked on row 1 in reverse. In fact, all of column 1 is going to be the inverse of row 1, so we can immediately fill in that column, then proceed with the rest of row 2. Similarly, you can fill in each row above the diagonal, then fill in the column with the same number with the inverse of its row. Then you total the rows, and the row with the highest total is ranked 1, next highest total is ranked 2, and so on.

We can clearly see that Shawna is the highest ranked person, with 4 points. Then we have a tie between Bill and Trent. That tie has been broken inside the matrix. If you look at row 2, where we ask if Bill is more cooperative than Trent, you find that the answer is yes, so Bill ranks one step above Trent. Similarly, there is a tie between Jane and Melissa, which has been broken in the matrix in Melissa's favor.

THE ANALYTICAL HIERARCHY

Dr. Saaty has extended the application of paired comparisons to include cases in which some aspects of the problem are quantitative and others are qualitative. Because the analysis involves matrix algebra, it is a challenge to do manually. So Dr. Saaty developed a software program called Expert Choice™ to do the analysis. It is available from Expert Choice, Inc. (call 412-682-3844 or download a demo version by visiting their Web site: http://www.expertchoice.com).

Using the Expert Choice software, I ranked employees as was done in the preceding section. As before, Shawna ranks number 1 and Melissa ranks at the bottom.

Figure 16–2 is a printout from Expert Choice showing the paired comparison matrix, together with a bar graph of their rankings.

This is a very simple example, and Expert Choice is not needed to do the employee ranking, but its use shows that it arrives at the same outcome as a manual paired-comparison. For more complex problems, the software is invaluable. Applications include choosing software, choosing computers, selecting project strategy, and so on.

DECISION ANALYSIS IN PROJECTS

Most decisions in projects involve committing resources, such as time and money. In the early stages of a project, you may be doing a feasibility study involving technical and economic viability. As project planning begins, risk analysis becomes important. Finally, there are the day-to-day decisions that must be made during the implementation of the project, through the closeout phase.

Although many situations will always involve a subjective evaluation of possibilities, Expert Choice and decision analysis methods are designed to help sort through a complex array of choices. Psychologists have found that humans can only deal with seven ± two bits of information at one time—that is, from five to nine. Some individuals can deal with nine, others with no more than five. When situations involve consideration of more than nine elements of information, we become overwhelmed. In this case, decision analysis is helpful.

F I G U R E 16–2

Matrix with Bar Graph Rankings

Rank employees using cooperativeness as a criterion

Node: 0

Compare the relative IMPORTANCE with respect to: GOAL

1 = EQUAL   3 = MODERATE   5 = STRONG   7 = VERY STRONG   9 = EXTREME

#	Left	9	8	7	6	5	4	3	2	1	1	2	3	4	5	6	7	8	9	Right
1	Jane	9	8	7	6	5	4	3	(2)	1	1	2	3	4	5	6	7	8	9	Bill
2	Jane	9	8	7	6	5	4	3	(2)	1	1	2	3	4	5	6	7	8	9	Shawna
3	Jane	9	8	7	6	5	4	3	2	1	(2)	3	4	5	6	7	8	9	Andrew
4	Jane	9	8	7	6	5	4	3	2	1	(2)	3	4	5	6	7	8	9	Melissa
5	Jane	9	8	7	6	5	4	3	2	1	(2)	3	4	5	6	7	8	9	Trent
6	Bill	9	8	7	6	5	4	3	2	1	(2)	3	4	5	6	7	8	9	Shawna
7	Bill	9	8	7	6	5	4	3	(2)	1	2	3	4	5	6	7	8	9	Andrew
8	Bill	9	8	7	6	5	4	3	(2)	1	2	3	4	5	6	7	8	9	Melissa
9	Bill	9	8	7	6	5	4	3	(2)	1	2	3	4	5	6	7	8	9	Trent
10	Shawna	9	8	7	6	5	4	3	(2)	1	2	3	4	5	6	7	8	9	Andrew
11	Shawna	9	8	7	6	5	4	3	(2)	1	2	3	4	5	6	7	8	9	Melissa
12	Shawna	9	8	7	6	5	4	3	(2)	1	2	3	4	5	6	7	8	9	Trent
13	Andrew	9	8	7	6	5	4	3	2	1	(2)	3	4	5	6	7	8	9	Melissa
14	Andrew	9	8	7	6	5	4	3	2	1	(2)	3	4	5	6	7	8	9	Trent
15	Melissa	9	8	7	6	5	4	3	2	1	(2)	3	4	5	6	7	8	9	Trent

Abbreviation	Definition
Goal	Rank employees using cooperativeness as a criterion
Jane	
Bill	
Shawna	
Andrew	
Melissa	
Trent	

Jane	.169	
Bill	.178	
Shawna	.219	
Andrew	.116	
Melissa	.143	
Trent	.176	

Inconsistency Ratio = 0.16

A typical decision analysis involves the following steps (Schuyler, 1995):

◆ Determine the decision alternatives.

◆ For each alternative, identify the possible outcomes and the outcome values.

◆ Assess the probabilities (or distributions) for the various chance events.

◆ Solve for the expected monetary value (EMV) of each alternative.

◆ Implement the best alternative.

As an example, suppose you have developed a project plan and are examining risk (see Chapter 15). You identify something that could go wrong. It can have a low, medium, or high impact on the project if it happens. To represent the possibilities, you draw a decision tree like the one shown in Figure 16–3.

F I G U R E   16–3

Simple Contingency Decision Tree

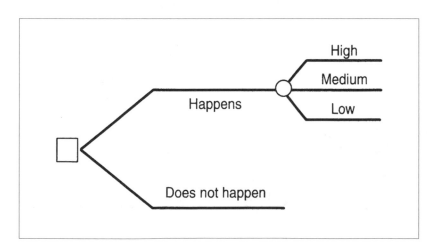

You believe that the probability of the event happening is only 30 percent (or 0.30). This means that there is a 0.70 probability that it won't happen. There are three options you can use to correct for the problem if it does happen, each with its own probability and associated cost. Using a decision tree, we can calculate the expected value (EV) of the risk if nothing is done to avoid it ahead of time. This is shown in the decision tree in Figure 16–4. Note that this is a cost impact to the project if it happens.

Whatever alternatives we consider must reduce the EV cost by more than the cost of implementing action. You could decide now to go ahead and apply option 1, rather than waiting to see if the risk materializes. However, it will cost you an additional $500 to implement option 1, whereas going with your current plan will cost nothing. Is this a good course of action?

Figure 16–5 shows the decision model in which we try option 1 initially. If we do apply option 1, we estimate that we reduce the risk of still having a problem from 0.3 to 0.1.

F I G U R E 16–4

Expected Value of the Risk If Nothing Is Done About It

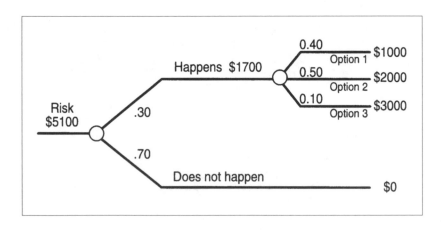

F I G U R E   16–5

Decision Tree Showing Option 1 Being Implemented Initially

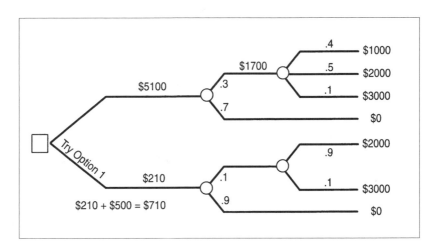

We also increase the probability of option 2 from 0.5 to 0.9. The expected value of implementing option 1 initially is $210, but since actually implementing the option costs $500, the total cost to the project is expected to be $710. Since this is significantly less than the $5,100 expected value (cost) to the project if nothing is done, it is clear that implementing option 1 from the very beginning is a good move.

If you want to go beyond decision analysis, you might want to consider preference theory. Since not all managers have the same attitude toward risk, preference theory allows the individual to tailor expected value computations to his or her own inclination to take risk. See Hammond (1975), for example.

SECTION THREE

PLANNING

17
CHAPTER

Developing a Shared Understanding of a Project

The first title I wrote for this chapter was "How to Develop a Shared Vision with Your Team." I changed it to "Developing a Shared Understanding of a Project" because the word "vision" has been used by so many people in so many ways that when people hear it, they are put off. We want all members of a project team to be going in the same direction, heading for the same destination. I don't care whether you call it "vision" or "peanut butter," there must exist a shared understanding of the project or you will not achieve the result you want.

> A primary purpose of planning is to produce a shared understanding of the project in the team.

The difficulty of doing this should not be taken lightly. It no longer surprises me when project managers tell me that they have been working on a project for three months and just learned that key members of their team are not on the same page with them. I have seen it time and time again. I am also not surprised, when I suggest to a team that we write out the mission statement and vision statement, that they protest that this is not necessary. "We all know what the mission is," they say.

My response is that if this is true, it is a mere formality to put it on paper and will only take a few minutes. I insist that we do it, because I know they are usually wrong in believing that a shared understanding exists, and even if they are right, there is no harm in doing the exercise. Never once have we been able to write a clear statement in a few minutes. If there are six people or twenty people in the room, you have almost as many perceptions of where the project is headed.

The other thing that I have found, as I suggested at the beginning of this chapter, is that different meanings of words like vision and mission have been used, so confusion is rampant. I want to clearly define what I mean in this chapter. I don't propose that my definitions are gospel and that everyone else is wrong. I simply know that unless we all agree on the meaning of the words we use, we can't possibly communicate with each other.

MISSION, VISION, PROBLEM STATEMENT

If you refer to the first two steps of my model for managing projects, which I have extracted and show in Figure 17–1, you will see that a project almost always begins as a concept, which must be turned into a concrete definition of what the project is going to be. I have also found that most projects tend to fail at this step. The reason is that people want to "get on with it" and do not want to spend time on this step. As I have said, they usually think they all understand and agree on what they are going to do, so there is no need to waste time going over ground that they have already covered.

F I G U R E 17–1

Steps 1 and 2 from the General Model

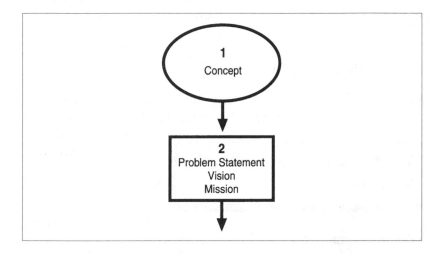

You will see in Figure 17–1 that three things must be done. A problem statement, vision, and mission statement must be developed. Why a problem statement? Because, as J. M. Juran has said, a project is a problem scheduled for solution. That is, every project is done to solve a problem that the organization has. However, we do not mean problem in the negative sense necessarily. Developing a new product is a problem, albeit a very positive one.

PROBLEM OR PROJECT DEFINITION

The team cannot develop a vision for the project until they understand the needs of clients. Chapter 18 covers defining clients' needs in more detail, so I will not say much about the process here. Suffice it to say that you must begin by identifying key project stakeholders, then identify their needs. A stakeholder is anyone who has a vested interest in the project.

These include customers, contributors, senior managers in your organization, key suppliers, and so on. Key stakeholders are those with the greatest influence on the project. Once these have been identified, you can examine their needs.

DEVELOPING A VISION

Once you formulate a problem statement, you next should develop a vision for the situation that would exist if the problem were solved. There are two reasons for this. One is that you won't know the problem is solved unless

> **Vision:** a positive mental image of the future.

you understand the conditions that would exist if it were solved. Second, having a vision for the desired end state creates a driving force that pulls or drives the team toward the final result. A shared vision can be a powerful motivating force and should not be underestimated in this regard. It lends a sense of purpose to a team, and purpose itself is very powerful. The mission for the team, in fact, is to achieve the vision. This is shown in Figure 17–2, compliments of my colleague John Carretti of Chesapeake Company.

To add more substance to the idea of vision, Peg Thoms (1997) has written, ". . . a shared vision refers to an image that a group of people—for example, a project team—hold in common, an image of how the project will look, work, and be received by the customers when it is completed. Technically, it is unlikely that all of the people in a group will have exactly the same mental image, but it will be similar if the vision is developed as a group" (p. 33). The key here is that the vision be developed by the group—the *entire* group, if possible; not the elite members alone, but all of them. The reason is simple: Unless every member—from

The Relationship between Problem Statement, Mission, and Vision

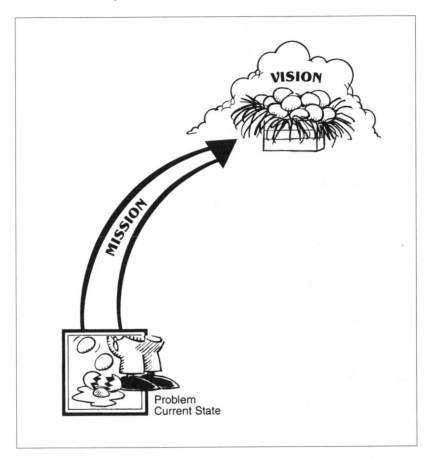

the lowest-status to the highest-status member of the team—shares the vision, fragmentation of effort is likely to occur at some step in the project.

The common complaint in large teams is that this is impractical. "You can't get 50 people together in one place to work on vision," howl the protestors. "It's impractical!" I'm sorry, that is not true. Practitioners all over the world have done so with groups much larger than 50, and the results are outstanding. In fact, there is no other way to achieve the same result that is accomplished by having the entire group work on developing a shared vision. When a few people work on a vision and then try to communicate it to others, it just never has the same impact. People to whom the vision is communicated either (1) don't get it, (2) don't agree with it, or (3) don't buy into it, because "it is *their* vision, not ours." When they participate in developing it, however, it is "ours," not theirs, and commitment is the result of that ownership.

No doubt, it is difficult to identify all members of the team from the very outset of a project, so some of the later additions will not have participated in formulating the vision. However, if most of the group was involved, they will collectively be able to communicate the vision much better than could be done by the project manager alone. In fact, a shared vision that is important to a group is contagious. In no time at all, new members of a team will be "infected" by it.

HOW TO DEVELOP A SHARED UNDERSTANDING

When a core project team is formed, you should explain the assignment and the overall objectives of the organization for the project. Let them know that there will be another meeting in a few days to develop a shared understanding of the project. I personally prefer to avoid the words vision and mission because they carry negative baggage. The term "shared understanding," on the other hand, is more palatable. Or I might say that we are going to meet to be sure we are all on the "same page together" in our understanding of the project.

The meeting to develop a shared vision should be well planned and well managed. If possible, a facilitator skilled in group process should lead the team through the steps. The process that I am going to outline is a derivative of what is called the "future search conference." The format was originally developed by Emery and Trist in the 1950s and has been used worldwide with all kinds of groups to plan future outcomes. Perhaps one of the strongest advocates for future search today is organization development practitioner Marvin Weisbord (Weisbord and Janoff, 1995).

The idea behind the future search meeting is very simple: The best way in which an organization can arrive at an ideal future is to get the entire membership together in one place and let them plan that future themselves. Note that the group should begin by designing the *ideal* scenario, and then, if necessary, they

> The best way an organization can arrive at an ideal future is to have the entire membership plan it themselves.

can settle for less. It is always easy to give up things if need be. It is harder to go the other way.

For groups larger than nine, subgroups are formed. The guiding rule is that working groups should be sized between five and nine, so for large groups, small subgroups are set up. The facilitator gives them assignments, which are always time limited. The groups need ample working space so that they are not on top of each other when they do their assignments, so a large room is necessary. Alternatively, break-out rooms can be used. Each subgroup also needs a flip chart and lots of colored felt markers, drafting tape, and any other media that can be used for creative thinking.

The first step in the process is to identify all attributes of the project deliverable. If it is a product, what will it be like? How will it work? How will the customer use it? How will it compare to other similar products? If the project is to move a facility, the questions might be: How would we conduct the ideal move? Who would move various departments? How would the timing work? How do we move people so they can be functional immediately after the move?

The best "tool" for identifying all attributes of a project outcome/deliverable is probably the mind map. You begin by writing the name of the project in an oval, then start listing major attributes around it. These will, in turn, make you think of related ideas, which are clustered around the major attributes, and so on, until everything has been covered. There is an example in Figure 17–3. If you would like to read a book on the many uses of mind maps, I highly recommend Tony Buzan's *The Mind Map Book* (1993).

F I G U R E 17–3

A Mind Map for a Project

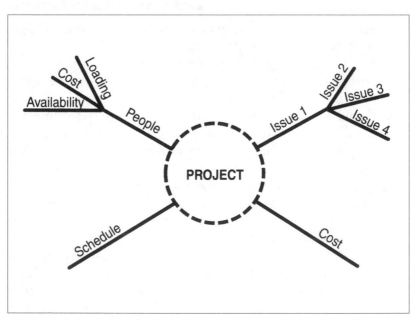

Once the mind map is finished, you can have the group describe the ideal scenario, which would optimize all attributes that have been listed in the map. There are creative ways to do this. Draw a picture of a product, write a commercial and present it, or design a brochure. If the project is moving a facility, put on a skit that demonstrates how the move is to be accomplished. For other scenarios, the group might write songs, poems, skits, raps, and so on. These are all presented by the subgroups for the others.

I once worked with a group of school principals to design the ideal school. They went away in their subgroups and wrote songs, skits, and a Charles Kuralt-like "on-the-road" interview. These were then presented. The amazing thing about this process is that the core ideas presented are usually very similar. You would almost swear that the groups colluded to develop their presentations. Furthermore, by the time all groups have finished, you have a wealth of ideas that can now be drawn on by the entire group. These can now be incorporated into the overall end result.

The process creates an enormous amount of energy. Recently I co-facilitated a version of one of these on a Saturday, and at 3:00 p.m. people were at a higher energy level than you would ever expect after working all day. And they understood their project much better than they ever would have if we had merely communicated it to them. In addition, the subgroups developed several good strategies, so that the project manager will now be able to work with them to select the best strategy to be implemented later on.

COMPLETING THE PROCESS

The team now has an ideal vision for the project. Naturally, we generally cannot "go for broke" in most projects, so we will probably forego some attributes. One way to do this is to place those attributes in three categories. These are labeled

F I G U R E 17–4

Problem Statement, Vision, Mission

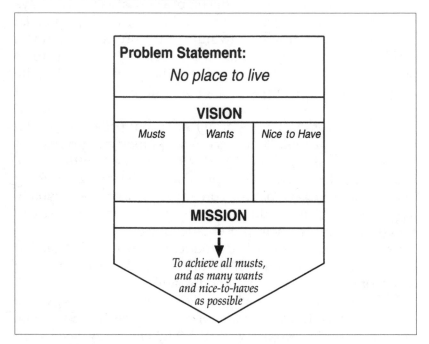

must-have, want, and nice-to-have. I have shown this in Figure 17–4, to illustrate the relationship between problem statement, vision, and mission in a slightly different way than was done in Figure 17–2.

Having done all of this, you can now proceed to step 3 in my general model of managing projects, which is to develop a project strategy.

18

CHAPTER

Identifying Customer Requirements

Every project team has the same ultimate mission that an organization has—to meet the needs of customers. In case you still have not resolved for yourself the apparent conflict between making a profit and meeting customer needs, perhaps this will help: The primary *motive* of a business is to make a profit. Its *mission* is to meet customer needs. Naturally, they must both be accomplished. The difficulty is that if we get focused on

> The *motive* of a business is to make a profit. The *mission* is to meet the needs of customers.

profits as our mission, we may do short-sighted things that will make us more money in the short term but cost us our customers in the long term.

As an example, a restaurant needs to turn its tables as fast as possible during lunchtime to maximize its sales. So the manager tells the chef, "Don't take too long to prepare each meal. Keep it short. Turn up the temperature on the stove so the food cooks fast." He also tells the serving staff, "Get them in and out as fast as possible."

Of course, the end result is that the food is poor quality and the serving staff borders on being rude. Sooner or later, word gets around and the business dies.

WHO IS THE CUSTOMER?

The next point that is important is to define "customer." Essentially, a customer is defined as anyone who uses what the project team produces. That means that there can be more than one customer. A product development group produces prototypes and drawings for manufacturing to use to make the final product. The manufacturing department is a customer of the design team. So is the ultimate customer, who buys the product. Each has different needs. The design team has to meet all of those needs.

The following definitions might help in understanding the different categories of customers and their needs. There are three categories:

1. *Internal customers* are those people inside your company who use something you produce. Often they are next-in-line. For a product-development group, this would be the manufacturing department, which takes the drawings for a new product and actually makes the product from those drawings.
2. *Intermediate customers* are usually external to the company but not the final end-user of the product or service. They will typically be distributors of products.
3. *External customers* are considered to be the users of the product or service being delivered by the company.

In some cases, it might be better to say that we must satisfy all "stakeholders" for a project, since we will eventually be judged by them. A stakeholder is anyone who has a vested interest in the project. This includes contributors, actual customers, financial people who are funding the project, and perhaps the community outside the organization.

If we are to meet the needs of our customers, however, we must have some way of

> **Stakeholder:** Anyone who has a vested interest in the project.

knowing what those needs really are. This is easier said than done. If you ask the customer, you can't always get a good answer, because the customer really isn't sure what she needs. All she knows is that she has a problem, and she is hoping you can solve it. This means, of course, that you have to translate the customer's needs into a solution.

Note that we are also using the word "needs" to mean both actual needs as well as what the customer *wants*. Following the restaurant example, I might need nutritious food and want it to taste good. I might want to be treated a certain way by the serving staff. Taken together, these define for me the *quality* of the experience I have with the restaurant. Deming and others have said that *only* the customer can tell you what qual-ity means. So when we are doing a pro-

> **Principle:** *Only* the customer can tell you what quality is for the product or service you provide.

ject in which we try to satisfy the customer, we are sure to have to meet her needs, wants, and expectations.

In some cases, we are solving a problem for the customer. Here again, the customer might not know exactly what the problem is. You must sometimes begin with the *symptoms* that tell the customer she has a problem to begin with. I say this because it is through symptoms that we know we have problems. For example, someone says, "Sales are down this month." That is a symptom of a problem, not the problem itself. Until we know what is causing sales to slump, we cannot correct it. It could be the sales staff has had a number of illnesses, or the market is depressed just now, or perhaps a competitor is undercutting your price.

The thing is, the way a problem is defined determines the approach that we will take to solve it, so it is vitally important that we define the problem being solved by the project, or identify customer needs, wants, and expectations, before we go beyond step 2 in the flowchart.

> **Principle:** The way you define a problem determines the approach you will use to solve it.

In fact, failure to properly handle step 2 is the cause of many project failures. I often say that projects don't fail at the end, they fail at the beginning. Quality time spent on this step will pay dividends later on.

THE NEED FOR FIRSTHAND UNDERSTANDING OF THE CUSTOMER

I believe that every member of a project team should have a firsthand understanding of customer requirements. In saying this, I have absolutely no intention of usurping the role of the marketing department or any other group that is responsible for telling you what the customer expects of you. Those individuals have an important role to play.

However, in the typical scenario, the marketing department has someone interview customers, conduct a focus group or survey, and then develop a written description of what the customer wants. Invariably, the marketing person has to *translate*, because the customer often does not know what he or she wants. She only knows that she has a problem that must be addressed and is looking to the provider to develop a product or service that will solve that problem or meet her need. This means that the marketing group can *mistranslate* what they think the customer wants.

In any case, the marketing department develops their specification and it is passed on to the product development group. Now another translation takes place. The product developers interpret the written spec into what *they* think it represents as a product, and there is room for another error. Is it any wonder that by the time the customer gets the final result, it is nothing like what she wanted?

The importance of understanding the customer firsthand was brought home to me about three years after I started my career as an engineer. I worked for a small company that made land-mobile radio equipment, and we sold some units to the police department of a major city. They had some technical difficulties with one of the radios, and I was sent to correct the problem. While I was working on the radio, I was approached by a very large police officer.

"You work for Aerotron?" he asked.

I told him that I did.

"Good. I'd like to give you some feedback on this handheld unit," he said.

"Okay," I said.

"You see these little tiny knobs?" he said, pointing to the top of the radio.

I nodded my affirmation.

> "The real problem with this radio is that when you hit somebody with it, the case cracks, and you can't call for backup."
>
> —Police Officer

"You can't get a hold of these little knobs when you have a hand as big as mine," he said, holding up a big paw. "Especially when you have gloves on," he continued.

I told him he had a good point.

"You know what the real problem is with this radio?" he asked.

I didn't.

He looked me directly in the eye and said, "When you hit somebody with this thing, the case cracks, and you can't call for backup."

ಬಿ ◆ ಛ

**If you can't
call for
backup, you
really have a
problem.**

ಬಿ ◆ ಛ

I said something to the effect that we hadn't designed it to be used as a billy stick.

"Maybe not," he said, "but when somebody jumps you in an alley, you hit him with whatever you have handy. When it's the radio, and the case cracks, then you can't call for backup and you've really got a problem."

Now, like it or not, this is a real-world situation. The radio design was changed to make it withstand a higher impact, and the problem was apparently solved. Consider, however, an engineer who is shown the impact spec without understanding the reason for it.

"What idiot wrote this?" he says. "We aren't supposed to be designing a club!"

Little does he know.

Over the years I have experienced numerous incidents in which firsthand understanding of the customer has made a significant difference in how designers develop products. One scientist that I know visited a lab in which his products were used and came away totally transformed. He got so many new ideas that it will take him years to develop all of them.

SOME CAUTIONS

Since I believe strongly in firsthand understanding of customers, I encouraged one of my clients to start a customer involvement program (CIP). The program was designed to get technical people into the field to visit customers. They usually went along with a sales or marketing person. The first mistake we made, however, was that we didn't teach the techies to

> Before you send employees to the field to talk to customers, teach them to *listen.*

listen. So as soon as a customer made a critical comment about a previous product, the technical person got defensive, started explaining why the customer was wrong, and lost the opportunity to learn from what the customer had to say.

Another problem is failing to distinguish between customer requirements and product features. A study conducted by Product Development Consulting and the Business Roundtable was reported in the *PM Network* April 1995 issue. Although this study is quite old, the findings are still relevant today. They surveyed 4,000 companies in a wide range of industries, including electromechanical systems, medical, aerospace/defense, components, automotive, computer, and services. One-third of the responses were from "best-in-class" companies, this being based on sales volume and market share. This group was contrasted with average performers to determine differences in practice.

The best-in-class pass on requirements. The others specify features. For example, there is a significant difference between telling a designer that the customer wants to be able to change channels in the dark and telling him to "put a light on the remote." The customer requirement allows the designer to exercise some creativity in solving the problem, whereas the other is a rote solution. As Sheila Mello, a principal at Product Development Consulting, remarked, "Given a directive, engineers are destined to produce 'me-too' products. But when provided with an in-depth view of customers' needs, they are likely to create 'delighters'" (*PM Network,* April 1995, p. 49).

> We must distinguish between customer requirements and product features.

Another interesting finding from the study is that understanding customer needs does not necessarily mean interviewing more people. On average, best-in-class companies were found to gather data from around 10 customers, compared with 24 for average performers. Furthermore, the best companies were more likely to interview customers in-depth rather than to use focus groups. The problem with focus groups is that members of the group influence each other, so you don't know for sure if a customer really had a specific need or it just sounded good when someone else said it. Also, by conducting interviews at the customer's worksite, the interviewer can gain firsthand knowledge of the environment and how the customer might apply the product. This was one of the things that struck the scientist mentioned earlier. He saw how the customer actually worked, and this gave him a lot of ideas on how to improve the design of his products.

Finally, the study found that best-in-class companies focus on the total product, taking into account various factors that influence product success, such as product-specific sales and service strategies. The less effective companies tend to focus only on product development skills and technology core competencies. The bottom line is that businesses that want to become market leaders must develop a companywide vision of their customers' complete needs.

THE NEED FOR CONCURRENT PROJECT MANAGEMENT

Not only are there problems in understanding outside customers, but problems in meeting the needs of inside customers as well. When the marketing department develops a product specification and hands it off to product developers, who have no direct contact with customers, we say the specification has been "thrown over the wall." In fact, in a typical product development scenario, you have a sequence like the one shown in Figure 18–1.

F I G U R E 18–1

Groups Involved in Product Development

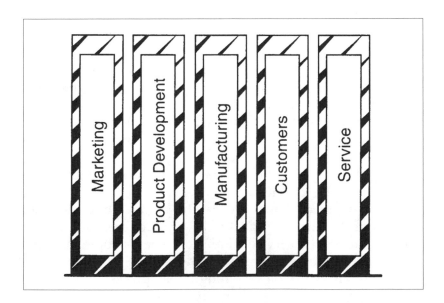

Now, before you say, "I'm not in product development, so I can skip this," let me suggest that you read on. I believe what I am going to discuss applies to all projects.

The walls between the various groups should be thought of as the walls of silos, not cubicles. The reason is that you can see over a cubicle wall and even converse. The walls of a silo are too tall to permit conversation, so when people work in silos, they are isolated from the rest of the world.

As I said above, in this situation, marketing throws the product spec over the wall to product developers, who look at it and break out in hives. They throw it back over the wall to marketing, protesting that they can't possibly develop a product with *these* specs to sell for the desired price. This process might go through several cycles before a spec is finally agreed upon.

Then the product developers design the product and throw their drawings over the wall to manufacturing. The people in manufacturing look at the drawings and throw them back over the wall to product development. "We can't make this thing in our plant," they protest.

"Not our problem," say the product developers. "We designed it. You guys have to build it."

This also goes through several cycles, and occasionally some redesign is necessary before manufacturing agrees that they can build the product.

Then the product is shipped. The customer takes one look at it and says, "What is this? Who came up with this idea? This isn't what we need."

Again, the product might have to go back for more redesign to solve this problem.

Finally, the customer accepts the product, but this is not the end of the line. Eventually, the product breaks. The customer takes it to a service shop. The repair people take one look at it and they also break out in hives.

"We can't work on this thing!" they protest.

As a real-world example, certain cars and vans were so designed that the spark plugs could not be reached without pulling the engine out of the vehicle or cutting a hole through the firewall. Wouldn't that be a shock if you were the customer? You take your car in to have the plugs changed, which should be a routine servicing job, and the mechanic tells you it will cost about $500 dollars in labor to take the engine out—just to change a $5 plug!

One auto company solved this problem in inimitable style: They put a platinum-point plug in the one position that couldn't be easily reached. You don't have to change that type of plug but once in 100,000 miles, though—and hopefully, by then, you will have traded the vehicle and it will be someone else's problem!

This entire throw-it-over-the-wall scenario is ridiculous, and fortunately many organizations abandoned it long ago. However, I find it is still alive and well in entirely too many companies. If yours is one of them, I urge you to practice concurrency, as shown in Figure 18–2.

The only way to solve the problem is for everyone involved—from concept through final disposal of the product—to be involved in the process throughout. This is why the process is called *concurrent*—everyone is involved at every step.

This way, manufacturing can provide guidance to product development on how the product should be designed to make it manufacturable. And service can do

> Rather than abandon concurrency because of its difficulty, learn to manage consensus.

the same so that it can be repaired when it finally breaks down. And the customer can give guidance on how the product should be designed in order to best meet her needs.

This practice is exemplified by the process employed by Alan Mulally to manage development of Boeing's 777 airplane.

F I G U R E 18–2

Concurrent Project Management

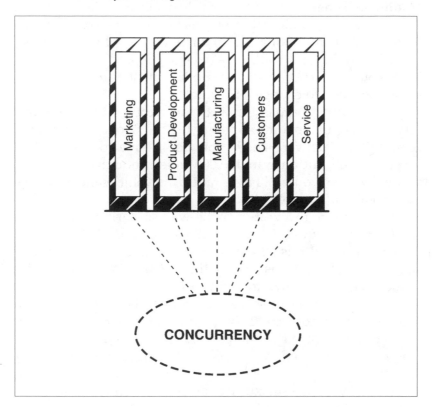

It was dubbed the *working together* approach, and was actually modeled after a process developed by Lew Viraldi to manage the Taurus program at Ford. In fact, Alan Mulally joined Ford in 2006 as CEO, and is now implementing the working together model throughout the organization. See my book, *Working Together*, for details on this approach (Lewis, 2002).

The problem—as you know if you have ever tried this approach—is that it is extremely difficult to make it work. As Dilbert has said in one of Scott Adams's cartoon strips, "The difficulty of getting agreement goes up as the exponent of the number of people involved." So the inclination is to throw out the process and go back to throw-it-over-the-wall.

That is the wrong response. Rather than throw out the process because it is difficult, we need to learn to manage consensus. Unfortunately, we find that many people don't seem to know how to do this. They generally resort to majority rule, by voting, and this always leads to problems if the issue is a serious one. A couple of things are likely to happen. One, as soon as a problem crops up, the outvoted members will say, "I told you so." Second, even if there are no problems, the dissenters will often refuse to support the majority approach or may even try to sabotage it to prove that they were right.

But how do you get everyone to agree on anything?

You don't. That is too high an order. What consensus must mean is that every member of the group is able to say, "While I don't entirely agree with the majority, I have heard you, and you have listened to me, and I am willing to support the approach you want to take."

This is the best you can do with a group. The key word is *support*. Every member must be willing to say she or he will support the approach. If someone can't do that, then you need to try to find an alternative that everyone can support or try to convince the person to go along with the majority, or—in some rare cases—just overrule them. It's not a good thing, but you occasionally have to do it. Naturally, if you need the person's support later on, you aren't likely to get it.

USING THE QUALITY FUNCTION DEPLOYMENT MATRIX

One tool that is helpful in understanding stakeholder requirements is the quality function deployment matrix (QFD). It is sometimes called the "house of quality." The name itself is enough to scare anyone to death. Quite simply, it should be called a correlation matrix, in which we look at customer concerns (whether they be needs or wants) and product or service features and ask which of these have correlations.

In *The QFD Book* (1993), Guinta and Praizler suggest that QFD should be used to answer three questions:

1. What are the qualities or characteristics that the customer wants?
2. What functions must this product serve, and what functions must we use to provide this product or service?
3. Given the resources that we have available, how can we best provide (deploy) what our customer wants?

QFD is used to translate broad product requirements or specifications into specific action assignments. This is done through the use of a number of matrices. It helps teams determine the right methods, tools, and order in which they should be used. Note also that you do not have to be developing products to use QFD to advantage. You can be developing a new service or trying to solve almost any kind of problem. In fact, throughout the remainder of this chapter, the term *product* will be used to mean product or service in general.

When QFD is used properly, it results in shorter product development cycles (or less time to solve problems), provides lower costs and greater productivity in making products, and helps us break out of the paradigm dictating that higher quality products mean higher costs. In fact, improving quality of a product usually leads to lower production costs. The reason—elimination of scrap, rework, and warranty costs.

A major benefit of QFD is that it virtually eliminates the throw-it-over-the-wall approach discussed earlier, because it brings together people and data from many places—customers, marketing, product development, manufacturing, field service, and so on. By using this collective knowledge, companies can identify what will work and what won't. Since as much as 80 percent of project cost is determined in this early phase, the QFD assessment can greatly reduce program costs and development time—simultaneously!

According to Guinta and Praizler, companies that use QFD for product development have achieved a 50 percent reduction in costs, 33 percent reduction in development time, and 200 percent increase in productivity (1993, p. 14).

Although the full-blown QFD process can get fairly complicated, the essence of the approach is simple. Customer needs are correlated with product or service features. I am using the word *need* to stand for musts, wants, and nice-to-haves that were discussed in Chapter 17. Furthermore, the customer ranks his needs so that the project team can be sure to satisfy them in order of importance. If trade-offs must be made, we can do so with the low-priority items rather than the high-priority ones.

As an example of a QFD matrix, consider Figure 18–3. This matrix is for a hotel. Down the left side we list customer needs. In this case, we have a mixture of musts, wants, and nice-to-haves. Across the top, we list some features of a hotel that might satisfy customer needs. In each cell, we put a +, *, 0, – or – – to indicate the relationship between the feature and the customer need. A + means that there is a positive correlation between the feature and satisfaction of the need. A * is a strong positive correlation. A 0 means no relationship. A – sign is a negative. That is, there is actually a negative relationship between the feature and the customer's need. Finally, a – – is a strong negative correlation.

We can see in Figure 18–3 that the customer's most important concern is security—but none of the hotel features correlate with security. Clearly, the team that did this analysis has missed something and now must go back to the drawing board. Also, notice that convenience is negatively correlated with quietness. If the hotel is near a freeway, it is convenient, but the freeway noise might be a problem.

One of the key ideas of QFD is that we should give the customer those features that have correlations *with things he*

F I G U R E 18–3

QFD Matrix for a Hotel

+ = CORRELATION ∗ = STRONG CORRELATION 0 = NO CORRELATION	Individual Temp. Control	Lighting	Furnishings	Cable TV	Room Service Menu	Courteous Staff	Airport Courtesy Van	Rank
Comfort	∗	+	∗	0	∗	0	+	2
Service	0	0	0	0	∗	∗	∗	3
Price for Value	∗	∗	∗	∗	∗	∗	∗	5
Security	0	0	0	0	0	0	0	1
Able to Read or Work Comfortably	0	∗	∗	0	0	0	0	4
Access to Telephone / Computer	0	0	+	0	0	0	0	6
Convenience	0	0	0	0	∗	0	∗	7

cares about and not give him things that he either cares nothing about or that at least have very low correlations! I have known product developers who wanted to incorporate a feature in a design because they thought it was nifty, but the customer didn't want it and would have to pay for it if it were included. We need to be customer-driven, not designer-driven. This process of incorporating features into a product simply because the engineer thinks they are desirable is called "gold plating" in the *Project Management Body of Knowledge* (PMI, 2004).

Interestingly, in recent years the hotel industry has come to an astonishing realization. Customers actually want comfortable beds in their rooms! Who would have believed it? (I'm being sarcastic, of course.) Their response has been quite admirable—they are replacing older beds with new plush ones that really are very comfortable.

One problem with QFD is that you can generate an enormous amount of data that can quickly become overwhelming. You don't want to go into analysis paralysis and get nothing done, so you have to use judgment as to when the analysis should be stopped.

As I said earlier, QFD can get very involved in its full-blown form. For an in-depth treatment refer to Guinta and Praizler's *The QFD Book*.

19
CHAPTER

Managing Resources
in Project Scheduling

It has been estimated that of the million people who have bought Microsoft Project, only a few percent are using the resource leveling feature. I would concur with that estimate. Of the thousand people who attend my classes every year, only a small number are doing much with resource allocation. They have tried assigning people to tasks, even leveling them, but the situation is so complex that many of them give up.

> If you can't manage resources, your schedule is unrealistic.

The problem is, this is the key to meeting a schedule. If you don't have adequate resources, your schedules are not realistic, and in my opinion, a wrong schedule is worse than no schedule because it sets up an unrealistic expectation that causes frustration when the deadline is missed. As you may know, developing critical path diagrams involves a hidden assumption that you have unlimited resources. This is because each task is estimated independently of the others.

Then when you do your diagram, you are supposed to show what is logically possible to do. At some point, you have two tasks that can logically be done in parallel. However, the same person is assigned to both of them. If that assignment is full time on each, then you have the individual double-scheduled, which won't work. The hidden assumption was that you had two persons available, when you really only had one. So, unless you manage the allocation of resources, you wind up with a schedule that can't be met.

ASSIGNING RESOURCES TO TASKS

The first problem in scheduling is estimating task durations. This is discussed in detail in Chapter 28. We must begin with the number of working hours (or days or weeks) that will be required to complete a task with a certain person assigned to it. If you can't assign a specific person to a task at the planning stage because you don't know who will actually do the task when the time comes, then you will have to assign a *skill-category* to the task. This means that you would assume the person assigned is going to be someone from the required discipline having a certain level of skills. Members of that discipline would then have to estimate how long the task would take a person having those skills. It isn't perfect, but it's the best you can do sometimes.

> What does full time really mean?

Next you have to ask if the person will be assigned to the task on a full-time or part-time basis. Let's begin by assuming a full-time assignment. The person will work on the assigned task and nothing else until it is complete. I know this is very unrealistic in most organizations. Most people are working on many assignments at once. Still, we'll start with this scenario just to show that even with the best of situations, there are still problems to resolve.

The first problem is, what do we mean by full time? If we assume we are scheduling people to work a standard 8-hour day, 40-hour week (which you really should do—keeping overtime in reserve as a way of handling unexpected problems), then you could say that a task requiring 16 hours of working time would span two days. However, this assumption would get you into trouble. If the working time required is really 16 hours, it will take more than two days to accomplish it, because nobody works 8 productive hours each day.

Industrial engineers reduce the 8-hour day by 20 percent to account for what they call *personal, fatigue,* and *delays* (PF&D). People need to take occasional breaks (personal), they get tired (fatigue), and their work is held up by other people, unavailability of materials, information, or other resources (delays). Thus, a standard 8-hour day yields only 6.4 hours of productive work. This means that our 16-hour task will span 2.5 days. If the person starts first thing Monday morning, he will finish around noon on Wednesday.

At this point, we better evaluate the assumption that people are available even 80 percent of their time to do productive work. I was told by a fellow that his company became frustrated because they missed so many project deadlines and couldn't understand why. They seemed to have enough resources, based on the 80 percent assumption.

> Typical availability of knowledge workers for project work is 40 to 60 percent.

As a test of their assumption, they gave each project member a log sheet and told them to record, once an hour, what they had been doing during the previous hour. They did this for two weeks. To their surprise, they found that many of their team members were working on project assignments only 25 percent of the time! No wonder nothing was getting done on time! With people working on projects only

25 percent of the time, rather than 80 percent, the calendar time required to finish a task is at least 3.2 times longer than planned.

Since he told me this, I have surveyed several hundred people informally, and they tell me that they experience similar situations. At best, they tell me that the availability of people to do project work is about 50 to 60 percent.

What robs us of their time? Many factors are involved. Just to list a few, meetings that have nothing to do with the project, nonproject assignments, training classes, interruptions from people, helping people work on other assignments, working on proposals for future projects, working on next year's budget, and solving problems in old projects that you thought were complete, but you're the only person left who knows anything about it. One factor that stands out as a major issue is sharing a person with other projects. We will discuss this one in more detail later on.

The lesson, of course, is that you must be realistic about how much time a person has available to work on your project or your schedule will be grossly inaccurate. The only way to assure anyone is available to work 80 percent on a project is to tie them to a desk and keep them there. In factory environments, though, 80 percent availability is often the norm, since the worker's situation is essentially that he or she is not free to wander around or be assigned other to other tasks. For knowledge workers, however, 80 percent availability is unrealistic.

THE EFFECTS OF MULTIPLE PROJECTS ON PRODUCTIVITY

Another reason why resources are not available more than 80 percent of the time is that they are shared with other projects. Informal surveys of my seminar participants indicates that most of them have team members working on two to six projects at the same time, with the norm being about four projects.

This means that team members are available to work on a given project only 20 percent of the time.

If this were a linear effect, it would be bad enough, but it is not linear. To illustrate, suppose I assigned you a task that you could complete in six working hours if you could work straight through until you finished it. Of course, this is a pretty long stretch, so you would probably work three or four hours in the morning and finish it in the afternoon. Would it still take six hours? No. The reason is that you would have to spend a few minutes getting reoriented to the task after taking a break. It may be only a few minutes, but it does reduce your productivity.

Now suppose, because of working conditions, that you have to work on the task two

> Setup time adds no value to a process. Eliminate setup time and improve productivity.

hours today, another two tomorrow, and two more the third day. Now the task will take even longer than it would by splitting it into two chunks. The reorientation time is called *setup time* in manufacturing, and we learned years ago that setup time is a total waste. Every minute of setup time eliminated is a minute gained for productive work.

This shows why we have problems with multiple projects. People are constantly shifting back and forth from one project to another. Time management studies have found that if you get interrupted by a person (face-to-face or by phone) while you are working on a task, you may need 15 to 20 minutes to get reoriented to it. If you get interrupted three times in one hour, you may lose most of that hour, even though each interruption lasts only five minutes.

Not only do you lose productivity because of setup time, but consider the time people spend in meetings—usually a minimum of one hour per week for each project. And, as we know, many meetings are virtually nonproductive, so having people work on several projects at once also increases time wasted in meetings.

Experience has shown that there are big gains to be made by reducing the number of projects that people are working on. One company found that by having people work on one project as a primary project, with a secondary project that they could work on if they had some dead time, their productivity nearly doubled.

It can be very hard to get senior management to buy into this notion. They get trapped into thinking that everything must be done at once, not realizing that if they would prioritize projects and do them in priority order, they would get everything done in the same calendar time and at higher efficiency and higher quality.

QUEUING THEORY AND RESOURCE MANAGEMENT

Another factor that adversely affects projects is the lean-mean paradigm that is so prevalent in organizations today. As a brief historical perspective, you might think back to the 1980s and remember that many companies had layer upon layer of management. This was probably the ultimate consequence of the belief that a manager could only directly supervise about six people. Over time, organizations became pyramidal—one manager had six people reporting to her, and each of them in turn had six people reporting to them, and so on.

This might have been necessary in the early days of the industrial revolution, when many workers had little education and required a lot of supervision, but it had ceased to be true by the 1980s. Nevertheless, we clung to it, because the paradigm was that span of control should be limited to six direct reports, and that was that.

Then people began realizing that this was no longer true, and a wave of reductions in middle management followed. The metaphor was that we were getting rid of *excess fat*, and we were. The result was highly positive for business: The bottom line showed *immediate* improvement, and rightfully so. If you eliminate costs without affecting sales revenues, you have automatically increased profits.

Because that first dose of cost-cutting felt so good, managers were quick to apply more of it. When you find something that works, it is natural to try it again, so they did. Now we

> A lot of organizations have focused on "trimming fat" to the point that they may die of anorexia.

are in the midst of the lean-mean paradigm. Companies have cut every expendable person they can identify.

Trouble is, some of them long ago got rid of *all* the fat, so now they're cutting muscle.

In addition, since this is a biological metaphor, we know that you don't want to remove all of the fat from any organism. The fat provides reserve energy for hard times. But we have failed to realize this.

So, what does queuing theory have to do with the situation? Queuing theory deals with things like highway capacity, production line capacity, and so on. If you have ever tried to get onto a major highway during rush hour, when everyone else in the whole world was also trying to get onto it, you understand what hap-

> Insanity is defined as continuing to do what you've always done and expecting to get a different result. I think mindlessness is continuing to do something that has worked in the past and expecting it to get the same results as it always has.

pens when any system is at its limits. The amount of time you must wait to get onto the highway gets very high at

F I G U R E 19–1

Waiting Time as a Function of System Utilization

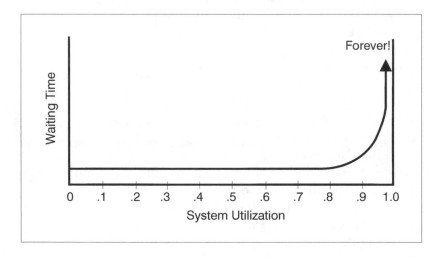

rush hour. At other times of the day, it is insignificant. Figure 19–1 shows how this works. As the capacity of a system approaches 100 percent, the waiting time to use that system approaches infinity!

This same idea can be applied to a resource pool. As we load people up to their limit, the time new projects must wait to be started approaches infinity. Yet many managers think that the only way to be productive is to keep people working at 100 percent (or even greater) capacity. And when people try to say they're overloaded, some of the very macho managers tell them to quit complaining, they're lucky to have jobs.

THE WONDERFUL BENEFITS OF OVERTIME

When faced with the fact that there are only so many hours in the workday to get things done, we respond by having people work overtime. In many organizations, professionals are expected to work 50- and 60-hour weeks routinely. After all, they're paid the big bucks, and we want to get our money's worth from them.

Here, too, we are being penny-wise and pound-foolish. Studies show that after people have worked 10 to 15 hours of overtime each week for several weeks in a row, their productivity drops back to what they would normally do in 40 hours, and their error rates go up.

> After working several weeks of 50 to 60 hours, productivity falls to the normal 40-hour level and errors go up.

This is true for both factory workers and knowledge workers. It is possible to work overtime for one week and gain productive output. But people get tired after so many weeks of this, and fatigue takes its toll on performance.

For this reason, it is very bad practice to plan a project so that long stretches of overtime are required to meet the original end date. Not only will productivity drop rapidly, but if unforeseen problems occur, you can't use overtime to solve them, as people are already working all they can stand.

To see the effect of overtime, consider Figure 19–2. While this represents construction work, you can be sure that similar effects exist for other kinds of work. For recent research on the overtime-productivity relationship, see also Brunies, 2001.

Figure 19–3 shows the impact of having too many workers on a construction site. While this might seem to be restricted *only* to construction, how about problems that people encounter with having too many people in a department, too few desks, too little office equipment, and so on? I believe it is a similar effect. These are all factors that we should consider in trying to accelerate projects.

F I G U R E 19–2

Decline in Productivity with Overtime

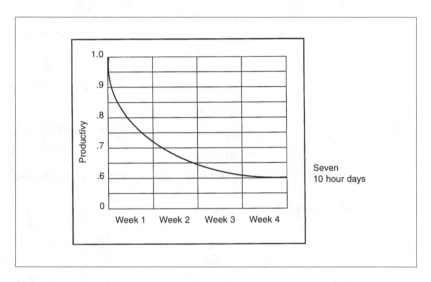

F I G U R E 19–3

Decline in Productivity with Site Loading

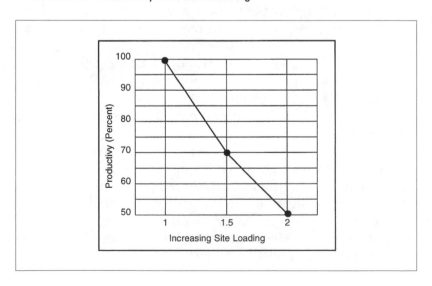

THE NEED TO SHARPEN THE SAW

Stephen Covey, in his book *The 7 Habits of Highly Effective People,* says that effective people spend some time sharpening the saw. They do not work all the time. His metaphor comes from the fact that if you saw wood for an extended period without stopping to sharpen the saw blade, it gets dull and won't cut very effectively any more. Over a period of time, the woodcutter who keeps his saw sharpened will generally cut more wood than the one who does not.

It has always struck me as odd that many companies treat their capital resources better than their human resources. When I was in college, I worked summers in a shipping department that was housed in an old cotton mill. Those

> We treat our capital resources better than we do our human resources.

old mills were not air-conditioned, and in July the temperature in North Carolina can easily be 95 outside, which results in an inside temperature of 100 to 105 degrees. Needless to say, you can't move at extreme speed in that temperature, or you'll have a heat stroke.

In many old factories, air-conditioning was out of the question. Costs too much, was the belief. Yet people were moving at a snail's pace. I always thought the increased productivity that would have been achieved in an air-conditioned building would far offset the cost. But what do I know?

Then along came computers and computer-controlled machinery. These may fail if they get too hot, so guess what—they have to be housed in air-conditioned offices. On top of that, in the 1960s, when the computers were being installed, smoking around them was banned—yet you could puff away around your coworkers.

The message here is simple: If you want to get maximum value from your most valuable resource of all—a human being—you must make it possible for him or her to sharpen the saw once in awhile. This is not just a soft-hearted humanitarian plea; it just makes good business sense!

APPROACHES TO RESOURCE LEVELING

Consider the bar chart schedule shown in Figure 19–4. Activity A is a critical path task. Activity B has a duration of three weeks and has one week of float. Activity C has a duration of

F I G U R E 19–4

Bar Chart Schedule with Resources Overloaded

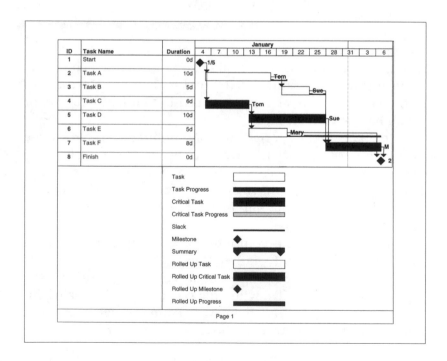

two weeks and has three weeks of float. These durations are based on having two people available to work on A, one on B, and one on C, full time for each task.

However, we only have three workers available. This clearly means that the job cannot be completed as scheduled.

Note that I am assuming what would be called *generic* or *pooled* resources in this example. Generic resources are people who can all do the same work. This is possible in some crafts, such as plumbing, carpentry, or electrical wiring, but would often not be true for specialists, such as engineers, certain machinists, and other professionals. In the case of specialists, you must assign specific individuals to tasks. We will consider that case further on.

Now suppose you were going to manually allocate resources so that no one is overloaded. How would you go about it? Well, you might begin by assigning two people to Activity A, since it is on the critical path. We know that if this task is not completed on time, the project will slip, so we must begin here.

This leaves one person to do B and C. It occurs to you that you might assign that person to work on each task half-time. If you do that, you will have to double the durations of each task, which would work for C, since it has enough float, but would not work for B. Doubling durations, of course, assumes that time is a linear function of resources assigned, which is itself a faulty assumption in many cases.

Since changing durations appears unfeasible, you might next ask, "Since I need another person, maybe I can just get one and be done with it." So you ask the powers that be in your company, and they tell you that three people is all you can have. You still are in a bind.

Next you might try assigning that one person to either B or C, but which one? You might think that you should assign the person to B, because it is longer than C. It turns out that B is the correct choice, but you have made it for the wrong reason. It is best to consider the float available to each task. You

did this when you assigned two people to task A, which has
no float. The most common rule for assigning resources is
called the *minimum-float* rule. Assign resources to those tasks
that have the least float, then the next least, and so on, until resources are exhausted. Then those tasks that have float and no
resources can slip without (hopefully) impacting the deadline.

It is easy to see in Figure 19–4 that this works very
nicely. Activity C has enough float that you can slide it over
to the point at which task B is complete, and then resources
will be available to do task C. Fortunately, this happens just
at the point where C runs out of float. This is shown in Figure
19–5. Note also that because activity C has run out of float, it
is now on the critical path. This is shown by making its bar a
solid color.

You will realize that this is a very clean example. It never
happens this way in the real world! What *will* happen is that
task C will run out of float before B is complete, and now you
have a dilemma. If you slip C any more, it will cause the project deadline to slip. What do you do in that case?

F I G U R E 19–5

Bar Chart with Resource Overload Resolved

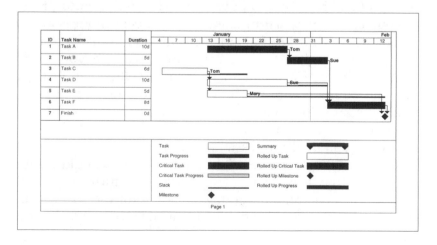

TIME-CRITICAL VERSUS RESOURCE-CRITICAL ALLOCATION

In the above example, we assumed that you were allocating resources manually, that is, without benefit of a computer. Ultimately, however, this is impractical. As the number of tasks and resources increases, the solution to overloads becomes very difficult, and a computer programmed to level-load resources will be required. The most common allocation rule (or heuristic, as it is sometimes called) is the minimum-float rule that we applied in the previous example.

In addition, the computer must be programmed to do either time-critical or resource-critical leveling. Under time-critical conditions, once a task runs out of float, the program will stop moving it, since to do so would slip the end date for the project. When this condition exists, you will have to find a way to deal with the remaining overloads. It may be that you can work people overtime for a brief spurt to resolve the problem, since working someone overtime is equivalent to adding resources to the project.

20 CHAPTER

Scheduling Uncertainty in Projects

In projects where most activities are fairly well defined, scheduling is straightforward. You estimate durations, work out the sequencing of tasks, and use the computer to find the critical path and calculate slack. But this is not true for projects that have activities that can branch in several directions, based on the outcome of a given task. This is typical of research projects. You run an experiment. Depending on the outcome, you may run another experiment, start a new task, or abandon the work altogether. Such junctions in projects are called *conditional branches,* and they defy our best efforts to schedule them *deterministically.*

DESIGN OF EXPERIMENTS

Somewhat related to conditional branches is the situation in which you are not quite sure how to make something work. You try an approach and it doesn't work, so you try something else. It doesn't work either. Several questions arise. How many iterations do you try before you give up? How do you determine in which order to try things? How do you know that you didn't miss the exact combination of things that would have solved the problem? And, perhaps most important for project managers, how do you schedule such a situation?

This kind of problem is encountered frequently in engineering design and science projects of various kinds, such as pharmaceuticals. I can always tell that a person is dealing with this kind of problem when he asks me, "How do you deal with a loop in a schedule network?"

"Why do you have a loop?" I ask.

"Well, I'm trying to find just the right combination of insulator and contacts to make a circuit breaker that will have a certain capacity. You try one combination and it doesn't work, so you have to try another and another until you finally find the right one."

When one engineer asked me about this, I said, "Why don't you use design-of-experiments?"

"Somebody told me it was more expensive than just trying different combinations," he said.

"Somebody misled you," I said. "Unless you are just plain lucky and hit the right combination the first try, design-of-experiments [DOE] is always more cost effective. Besides, without using DOE, you have no way of knowing if your approach is really the best one or just one that happens to work. With proper DOE, you can answer a host of questions in a fairly short time and have a very robust outcome."

> Design-of-experiments is always more cost effective than cut-and-try.

He was convinced, and sure enough, the outcome of his work was very positive.

I was asked this same question by a scientist. He wanted to know how to schedule loops when doing critical experiments. I asked him, too. why he didn't use DOE. His response floored me.

"What's that?" he asked.

This was when I learned that life sciences majors do not routinely receive training in statistical procedures. (This is also true in some engineering programs.) So project managers need to be aware of the approach so that they can suggest its use when it is appropriate.

The approach that these individuals mentioned above were suggesting is equivalent to a loop called "design-test-redesign," which can go on for an undetermined number of cycles. Standard PERT/CPM scheduling software will not handle loops. In fact, if you accidentally insert a loop into a critical path diagram, most software programs will immediately tell you that you have a logic violation and must correct it before the program can identify the critical path.

Some sophisticated scheduling programs can handle conditional branches and loops, but they are mostly used by defense contractors, run on mainframes, and, as far as I know, are not available in microcomputer versions. So you can't handle these situations with scheduling software.

However, you don't need to, for the answer to the design-test-redesign problem is to employ design-of-experiments to answer your questions. This merits a seminar in itself, and I don't intend to go into detail on design-of-experiments in this book, but I do want to outline the basic procedure.

Suppose you were managing a project to determine the combination of fertilizer and seed variety that would produce the best crop yield. You plant a field with combination F_1S_1 (fertilizer 1, seed 1) irrigate it, and when it is harvested, you record the results. Next season, you plant a field with combination F_1S_2 (fertilizer 1, seed 2), harvest it, and record the results. You continue this process until you have tried all the combinations available to you.

However, if there are numerous combinations, you will be a very old researcher by the time you've finished. Besides that, you have not controlled for some major factors that affect crop growth—sunlight, rainfall, and temperature. (Even if you irrigate, the rainfall variation will still be a factor.) Fortunately, there is a better way. In Figure 20–1 you will see a field that has been divided into a number of equal-area plots. In each plot, you plant a different combination of fertilizer and seed. At the end of the season, you harvest all of the plots and see which one has the best yield. In this way, the sunlight, rainfall, and temperature will have been uniformly distributed across all of the plots, so their effects are controlled and cease to be a factor in different crop yields. Now you can definitely tell which combination of seed and fertilizer is best.

Another example: Suppose your project is to determine if sales of a product can be increased best by a sale, combined with a particular advertising campaign, or by a giveaway and a different advertising approach. You would have four possible combinations of these options. They could be represented by S,A_1, S,A_2, G,A_1, and G,A_2. Now, the problem is that people differ greatly in their responses to various options, so unless you have a way to account for the variability in people, you can't answer the question.

F I G U R E 20–1

Field Planted with Different Combinations of Fertilizer and Seed

F_1S_1	F_1S_2	F_1S_3	F_1S_4	F_1S_5
F_2S_1	...	...	...	...
F_3S_1	...	...	...	...
F_4S_1	...	...	...	...
F_5S_1	...	...	...	F_5S_5

To test this situation, you need four groups of people so that you can administer to each a different *treatment*. This is shown in Figure 20–2. Groups 1 and 3 will be exposed to the sale and both ad approaches, while groups 2 and 4 will be exposed to the giveaway and the two ad approaches. To determine which combination is most effective in increasing sales, we measure how much product is sold to each group after they have been exposed to the various treatments, then we do an analysis of variance, or ANOVA. If the variation in sales *between* groups is greater than the variation *within,* and if that difference is statistically significant, then we can say that one treatment is better than the others.

By statistically significant, we mean that the difference would not have a high probability of occurring by chance alone, so that most likely we can account for it because the treatment actually caused the variation.

Good DOE is an extremely powerful way to answer questions that cannot be answered any other way. However, the design should be set up by someone very well schooled

F I G U R E   20–2

Test of Various Combinations of Sales Campaigns

	Sale	Giveaway
Ad 2	Group 1	Group 2
Ad 1	Group 3	Group 4

in principles of statistics, because it is easy to contaminate your results through an inappropriate procedure. We assume in the above experiment, for example, that the population is randomly distributed through the four groups for age, race, and sex. But suppose we actually did the group 1 treatment in an area that is inhabited largely by retired persons. Then we have contaminated the experiment, because the assumption is that all four groups are homogeneous—that is, all the same. If group 1 is mostly retired persons and the rest of the groups are mixed in terms of age, then we would expect the behavior of people in group 1 to differ from that of the other groups. (This is analogous to having a small area of a large plot of land that is very alkaline, whereas the rest of the plot is not.)

DOE does not guarantee that you will answer your questions in one pass, but it improves the likelihood. Furthermore, once you have done a number of such experiments, you begin to build a history on how long an experiment typically takes, and you can estimate durations with better accuracy. It will never be as good as well-defined tasks, however.

SECTION FOUR

CONTROL

21

CHAPTER

Tracking Progress to Achieve Project Control

If you are going to keep a project on schedule, within budget and scope, and meet quality requirements, you must have a way to measure where you are for each variable of interest. This is much easier said than done. When you are doing work that has some tangible nature, you can measure progress fairly well, but when you are trying to measure knowledge-work progress, it gets more difficult.

DEVELOPING PROJECT METRICS

There are some guidelines on developing metrics that should be followed. Otherwise, you can fool yourself. Metrics tend to encourage people to behave in ways that make the measures most favorable. For that reason metrics must be chosen to encourage the behavior actually desired by the organization. Otherwise, you will encourage people to do what you *don't want!*

> **Metrics:** Measures.

Marvin Patterson (1993) relates several examples of problems being created because of metrics. In one instance a company wanted to measure the productivity of keyboard operators, so they attached keystroke counters on the keyboards. One day the supervisor of the group walked in during lunch hour and noticed one of the operators having her lunch, while holding down the spacebar on her keyboard with her thumb. Because holding down a key causes it to generate a continuous stream of characters, she was generating a lot of keystrokes, but none of them were useful!

> What kind of behavior are you trying to encourage?

Another company wanted to set up incentives for their divisions to develop more new products in less time. They told their executives that they would receive bonuses based on how many new products their units produced each year. One division caught on to the fact that corporate tracked new products by way of new part numbers in their catalog. They quickly began repackaging old products, assigning a new part number, and for a couple of years, they collected bonuses without actually producing anything new!

For a set of metrics to be effective, they must meet four criteria:

Relevance

The metric must provide information on factors that are *important* to the project. Collecting data that are not important is a waste of time. For example, it may not matter very much how many changes an engineer makes to a design *before* it is released, but it certainly makes a difference *after* it is released.

Completeness

The set of metrics should include *all* factors important to the project. If you leave one out, the others will be optimized, but at the expense of the one omitted. "Every important aspect of the operation under scrutiny should be measured" (Patterson, 1993, p. 29). While we want the minimum number of metrics that will do the job, nothing should be omitted that is critical to success.

Timeliness

Timeliness is a function of how quickly the project can change. Nyquist sampling criteria state that if something is changing and you cannot monitor it continuously, then you must sample at least twice as often as the change occurs in order to know what is happening. Thus, if a project can change once weekly, you would have to measure it twice weekly. (This will be discussed in more detail later in the chapter.) Measures need not be absolutely precise to be useful, but they should be timely enough so that decisions based on them are effective. Failing to get information in a timely fashion is like having someone navigate for you while you are driving, and a second after you pass a turn, your errant navigator says, "Oops, you should have turned back there!"

Elegance

Metrics can seriously burden a project because of the serious overhead cost incurred. For that reason, they should be designed to provide a maximum level of insight into the project with a minimum amount of data. This is commonly called the KISS principle—keep it simple, Sam. In my view, I want to do the absolute minimum that will allow me to successfully control project progress.

KINDS OF METRICS

There are at least three kinds of metrics that are important in projects: *process metrics, personnel performance metrics,* and *management performance metrics.*

Process Metrics

Processes have attributes called *state variables*. These are analogous to the state variables of a physical system, such as a spring-mass system. The states of such a system are the positions and velocities of the masses in the system. You can predict the behavior of the system if you know the parameters and state variables at any given time. Project management processes have similar state variables. If these can be established, they will serve as process metrics, which can be tracked so that the process can be understood and controlled.

Some examples of project metrics that are important are shown in Figure 21-1. However, you have to apply these with caution. For example, when you ask people to do a job faster, they will sometimes do poor work in order to finish faster. I have seen this happen in product development especially. The admonition must be, "Do it faster without sacrificing quality."

The number of scope changes is also not a good measure unless you factor in the impact on the project of the change. You could have several small scope changes that make almost no difference to the job. Or you could have just one change that almost sinks it.

Customer satisfaction is an excellent measure, if you can get that information. As was mentioned in Chapter 9, success

F I G U R E 21-1

Metrics Appropriate for Projects

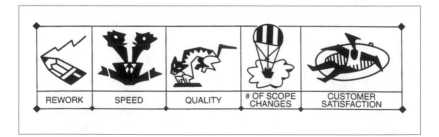

| REWORK | SPEED | QUALITY | # OF SCOPE CHANGES | CUSTOMER SATISFACTION |

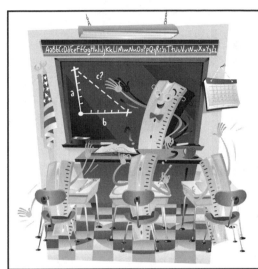

You must have
a way to
measure
where you are
for each
variable of
interest.

of projects is generally a function of whether customers are happy with the outcome, so it is really *perceived success* that we are looking at.

It is outside the scope of this book to address personnel and management performance metrics. Our focus will be on process metrics only. Later in this chapter, we will use other measures of progress to keep the job on track, including earned value measures.

THE TYPICAL PROGRESS REPORTING SYSTEM

I recently sat through a project status reporting meeting held by a client. It essentially went like this:

"How is project x?"

"It's okay."

"Good, let's move on to project y. How's it doing?"

"Okay."

You get the message. There are four variables that we care about, as has been discussed in previous chapters: cost,

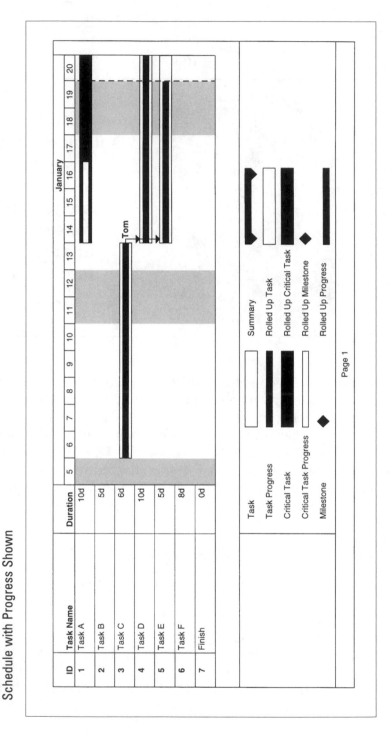

F I G U R E 21-2

Schedule with Progress Shown

performance, schedule (or time), and scope. Saying that a project is okay does not tell us anything about the status of these variables.

A step above the system of reporting progress as okay/not okay is to report schedule performance only. This is done as shown in Figure 21–2. This report is from Microsoft Project®, but most scheduling software reports progress in a similar way. The smaller bars that run inside the schedule bars show your schedule performance to date.

In this example, the date on which progress is being measured is January 20. The shaded areas at January 5, 11, 12, 18, and 19 are weekends, during which no work is being done. From this report, we can see that the tasks have the status shown in Table 21–1.

The problem with this report is that the information is very limited. First of all, we know nothing about performance or scope. We must take for granted that the quality of work being done, as well as the scope of work, are correct. Furthermore, we know nothing about what was done to achieve the result—that is, we don't know the cost, whether it is expressed in monetary terms or working hours expended.

There are companies that don't track project costs in any form. They consider that the people doing the work are on

T A B L E 21–1

Task Status for Sample Schedule

Task	Status
A	Behind one day
B	Not started
C	Complete
D	One day ahead
E	Right on target

the payroll, so it doesn't matter. I'm sorry, it does matter. Every hour spent on one activity is an hour lost to some other work that might be done. Only someone with an endless pot of gold can be in a position to disregard costs.

> Knowing that a person has worked twice as many hours as planned, even though he is on schedule, tells me he might be in jeopardy.

In any case, knowing that a person is on schedule but has worked twice as many hours to get there as he had planned tells me that his work is not going well and that the project may be in jeopardy. The sooner I know this, the sooner I can address the problem and make a decision about what to do. Conversely, if I find that a person is only taking half the time to get the job done, then I can begin to think about what this will ultimately mean to the project. So whether you know about labor costs or not does not matter. You can always track hours expended and make adjustments based upon that data.

EARNED VALUE ANALYSIS

Measuring progress using earned value was first done in manufacturing as part of standard cost systems. It goes like this. Suppose you are making widgets, and each widget has a value of $50. You are supposed to have made 1,000 of them by noon today. When I check with you, I find that you have only made 800 widgets, all of them good. How much are they worth to me? Clearly they are worth $800 \times \$50$, or $40,000. I tell you then that I will give you credit for having produced $40,000 worth of widgets for me, and I call this *earned value*.

How are you doing? Well, since you have made only $40,000 worth of widgets and you should have made $50,000, you are behind schedule by $10,000 worth of widgets. What that represents in time is a function of how many widgets you

---

THE PURPOSE OF VARIANCE ANALYSIS

When progress is monitored, three questions should always be asked:

1. What is the actual status of the project?
2. What caused the deviation (when there is one)?
3. What should be done about it?

It is not enough to simply monitor progress in a project. When a significant deviation from plan occurs, *something* must be done in response. There are three responses that can be made:

1. Ignore the deviation.
2. Take corrective action to get back on target
3. Revise the plan.

Note the word *significant*—what is meant by significant should be determined in the planning stage of a project. In general, a deviation should exceed at least 5 percent to be considered significant, as most control systems cannot maintain a tighter tolerance.

---

can make per day. If you can normally make about $5,000 worth of widgets per day, then you are behind by two days.

With this comparison, I know the schedule status of the work you are doing, but I don't know how much effort you have spent to make the 800 widgets. Do I care? You bet! If you are working too many hours, my costs rise and that affects my profits. So I ask how many hours you have worked to produce the 800 widgets.

"You don't want to know," you say.

"Maybe not," I reply, "but I have to know, so tell me the bad news."

"Well, we've worked 1,200 hours to produce the 800 widgets, and our loaded labor rate is $50 per hour, so the labor cost is $60,000." Now I know how bad off I am. You have produced $40,000 worth of widgets for me and spent $60,000 to do it, so you are overspent by $20,000 on labor. In fact, not only are you overspent, but behind schedule as well. This is the worst position you can be in. It is bad enough to be overspent but to be behind on the work as well is really a problem.

Note that these measures do not involve material costs. The true cost of a manufactured product, building, or road is the material and labor costs combined. Do we care? Of course. However, what we are tracking is *work progress*, and we track material costs in another account.

Loaded labor rate: Direct labor cost plus overhead. To salaries, you add the costs of heat, water, lights, benefits, and so on, to get loaded labor rates.

We would also do the same with capital and other expenses in projects.

There seems to be some confusion about the word "value." Isn't the value of a widget what I can sell it for? Yes, but there are two uses of the word involved here. If you are working for me and I pay you $50 per hour, loaded labor, I value every hour that you work for me at $50. If I can only sell what you produce in an hour for $50, I don't have a profitable enterprise. This is why I am concerned if you take longer to do your work than we have estimated. If we estimated that it would take an hour and it actually takes an hour and fifteen minutes, then at a $50 per hour labor rate, the actual cost of labor would be $62.50. That will decrease my profit by $12.50. So I definitely care about the value of the work that you do for me.

I know a project management consultant, a specialist in software, who objects to earned value analysis being applied to software. He says that there is no salvage value in unfinished code. That may be true, but it misses the point of progress measures. Every step in a process should add value. If it does not, it should be eliminated. Nobody sets out to create salvage value in the first place. Salvage value is a measure of what you can get if you abandon a project. What we want to create is end-result value!

Using the consultant's argument, I could say the same for almost anything. There is no salvage value in unfinished buildings or roads. Using earned value to measure progress is like saying that you are halfway to a destination. There may be no salvage value in being partway to a destination, but it tells you how much further you have to go and whether you are making reasonable progress. If you

> Nobody sets out to create salvage value. What we want is end-result value!

had estimated that you were going to average 50 miles per hour and find that you are actually only averaging 25 miles per hour, then you aren't doing very well. You can expect that your trip is going to take twice as long as you planned unless you can get your average speed up to a higher level.

THE MEASURES USED

When we estimate that you can make 1,000 widgets for me by noon today, each with a value of $50, we call the $50,000 value of these widgets budgeted cost of work scheduled, or BCWS. This is your target. Since control is exercised by comparing planned effort to actual, when I look at how many widgets you have actually made I can tell if you are on track and whether anything needs to be done if you are not. So when we find that you have made only $40,000 worth of widgets, we know that you are behind. The amount of widgets that you have produced is called budgeted cost of work performed, or BCWP. If we take the difference between the scheduled work and performed work, we have the *schedule variance*. This is written as:

Schedule Variance = BCWP – BCWS

For our example, we have:

Schedule Variance = \$40,000 – \$50,000 = –\$10,000.

That is, you are behind schedule by \$10,000 worth of work, which is indicated by the minus sign on the \$10,000 figure. This is standard accounting notation, to show an unfavorable variance as a negative.

In the same way, we said that we could compare what you actually spent to the target and have an idea about cost variance. We call the actual spending figure actual cost of work performed, or ACWP. *Cost variance* is calculated as follows:

Cost Variance = BCWP – ACWP

For our example, we have:

Cost Variance = \$40,000 – \$60,000 = –\$20,000.

Thus, you are overspent by \$20,000. Notice that the cost variance is a composite variance. You are behind schedule by \$10,000 worth of work. You have also put in \$10,000 more effort than we estimated, so the total cost variance is the sum of the two. This is shown in Figure 21–3.

TRACKING KNOWLEDGE WORK

This system works nicely for tracking tangible work. You can count widgets and inspect them to see if they are of good quality. Tracking knowledge work is a great deal harder. How do you quantify what you have done? For example, if you were writing a book estimated to run 300 manuscript pages and you have 100 written, are you one-third of the way there? No way. Or say you are writing code, thinking that there will be 10,000 lines when it is all finished. The program-

F I G U R E 21-3

Project Is behind Schedule and Overspent

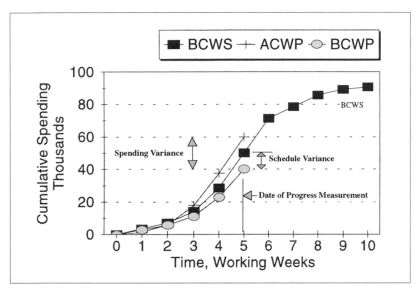

mers have written 8,000 lines. Are they 80 percent complete? I doubt it.

The problem with both of these examples is that they are at too high a level in the project. In order to track progress, you need to "chunk down" the work into increments that can be measured with some precision. In terms of the work breakdown struc-ture (WBS), you need to get down to a low enough level where work has durations that

> Knowledge work tasks should have durations no greater than one to three weeks.

do not exceed one to three weeks for engineering or pro-gramming, or possibly days for some tasks.

Let's see how this works using book writing as an exam-ple. I generally write chapter drafts, then come back and do fi-nal editing once all chapters are written. Many of the chapters

I can write within a day. The final edit might take a half day
per chapter. There are also figures to develop, and these are
generally done last. I can't tell from the beginning how many
figures I will have, but maybe I think it will be at least two
per chapter, and I estimate that they will require two hours
each to do. So I need 20 to 25 figures, at two hours each, or 40
to 50 hours for that part. Since I am working on this by myself, everything will be done in series; no need for a critical
path schedule.

My task list will look like Table 21–2.

T A B L E   21–2

Task List

Task	Time, Days	Total Days	BCWS
Write Chapter 1	1	1	400
Chapter 2	1	2	800
Chapter 3	1	3	1200
Chapter 4	1½	4½	1800
Chapter 5	1½	6	2400
Chapter 6	1	7	2800
Chapter 7	1	8	3200
Chapter 8	1	9	3600
Chapter 9	1	10	4000
Edit 1 & 2	1	11	4400
Edit 3 & 4	1	12	4800
Edit 5 & 6	1	13	5200
Edit 7 & 8	1	14	5600
Edit 9	1	15	6000
Index	½	15½	6200
Figures 1–4	1	16½	6600
Figures 5–8	1	17½	7000
Figures 9–12	1	18½	7400
Figures 13–16	1	19½	7800
Figures 17–20	1	20½	8200
Final Work	1½	22	8800

The nice thing about this system is that as each part is completed, I can see it, touch it, check it out. The question is, how do I value the progress I have made? The simplest system is to take a ratio between the total of 22 days and whatever has been completed to date. It isn't perfect, but it is better than nothing. So when I have completed Chapter 1, I get 1/22, or approximately 5 percent, credit. If I want to use earned value, I have to establish a BCWS baseline, which is shown in the final column of the table. I have valued my time at $50 per hour and consider a day to be eight hours, so each day I am supposed to accomplish $400 in work. This gives a linear rate of work, which is never quite correct but it is good enough for most purposes.

Now suppose at the end of the first day I don't have Chapter 1 complete. Should I get partial credit? You could estimate and assign a partial credit, but it is better to wait until the chapter is complete and then you get credit for the entire task. So let's say at the end of the second day I have finished both Chapters 1 and 2. If I plot my progress, it would look like the graph shown in Figure 21–4.

It turns out that at the end of the first day I have actually spent 12 hours writing, so my ACWP for that day is $600. This means that I am behind schedule and overspent. At the end of day 2, I am back on schedule but still overspent. Then I encounter a problem. I don't get to work on the book the next day, so BCWP and ACWP move horizontally. The next two days I do reasonably well. Then another two days when no work is done, so ACWP and BCWP again turn horizontal. At this point, even if I were to start making linear progress, the progress curves would fall below the BCWS curve. The point where BCWP reaches $8,800 is the forecasted end date for the project. It would be a two-day slip, as presently shown.

This same approach can be used in engineering design, software development, research projects, and so on. The proper approach is to break work down to very small increments, so

F I G U R E 21-4

Tracking Progress in Writing a Book

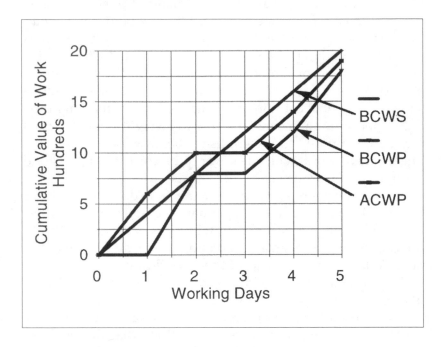

that some marker can be used to show that work is complete. In engineering design, for example, my first step might be a conceptual design, which I estimate will take one week. When it is done, I should be able to see it on paper. The next step is to build a model of the paper design. Time—two weeks. When it is finished, I can touch it. Next step, test it. Again, about one week. Result—a paper report on the test outcome.

Another example: I am doing scientific research. My first step is a literature review. Estimated time is about two weeks to identify papers to read. At the end of that period, I have a list of papers, and maybe even copies of them all. Next step, read them. Estimated time, two weeks. The reading pile should be empty at that time. Then I want to do some experiments. How long will they take? The ones I have planned will take a week, but after I see the results I may want to do additional experiments, so I can't plan this one as well as for the design project. In fact, this brings up a very important point—you should always separate development from discovery, be-cause discovery is very difficult to time-limit. That doesn't mean that you can't plan dis-covery projects, it

> Don't waste time doing detailed planning of work that will take place a year from now.

just means that it must be done in phases and no exact times can be placed on the overall project.

This also brings up a good point for most projects. If you are going to break work down to daily or weekly increments, you only want to do so for short periods. If a project is going to last for a year, you only want small increments for a few months at most, because you can't see very far ahead with any accuracy. To plan work that will occur a year from now to increments of weeks is a waste of time. Instead you do phased planning, as in the research project. As you get to the end of the first phase, you plan the next phase in detail, and so on. This is also called a rolling plan.

TRACKING EARNED VALUE GRAPHICALLY

You may want to present tracking data graphically so that you can see trends. Consider the curves in the graph shown in Figure 21–5. BCWS is the baseline plan for the project. It is derived directly from the scheduled work. ACWP is going high, while BCWP is going low; that is, the project is getting behind schedule and is simultaneously overspending. It does appear that BCWP is turning back toward the BCWS curve,

F I G U R E 21–5

Earned Value Curves for Project Echo

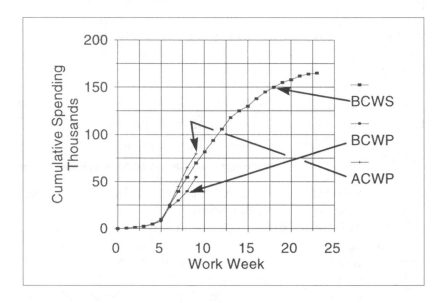

so perhaps the work will be caught up in a few weeks, but it may be at the expense of going over budget. Be careful about making linear projections of these curves to find the final state of the project, since most projects do not progress linearly, as shown by the BCWS curve.

All possible combinations of progress can be shown by these curves. In Table 21–3 are interpretations for most of the combinations. You should be able to figure out the few not covered in the table.

INDICES OF PERFORMANCE

The three earned value variables can be used to calculate indices of performance. One is called the schedule performance index (SPI), and the other is the cost performance index (CPI). These are calculated using the following formulas:

T A B L E 21–3

Earned Value Combinations

Combination	Status	Likely Cause
BCWP > BCWS and ACWP < BCWS	Ahead of schedule and underspent	Conservative estimate or lucky break
BCWP < BCWS and ACWP = BCWS	Behind schedule and spending correctly	Not enough resources applied to do the work
BCWP > BCWS and ACWP = BCWS	Ahead of schedule and spending correctly	More resources applied than originally planned
BCWP >BCWS and BCWS < ACWP < BCWP	Ahead of schedule and slightly underspent	More resources applied at greater-than-expected efficiency
BCWP < BCWS and BCWS > ACWP > BCWP	Behind schedule and slightly overspent	Too few resources applied at less-than-expected efficiency

> means "greater than"; < means "less-than"

$$SPI = \frac{BCWP}{BCWS}$$

$$CPI = \frac{BCWP}{ACWP}$$

The SPI is essentially a measure of work efficiency. If you are accomplishing as much work as you had planned to do, then your efficiency is 100 percent. If it is less than planned, you will have less than 100 percent, and conversely. The CPI can be thought of as spending efficiency—it is what you get for what you paid. If you buy $90 worth of goods and pay $100 for them, then your spending efficiency is 0.90.

If SPI and CPI are multiplied together, you get an overall measure of project performance called the critical ratio. The critical ratio then, is:

$$CR = CPI \times SPI$$

You can see that this number should be 1.0 if everything is going according to plan. If it is larger than 1.0, you are performing better than plan, and conversely. You can also see that the CPI could be a bit low and the SPI a bit large and still yield a CR equal to 1.0. That is, you are spending a little more than planned but getting more work done than planned, so that the net result balances out. The reverse situation could be true as well.

Meredith and Mantell (1985) suggested that the critical ratio can be plotted on a periodic basis and that control limits can be established so that determinations can be made based about project status. This is shown in Figure 21–6. If you are not familiar with control charts, you might want to consult one of the many texts on statistical process control, such as Juran and Gryna (1980).

F I G U R E 21–6

A Control Chart for the Critical Ratio

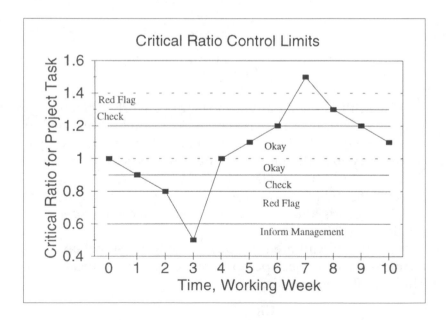

Most scheduling software packages offer earned value reports. Microsoft Project®, Primavera®, Project Workbench®, and others all do basic earned value reports. However, most do not employ the critical ratio. If you know how to program in Microsoft's macro language, you can calculate the CR. Or you can dump the earned value data to an Excel spreadsheet (like the one in Figure 21–7) and calculate it there. Use Excel to test the CR against the control limits shown in Figure 21–5, and place the words

F I G U R E 21–7

Spreadsheet That Calculates Critical Ratio

Earned Value Report

Project No.: 1201   Date: 20-Feb-95   FILE: BALIREPT.WB1
Description: Bali Book   Page_____ of _____
Prepared by: John Miller   Signed:

	Cumulative-to-date			Variance		At Completion			Critical	Action
							Latest		Critical	Action
WBS #	BCWS	BCWP	ACWP	Sched.	Cost	Budgeted	Est.	Variance	Ratio	Required
Recruit	900	900	930	0	(30)	900	930	(30)	0.97	O.K.
Travel				0	0			0	NA	NA
Pack	480	480	420	0	60	480	420	60	1.14	O.K.
VISAs				0	0			0	NA	NA
Staff				0	0			0	NA	NA
Survey	2,700	2,400	2,550	(300)	(150)	3,000	3,150	(150)	0.84	CHECK
Interview	1,500	1,500	1,350	0	150	1,500	1,350	150	1.11	O.K.
Reports				0	0	1,500	1,500	0	NA	NA
Local	1,800	1,200	1,200	(600)	0	3,000	3,150	(150)	0.67	RED FLAG
Photos	1,500	1,250	1,250	(250)	0	5,000	5,000	0	0.83	CHECK
Develop				0	0	1,250	1,250	0	NA	NA
Select				0	0	600	600	0	NA	NA
Print				0	0	1,000	1,000	0	NA	NA
Draft				0	0	18,000	18,000	0	NA	NA
Review				0	0	3,000	3,000	0	NA	NA
Revise				0	0	9,000	9,000	0	NA	NA
F.Edit				0	0	1,500	1,500	0	NA	NA
Captions				0	0	300	300	0	NA	NA
Typeset				0	0	2,000	2,000	0	NA	NA
Pasteup				0	0	3,000	3,000	0	NA	NA
Proof				0	0	3,000	3,000	0	NA	NA
				0	0			0	NA	NA
TOTAL	8,880	7,730	7,700	(1,150)	30	58,030	58,150	(120)	0.87	CHECK

NOTE: Negative variance is unfavorable ‖ If Critical Ratio < 0.6, INFORM MANAGEMENT!
    ( ) = NEGATIVE VALUES

"NA," "okay," "check," or "red flag" in the far right column. Then, by scanning that column, you can detect your trouble spots immediately.

FORECASTING FINAL COST AND SCHEDULE RESULTS

There are a couple of ways to forecast final results for a project. One is to replan based on what has been learned to date. Another is to calculate forecast results using earned value data. Perhaps it is best to do both.

The most common and widely accepted statistical forecasting method is a cumulative CPI estimate at completion. The formula for making this projection follows:

$$\$EAC = \frac{BAC - BCWP}{\text{Cumulative CPI}} + ACWP$$

Using this formula, we can calculate the $EAC for my book project. On day 7, the BCWS for my project is $2,800, the BCWP is $1,800, and the ACWP is $1,900. Inserting these into the formula gives:

$$\$EAC = \frac{8,800 - 1,800}{0.95} + 1,900$$

This calculates to an $EAC of $9,268, so the project will go over budget by $468, or slightly more than one day's work.

Fleming and Koppelman (1997) report that researchers have found the cumulative CPI to be very stable from as early as 15 to 20 percent into the project's time line. In fact, they cite Christensen (1994) as saying that the cumulative CPI does not change more than 10 percent once a project is 20 percent complete. In most cases, it gets worse, not better. One outcome of this finding is the certainty that a project already in trouble just 15 to 20 percent along the way is going to stay in trouble. The explanation is simple. Your plan was a forecast (estimate). If you cannot estimate accurately over the near term, then you aren't going to do any better over the far term. Thus, the earned value method gives early warning that a project is headed for disaster.

Forecasting your progress against the schedule is best done using critical path method. If you report progress against all tasks, the software will show the impact on the overall schedule. However, if a task has slipped and you now expect that its duration has changed, you

> If a project is in trouble 15 percent of the way along the horizontal time line, it is going to stay in trouble.

should revise the task duration, then let the software update your projection. It may be that changing the duration of a task that originally had float will now place it on the critical path. Of course, it goes without saying that anything on the critical path that slips will cause a one-for-one slip of the end date, unless it can be recovered somehow.

OTHER TRACKING METHODS

Another way to track a project is to use a run chart. You can plot any four of the project variables (P, C, T, S) using this approach. The chart in Figure 21–8 shows a plot of fraction of work completed each week for a hypothetical project called Echo. To plot the fraction of work completed, divide the amount of work completed to date by the amount of work scheduled to be completed. This could be called percentage of scheduled work actually completed and is equivalent to the ratio BCWP/BCWS. From this chart you can see that, starting in week 3, there is a downward trend. People are clearly having trouble. Then they somehow begin to recover and there is an upward trend that peaks in week 15, then falls back a bit. Since work following week 12 is being performed at a greater rate than scheduled, it is likely that the project will finish early, possibly by week 21, rather than as scheduled on week 23. This chart is highly unlikely to occur in

F I G U R E 21–8

A Run Chart for Project Echo

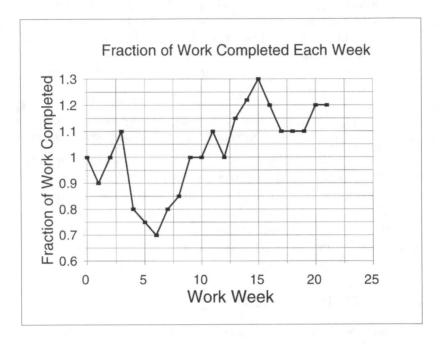

reality, because the team is in a lot of trouble early on, but it illustrates the approach.

There are two guidelines for interpreting run charts to detect meaningful systemic changes:

1. Since it is expected that there would be approximately the same number of points above the *average* line as there are below it, a good rule of thumb is that if there is a run of seven consecutive points on one side of the average, something significant may be happening and it would probably be a good idea to call "time out."

2. A second test is to see whether a run of seven or more intervals is steadily increasing or decreasing

without reversals in direction. As in (1.), such a pattern is not likely to occur by chance, thereby indicating [that] something needs to be investigated (Kiemele & Schmidt, 1993, p. 2–25).

To track quality, you might want to record rework hours. It is likely that most projects will incur from 5 to 40 percent rework. If you are improving your project management process, you should see a decline in rework. A run chart that tracks hours spent on rework is shown in Figure 21–9.

If you compare Figure 21–8 with Figure 21–9, you will notice that the curve showing rework hours is almost a mirror image of the progress curve. This suggests that one reason the team was not making good progress prior to week 10 is because they were making a number of errors that had to be corrected. After week 10, they had reduced the rework significantly, and progress reflects this. These figures would be for a very small team.

F I G U R E 21–9

A Run Chart for Project Echo Showing Rework Hours

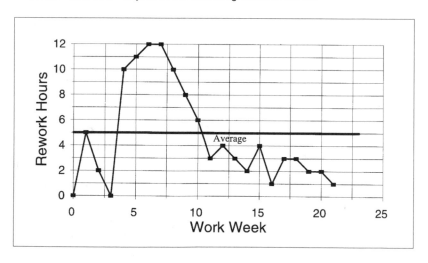

ɞ♦ʊ

You can track the influence of scope changes by looking at the dollar value of the extra work, or extra working hours.

ɞ♦ʊ

Other indicators of project quality might be documentation changes, engineering changes, design revisions, customer complaints, test failures, number of software bugs, and so on.

It is also useful to track the number of scope changes in a project, but you need to capture the impact of a scope change for this to be meaningful. You might be able to absorb a dozen small scope changes with almost no project impact, while a single change in scope might nearly sink the project. Since scope changes result in additional work, you can track impact by looking at the dollar value of the extra work required (or the number of working hours, if you don't have dollar figures). You can also show impact by any slip in schedule that results.

The other issue that should be addressed is the cause of the scope change. If the cause was an environmental change that no one could foresee, then it is probably legitimate—on longer duration projects, the world is going to change before you can finish the project. For instance, competitors bring out products that necessitate changes in your design. This is justifiable, although you sometimes should go ahead and freeze a design without the competitive feature, release it, and then start a new project to add that feature. It all depends on how critical that feature is for product sales.

On the other hand, changes required because too little time was spent up front in defining the project are wasteful changes that should be avoided in the future.

HOW OFTEN SHOULD PROGRESS BE MEASURED?

This question could be answered, "It all depends." If it is a long-duration project, it may be sufficient to measure progress monthly. On a job that has a duration of a few months, weekly might be in order. For a project that is going to last no more than a few weeks, such as a maintenance project, we would probably want to check progress daily.

If it were possible, we would like to monitor progress continuously. The reason can be seen by examining Figure 21–10. The essence of control is feedback. We compare where

F I G U R E 21–10

Variation in Project Variables

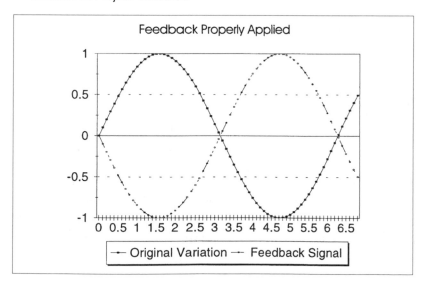

we are to where we are supposed to be, then take corrective action if deviations exist. In mathematical terms, if a deviation is represented by the sinusoid shown as a solid line in Figure 21–10, the feedback signal will be the dashed line. Because the dashed line is equal in amplitude and opposite in phase to the initial variation, the two curves cancel each other out. This causes the net variation to drop to zero.

Suppose the deviation represents project spending on labor. A positive deviation means that spending has gone too high, while a negative swing means it is too low. When it is too high, we are getting more work done than called for by the plan. This might not seem to be a problem, but it can be. Getting ahead on project work can sometimes create problems downstream. Conversely, if spending is too low, we are undoubtedly falling behind, unless the work is being done at greater-than-expected efficiency. This would also signal a problem.

We are dealing with an information gap. We learn about project spending through reports that often come from the accounting department, and these are sometimes received only monthly.

Suppose you receive spending reports monthly, and you have just received the latest one. It is shown in Figure 21–11. It says that spending was high for the month. You decide to cut back. The problem is, you are cutting back from this point forward. If the project is already entering a phase in which spending is going low, then your correction is only going to make matters worse. You would be better off doing nothing.

I said earlier that we would like to monitor progress continuously. What we are doing instead is sampling. In the case just mentioned, you get data for the project for an entire month. Suppose you monitor progress by going around to everyone and asking how they are doing. However, you don't do it every day. Perhaps the site is remote and you can only go there monthly. There are deviations taking place, but on the days that you visit the site, everything is right on target. This is shown in Figure 21–12.

F I G U R E 21–11

Delayed Feedback

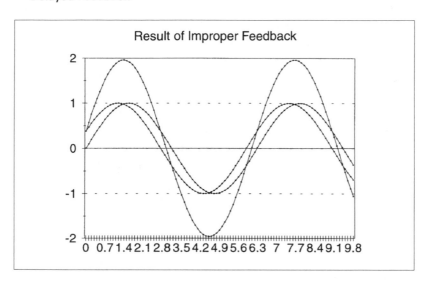

F I G U R E 21–12

Sampling at Zero Crossings

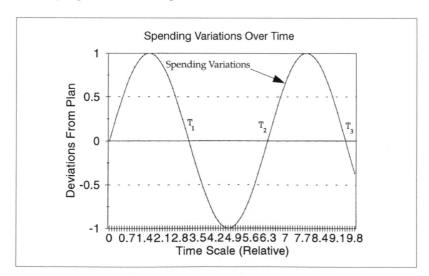

What you are doing is sampling at the zero crossings. This will cause you to report zero deviations, when, in fact, there are deviations taking place. The question is, how often should you sample to know what is going on?

There is a branch of communication theory that does offer some guidance. Nyquist established that you must sample at least twice the rate of change of the signal if you are going to have any idea what it is actually doing. If we add sample points T_4 and T_5, as shown in Figure 21–13, we will be able to tell in which directions the deviations are moving. We don't know if the deviation has the form of an instantaneous change (represented in Figure 21–14 by a square wave), or whether it varies sinusoidally or as a triangle wave (Figures 21–13 and 21–15). We do know that it isn't standing still!

F I G U R E 21–13

More Sampling Points

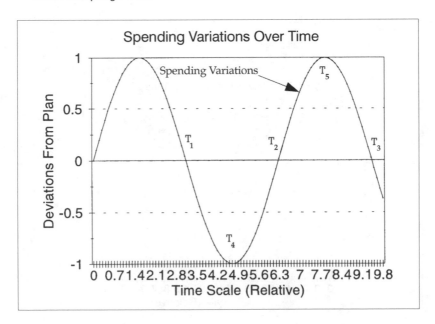

F I G U R E 21–14

Square Wave

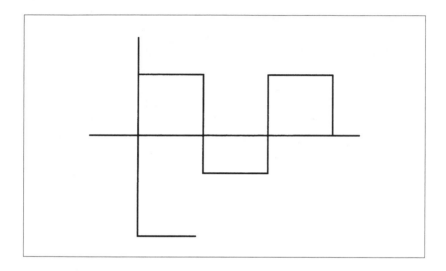

F I G U R E 21–15

Triangle Wave

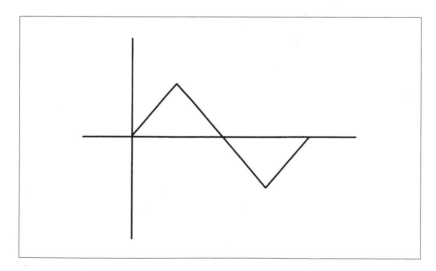

The only difficulty is, we don't know how often the deviations occur unless we first monitor continuously, and furthermore, it is not likely that the rate of change stays constant. So how do you apply Nyquist's sampling criterion?

If every member of your project team has a clear understanding of his or her work assignment and has a personal plan for doing that work, together with guidelines on acceptable variances, then the person can monitor his own progress and take corrective action whenever necessary. If a deviation goes outside acceptable limits, he knows to check with you, the project manager, or with his functional manager to decide what must be done. If this system is followed, then the person is monitoring himself continuously, and you can rely on sampling to discover any unnoticed glitches. Sampling becomes a check-and-balance to the system.

22 CHAPTER

Accounting and Cost Control

By Ben Thorp*

Cost control can be no better than the plan and the budget. Thomas Blackburn, Vice President of Kraft Operation, said to me once, "Without a plan, everything is a deviation." If the project manager is thinking about accounting and cost control and has uneasy feelings about the plan and the

> "Without a plan, everything is a deviation."
>
> —Thomas Blackburn

budget, then it is best to revisit those subjects using the principles discussed in other chapters. The four most common reasons for cost control issues are (1) poor budgeting, (2) uncertainty about cost status, (3) scope creep, and (4) unforeseen problems. Each one of these will be discussed using more familiar terms. Unforeseen problems will be largely covered under the subject of contingency.

---

* Former Vice President, Chesapeake Corporation, now retired.

CONTROL AGAINST BUDGET

The budget needs to be broken down into whatever level of detail is necessary to track the project. Reviewing the plan and the work breakdown structure should indicate the level of detail desired. The most common error is to not have enough detail or to not have it in the right place. For example, budgeting by area is not enough detail. One needs to break out major pieces of equipment, their installation, their connection to the process, their digital control (if any), service, and training. These areas may need more detail. Connection to the processes can have mechanical, piping, electrical, and instrument budgets. Breaking the whole project down by major equipment,

> Contingency funds should not be used to pay for sloppy estimating. They should be used to pay for undiscovered work.

etc., is not good enough unless it's a small project. There should be detailed budgets for each "unit operation." Sometimes, subunit operations are important. For example, in a solid fuel boiler, one subarea could be fuel storage and boiler feed. Another could be the boiler itself, and a third could be ash handling and distribution.

The budget log must be at least as detailed as the original estimate, and frequently more detailed. One must then track deviations from each line item to develop a sense of the total impact of being over on some and under on others. It is typical to be under budget on large single-item purchases (which come early in the project) and over budget on softer items like "installation" or "connection" (which come late in the project). This is because quotes are obtained for the larger items and the low bid is not usually used for the estimate. Items like installation or connection are factored or estimated from databases which may not be representative of the project at hand. These pluses and minuses must be tracked.

One way to do so is a budget adjustment entry (BAE), which is the fourth column on the spreadsheet after budget (see Figure 22–3). This budget adjustment must be carefully controlled, and a budget adjustment process (BAP) is recommended. A budget adjustment process is shown in Figure 22–1. A budget adjustment entry is shown in Figure 22–2. If the pluses and minuses for any one category (e.g., installation) or any one area (e.g., boiler) exceed the original budget, then the project manager needs to identify equal savings from budget or seek supplemental funding. *The use of contingency funds to make up for poor budgeting is not recommended.* Contingency, or management reserve, is for undiscovered work, as was discussed in Chapter 15. We will revisit it later in this chapter. This is an important principle that needs to be practiced with great vigor. Contingency is for unknowns, not for poor budgets.

COMMITMENT TRACKING

All experienced capital project managers know they must track their budgets as commitments are made. Waiting for bills to be paid and posted delays entry. Bills paid represents accounting, but this process is of little value in cost control. It's a little like not totaling the points in Saturday's game until Monday morning. The game is long over before the score is known. Accounting by bills posted creates significant *uncertainty* about cost status.

> You need to track your budget as commitments are made. Waiting for bills to be paid creates too much delay.

This uncertainty can cause inexperienced project managers to spend more than they should and can cause experienced project managers to spend less. Unfortunately, most plant, mill, and business systems do accounting on a bills-posted basis, so project managers must track commitments manually, using

F I G U R E 22–1

Budget Adjustment Process

BUDGET ADJUSTMENT PROCESS (BAP)

DEFINITION

Budget adjustment estimate (BAE) is a description and estimated cost of a change, which is to become an entry.

PROCEDURES

A BAE shall be prepared by the Project Engineer or his designee for any change or potential change that may result in the following:

    More than a $10,000* change in cost in the budget

    Equipment additions or deletions.

    Account additions or deletions.

    As requested by members of the project team.

The attached form will be used. Detailed estimates should be attached, as appropriate. Each estimate will be prepared in an unbiased and professional manner.

The BAE should be submitted to the Project Leader or Facility Department Representative for review and further submission to the Project Manager.

The Project Manager will determine if a Scope Change Request needs to be prepared, or dependent on approval levels, accept or reject the BAE.

A BAE log will be the responsibility of the Project Engineer or designee, along with a copy of all the backup, etc.

If the BAE is approved or disapproved and a Scope Change Request is not necessary, the Project Manager's secretary shall distribute approved copies to the entire project team and send the original to the project file kept by the Project Engineer or designee.

If the BAE requires a Scope Change Request, it should be returned to the Project Leader or Facility Department Representative for preparation of the Scope Change Request. The BAE should then be attached as backup to the Change of Scope. The Scope Change Request approvals shall then be followed.

USE

The BAE is used to recognize and document a change. It will communicate to all the team members the changes.

It will force discussions around the impact of a change.

BAE's should not be used to keep forecasted variances to a minimum.

*The level should be determined for each project.

F I G U R E 22–2

Budget Adjustment Request

BUDGET ADJUSTMENT ENTRY   NO. _____
FILE NO. _____

Location _____ Project Title _____

BAE Title _____

To: _____ Date: _____

From: _____ Estimated By: _____

Reviewed By: _____

Your approval is requested for the following change:

REASON FOR CHANGE (Including deficiencies with current situation)

DESCRIPTION OF CHANGE:

Budget Category	Estimate $ (Plus) or Minus			
	Equipment	Labor	Material	Total

Account No. _____   Previous BAE Total _____

This Change _____

New BAE Total _____

_____ Not Approved _____(Date)
_____ Not a Change of Scope   Estimate Accuracy m(+/-) _____
_____ Change of Scope

Approval of Requested Change

_____   _____ _____
Project Manager   Project Sponsor   (If over $100,000)

Type
_____ A = Facility Oversight   _____ D = Result of Detail Engineering
_____ B = Engineering Oversight   _____ E = Marketing Change
_____ C = Estimate Oversight

the fifth column (Figure 22–3) in their budget log. It can be done manually, special software can be designed, or current systems can be "adjusted" so that they enter the value of purchase orders in the commitment column.

Whatever system is used, this column must be kept accurate and up to date. It is the only way a project manager can know where her project is at any instant. It is a real-time method of understanding status against budget. (A literature search failed to reveal much written about the subject of commitment tracking or commitment accounting, but it is widely practiced and used.)

This method of tracking gets difficult if "open purchase orders" are used. Open purchase orders are an expediency which should be avoided for this and other reasons. It is also important to note that some "business enterprise" systems do not have a commitment tracking feature, and one is very difficult to

F I G U R E 22–3

Budget and Cost Control Log

Acme Company				
Project: Project Manager:				
Account No.	Description	Original Budget	Current Budget	Committed to-date

install because of the "tight integration" of these systems. Figure 22–3 shows important columns of our budget and cost control log as it has developed through this point in the chapter.

SCOPE CREEP

Scope creep is the single most important cause of a deviation from budget. The two driving forces are lack of detailed scope definition and a host of stakeholders wanting to make the project better, more efficient, or more operating-cost-effective. Scope creep can also be driven by the legislative process when new laws are passed or regulations added between the time the estimate was made and startup. Whatever the reason, it is important to have an effective cost control mechanism in place to deal with the *pervasive driving force of scope creep.* Figure 22–4 is a scope change log for a project.

F I G U R E 22–4

A Scope Change Log Form

Scope Change Log						
Project:						
Date	Nature of Change	Requested by	Impact to Project	Approval Document No.	Cost of Change	Paid for by

F I G U R E 22–5

Scope Change Process

SCOPE CHANGE PROCESS

DEFINITION

The Scope Change Process starts with a Scope Change Request (SCR).

A SCR is any discretionary change from the original Scope and estimate of the appropriation requisition.

PROCEDURES

A SCR will be prepared by the Project Leader or Facility Department Representative on the attached form, as requested by the Project Manager. The Project Leader shall obtain all stakeholders' agreement prior to submission of the SCR. The first step in preparing a SCR is preparation of the BAR.

After approval or disapproval, the SCR will be transmitted to all the team members by the Project Manager. Once notified of the approval, all parties will proceed with the changed work.

USE

A SCR shall not be prepared for items that are necessary to carry out the original intended Scope which are a result of new information such as detailed design, field information, regulations, estimating errors, etc.

The SCR shall be used to inform and gain the appropriate approvals prior to making any discretionary change in a project. A SCR should be prepared for items which do not impact the budget.

Figure 22–5 shows a scope change process, and Figure 22–6 shows a scope change request.

Project managers must be firm about this process. They must not permit any commitment or any expenditure until scope change approval is obtained. There are some gray areas between a budget adjustment and a scope change. Let's look at a couple of examples to understand this important difference. First, assume that a pump and motor used in the project was estimated for a feed rate of 5,000 gpm. If the process dictates it should be 6,000 gpm and this was a missed

F I G U R E 22–6

Scope Change Request

SCOPE CHANGE REQUEST	NO. _____
	FILE NO. _____
	PROJECT NO. _____

Location _____   Project Title _____

Scope Change Title _____

Purpose _____
_____
_____

As Proposed in AR Scope _____
_____
_____

As Proposed in Scope Change _____
_____
_____

Capital Cost (Increase) or Decrease $ _____

New Cumulative Scope Change Balance $ _____

Source of Funding _____

Approved

To $50,000	Date
To $100,000	Date
To $200,000	Date
To $300,000	Date
To $400,000	Date
To $800,000	Date

estimate, then the difference in cost is usually considered to
be a budget estimate. If someone wants the feed rate to be
8,000 gpm because more steam is needed for the old part of
the plant (when none was originally scoped), then this is a
scope change. It may be legitimate and it may be the right
thing to do for the
company, but the
project manager
must have the dis-
cipline and the
character to insist
on a signed scope change document. If it's "so right," then
those with approval authority will recognize it and formally
approve it.

All projects must have a control
mechanism to deal with scope
creep.

You can see that this gets to be an involved process. The
more detailed and specific the scope, the easier it is to judge
if it is a budget adjustment or a scope change.

Another example will indicate how outside forces can
impact decisions. Suppose a project manager gets a request to
install a backup pump that is completely redundant. If the request is for operational convenience, it's a scope change. If the
request is because the state or insurance codes require it, then
it is probably a budget adjustment, because the engineer
should have known code and allowed for the pump. Some
will call for the use of contingency funds, but as will be seen in
the next section, that is not the intended use of contingency.

CONTINGENCY OR MANAGEMENT RESERVE

The most useful definition of contingency is that it is money
set aside to pay for work or equipment that were unknown
and unknowable during estimating. This is a hard rule but
one that results in better estimates and control. If in the redundant pump example the code changed between estimating and construction, then the cost of the second pump was

unknown and unknowable. It requires a scope change, but the funding comes from the contingency budget. There are a host of project requirements that may be unknown at the time of budgeting. Experienced project managers know many of these areas and take great pains to evaluate them but cannot possibly evaluate all of them. Examples include:

1. Buried structures.
2. Soil conditions different from test borings.
3. Undetected soil contamination.
4. Conditions inside tanks.
5. Conditions inside structures.
6. Inordinate weather conditions.
7. Changes in workman's compensation or insurance rates.

The level of unknowns is higher in rebuild situations than new construction, and different contingency levels are frequently used. A good database can help document a reasonable contingency level.

There are a couple of "golden rules" regarding contingency. The first is worth restating. Contingency is for unknowns, not for errors of omission (it should have been known) or errors of budgeting. Second, one should never use more contingency than

> You should never use more contingency than the amount of work already completed in the project.

the amount of work already completed in the project. That is, if the project is 35 percent complete, one should have used no more than 35 percent of the contingency budget. Because most "unknowns" show up late in the project, some project managers have an even tougher rule of thumb. They say that the contingency used should be no more than half of the percentage complete, until the very end of the project. This means that if a project is 35 percent complete, one should have used no more than 17.5 percent of the contingency budget.

Saving contingency for the end of the project is an excellent idea for two reasons. First, one never knows what startup problems will be encountered. Startup problems must be resolved quickly, and you don't want to wait for funding changes during startup. Second, when the project is being closed, any unused contingency will be used to cover budget adjustment entries if the sum of the changes is greater than the original budget.

ACCURACY OF ESTIMATES

There is yet another reason for using different levels of contingency, which is not strictly part of cost control but which will be covered here because it can be a cost control mechanism. Experienced project managers know that the level of accuracy of estimates can be improved with increasing detail (and cost). Some firms have formalized this process. A system used by Dr. Jaako Pöyry and Paul Talvio, of Jaako Pöyry, Inc., as related to me privately, typically uses three levels. The first level, say E1, is a quick "back of the envelope" estimate based on similar projects. It generally takes a few hours or days to prepare. The E1 level is regarded as having a ±40 percent accuracy because even the exact site of the job may be unknown. This level of accuracy may be okay for evaluating alternatives or looking at the conceptual merits of an idea.

The second level, say E2, is a factored or parametric estimate. This level is regarded as having a ±20 percent accuracy and is used to judge feasibility, or to choose between closer alternatives. This estimate generally takes weeks to prepare.

The third level, say E3, is a "board quality estimate." It requires a site to be identified, flow sheets to be completed, and piping and instrument drawings to be done in as much detail as possible. Estimates are prepared from budget quotes. This means the three types of specifications (mechanical, life, and performance) must be developed. This estimate can take months and up to 3 percent of the total installed cost to develop. The E3 estimate is regarded to have an accuracy of ±10 percent.

The accuracy of any level is highly dependent on the accuracy of a database, and this illustrates the importance of establishing and maintaining an accurate database. Some clients require a +0, minus 10 percent level of accuracy, sometimes called E4. This requires more complete engineering, bid packages, and firm quotes, usually with guaranteed time limits. Even more funds may be required for this level of estimating.

The usual problem is that some marketing opportunity, competitive move, or cash surplus requires that a project be scoped and estimated for "board approval" in less time than "board-quality estimates" take. Engineers and estimators frequently complain when this happens but usually provide a number—an estimate. They frequently fail to communicate its accuracy, and when the project is approved, some unsuspecting project manager inherits a nightmare.

One solution is to communicate the accuracy of the estimate and get board approval for wide limits or make the adjustment in contingency. If the quick estimate is at an E2 level (±20 percent), then there will be 10 percent more unknowns than for an E3 level *because the E2 lacks detail.* Therefore, if E3 estimates have a contingency of 7 percent, an E2 can have the same total budget accuracy by having a contingency of 17 percent.

If the process is explained to the board and if the project is truly urgent, then workable budgets will be established. This "level of accuracy" budgeting shows one reason why the definition of contingency as "unknowns" is so useful, but the concept does require a level of estimating expertise that is sophisticated.

PROJECT ACCOUNTING

Figure 22–7 shows a portion of a budget log. Columns have been added for "expended to date" (bills paid), required to complete, projected final cost, and variance. Projected final cost is the sum of expended to date and required to complete, which *is always an independent estimate*. Please note that the budget log in Figure 22–7 is one detailed sheet on process construction. It is one of many sheets of the budget log. As you can see, the accounting process is quite detailed and takes professional financial skills to complete. Large projects require at least one full-time, trained financial person plus necessary support staff. This phase of project accounting is not covered in detail here.

F I G U R E 22–7

Portion of a Budget Log

Account no.	Description	Original budget	Current budget	Committed to date	Expended to date	Required to complete	Projected final cost	Variance over- or underrun

PROJECT AUDITS

It is an excellent idea for the project manager to request an "in-process audit" early in the project, say at the 10 to 20 percent of completion stage. This audit should focus on the project procedures established and practiced. The audit should answer two questions: (1) Are all of the established procedures adequate? (2) Are they being followed? This early audit will help the team understand the importance of the discipline of project management. It will help the project manager establish or strengthen any systems or procedures necessary to facilitate the discipline of project management. Since the purpose of the audit is partly training and strengthening, verbal feedback from the audit team to the project team can be very helpful if a positive environment can be created. With 80 to 90 percent of the project remaining, the team can make changes which will benefit the entire project. Holding this kind of a review at the 80 to 90 percent of completion stage is not helpful to the project or the team.

A final review at the end of the project is useful for accumulating learning and to record lessons for the benefit of the team members and future teams. This audit information can be added to the financial audit, which will be done typically 6 to 12 months after startup or commissioning. See Chapter 25 on conducting process reviews.

23

CHAPTER

Change Control in Projects

Any change made to a project during the implementation stage is likely to pose a threat to progress in some way. The impact can be to any one or more of the cost, schedule, performance, or scope targets. The project manager has a dual responsibility in dealing with changes: (1) to keep the client informed about the impact of the change, and (2) to protect himself and the team from being "beaten up" at the end of the project when they miss original targets because changes were made.

> Changes made to projects during the implementation stage always pose a threat to progress.

One of the most common requests for change during a project is additional scope. This can happen for three basic reasons:

1. The initial plan did not include the scope, because it was forgotten.

2. Something was learned about a technical issue during the project that suggested a change. Or work is
   discovered, such as asbestos removal, which was not
   known during the planning stage. (See Chapter 22.)
3. The world changes during the project life cycle
   and upgrades to the project are required to stay
   competitive.

The first of these can be avoided by doing a better job of
planning up front. The second two are pretty much unavoid-
able, but such changes should not be casually made. Everyone should understand the impact to the project before a
scope change is authorized. If the customer agrees that the
change is worth the impact, then a change to the plan is made
that will incorporate the scope revision, and all stakeholders
affected by the change will sign the change approval form. A
form for such use is shown in Figure 23–1.

This form has a feature not often seen on change approval forms. By checking a box in front of an individual's
name, you can indicate who must sign the form. I suggest
that a person sign a project approval only if he or she is taking responsibility for some aspect of the job. Signatures
should not be an ego thing. It takes a lot of time to route a
change request through an organization, and this can severely impact project responsiveness. It is useful to have a
project change board meeting on a regular basis if many project changes are being made in an organization. That way, a
change can be approved at the regular meeting—unless it is
urgent, in which case it can be walked around for signatures.

Another feature is the impact box at the top of the form,
which shows whether the impact of a change will be to
schedule, cost, quality, or scope. In some organizations, another field needs to be added. That is the impact on inventory. Is a change going to make obsolete parts in inventory,
which will then have to be scrapped? If so, what is the cost
impact, and can it be avoided?

F I G U R E 23–1

Project Change Approval Form

Project Change Approval		
Project Name:	Project Number:	Date:
Project Manager: Requested by:	Department:	Change in: ☐ Scope ☐ Schedule ☐ Budget ☐ Performance

Deviation Information

Description of change being requested:

Reason for change:

Effect on schedule:

Effect on cost (budget):

Effect on performance (quality):

Effect on scope:

Justification:

Class	Distribution of estimated cost deviation	The requested change is:	
Capital		☐ Absolutely necessary to achieve desired results	☐ Scope reduction that will not impact original targets
Noncapital		☐ Discretionary—provides benefits beyond the original target	☐ Scope reduction that will impact original targets

Required Approvals ☐

☐ Project Leader/Manager (type name)	Sign:	Date:
☐ General Manager (type name)	Sign:	Date:
☐ Concerned Dept. Manager (type name)	Sign:	Date:
☐ Controller (type name)	Sign:	Date:
☐ Concerned Vice President (type name)	Sign:	Date:
☐ President (type name)	Sign:	Date:
☐ Other (type name)	Sign:	Date:

CHANGES THAT NEED CONTROL PROCEDURES

The way to decide whether a proposed change needs formal approval is to ask whether it would alter any information on a document that has already been issued to authorize work. By this definition, a formal procedure should be applied whenever a change would affect:

> To decide if a change needs formal approval, ask whether the change would alter any information on a document that has already been issued to authorize work.

- ◆ The contract document or any of its attachments. Such a change would be called a contract variation.

- ◆ A purchase order that has already been issued. The change would probably be called a purchase order amendment.

- ◆ Any drawing or specification that has been issued for manufacturing, purchasing, or construction.

CONTROL PROCEDURES FOR ENGINEERING CHANGES

Before a proposed engineering change is approved, it is customary to assess the risks such a change might cause, including technical, manufacturing or construction, commercial, safety, reliability, time scale, costs, and inventory. This assessment must usually be done by a change board, since no one individual is likely to be able to assess the impact in all areas.

The project manager should designate someone to keep a register of all such changes and to record when they have been implemented. A standard change form like the one shown in Figure 23–1 would be used to request the change. When engineering documents are changed, revision numbers must be updated and logged. Before the advent of computer-aided engineering, it was easy to control drawing revisions because the master was housed in a central file. Now anyone can print out a drawing, and there is no assurance that it is the latest version unless the revision number is checked against the log.

> Before approving an engineering change, ask what risk such a change might cause.

Most organizations recognize a point in the design process beyond which a change will cause a serious impact on costs and/or progress. At that point the design is frozen. The change board will then refuse to approve any change to the product unless they are convinced that there are compelling reasons for doing so, such as safety or a customer-funded request. Ideally, even the customer should be bound by a design freeze, or should be made to pay heavily for violating it.

LOGGING CHANGES IN PROJECT SCOPE

In Chapter 15, I pointed out that management reserve is to be used to pay for undiscovered work, but this is only for internally funded projects. If customers ask for changes to project scope, they are usually required to pay for them. A log should be kept of all scope changes made in a project. The log should document the nature of the change, who requested it, the impact to the project, dates on which the change was incorporated, the number of the approval document that authorized the change, the cost of the change, and who pays for it. A suitable form was shown in Figure 22–4.

The form on page 319 should be used to authorize changes in project scope. Together with the log, these constitute a history of changes and causes of those changes for future reference.

24 CHAPTER

Managing Vendors in Projects

By Ben Thorp*

In projects that involve partnering with vendors, the vendor actually becomes a member of the project team in a sense. Such vendors must be managed exactly as you would manage any resource in your team. Naturally, you don't have direct control over vendors, but then you often don't have such control over internal resources either.

> **Owner:** The organization doing the project.

You also need to manage vendors when you have large capital equipment projects in which the vendor is delivering long-lead capital equipment. Because of the large investments in these projects, it is very important that all efforts between vendor and customer (namely your company) be well managed.

This is by no means meant to suggest that a "command and control" method is advocated, especially in a partnering

---

* Former Vice President, Chesapeake Corporation, now retired.

arrangement. A good partnering arrangement is only achieved by clearly defining goals, roles, and processes, and that is the focus of this chapter.

There are two points that need to be made. First, the accountability for all projects resides *totally* with the owner. Second, the most typical form of relationship between owner and supplier is contractual. This contractual arrangement must be well understood by the project manager and owner alike.

> To manage vendors does not mean to adopt a "command and control" approach.

The message to new project managers or sponsors is that the owner must take control of the process, which is shown in Figure 24–1. He must define the decision-making process and stakeholder roles. Major stakeholders include production, finance, engineering, technical, and vendors. Each of these stakeholder groups has its own culture and each needs to be addressed uniquely. Owners must take control by clearly and completely defining their needs and desires (musts and wants) and ensuring that they are in specifications, bid packages, orders, contracts, and the like. This will require owners to take control of agenda-setting in meetings so that the required output is obtained. Partnering or teaming is a preferred method of working, but it cannot take precedence over managing the project.

> **Sponsor:** The person in the organization who "drives" the project.

RESOURCE DOCUMENTS

There are three primary resource documents that need to be prepared as early as possible. The first is an *internal document*, which defines the level of approval, the time required

Owner Controls Process

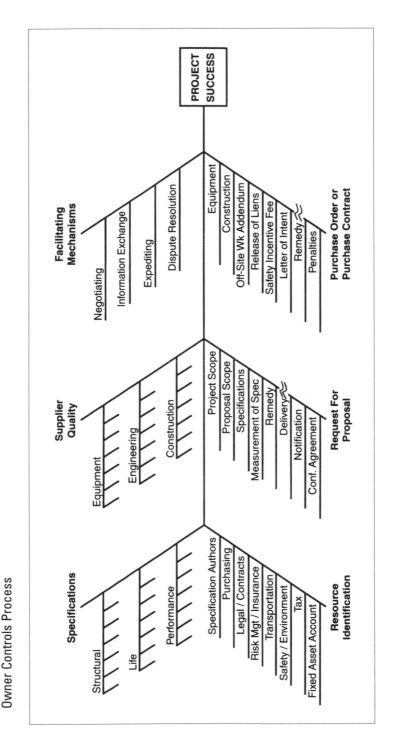

for approval, and the level of documentation needed for an approval to be granted. This simple document can save hundreds, even thousands, of hours of hunting down the right person for approval and in expediting delivery because the purchase order could not be issued in a timely manner. It can also save rework caused by the approving individual wanting to see more (or less) in order to sign. Does the approver want to see three bids, or just know that three bids have been obtained? Or is it satisfactory to know that the supplier has been the low bidder for the required quality on the last two jobs and the unit prices are the same for this job?

The second document identifies resources for the vendor management function, by name, either inside or outside of the owner's firm. Typical resources include individuals dealing with the issues shown in Figure 24–2.

F I G U R E 24–2

Issues That Must Be Addressed in a Project

Performance specification author
Safety
Purchasing
Transportation
Legal
Tax
Risk management/insurance
Fixed asset accounting

Every purchase order can have issues requiring input from one or all of these resources. Therefore, the resource needs to be *defined* and *available*.

The final document needed is a material coordination plan. This plan can be started early—around permitting—but can only be completed after all of the components are known. It can be a detailed description or a simple spreadsheet where each function (e.g., air permit), service (soil reports), or

F I G U R E 24–3

Sample Spreadsheet

Material Coordination Plan (Sample, abbreviated form)								
Project:						Date issued:		
	Requested	Purchased	Expedited	Received	Installed	Inspected	Checkout	Acceptance
Gen. Requirem'ts								
Site Work								
Foundations								
Masonry								
Carpentry								
Doors & Fixtures								
Finishes								
Equipment								
Mechanical								
Elec. & Inst.								
Piping								
Safety								
Environmental								

Instructions for use: List names of responsible parties in each cell and add any subcomponents of each item in column 1 from the work breakdown structure.

component (storm sewer) is listed. Columns would then be created for who will request, purchase, ship, expedite, inspect, construct, and approve. Where multiple ship-to sites are involved, another column will need to be added. See the example in Figure 24–3.

SPECIFICATIONS

The project team will need to discuss three very different types of specifications, namely:

Structural specifications
Life specifications
Performance specifications, including training

Historically, we have put emphasis on the structural specifications—typically type of material and strength or rigidity of the structure. Many firms have a comprehensive specification "library" for these. Those are still very appropriate. We are now adding to that certain life criteria for the product being delivered by the vendor. In automotive, we are talking about seven-year warranties on the drivetrain and 100,000 miles between tune-ups. There are industrial equivalents, which must be converted into specifications. Figure 24–4 shows some life issues which need to be considered.

F I G U R E 24–4

Life Issues for Deliverables

- ◆ Life of machinery
- ◆ Life of components
- ◆ Repair frequency
- ◆ Interchangability of spares
- ◆ Minimum spare inventory

However, the most critical specification for production machinery is *performance itself*. Specifications are normally written by engineers, but performance requirements are usually best understood by operations personnel, so this is an area that requires a team effort. Throughput models and run-rate models are sometimes helpful. That is, given certain input raw materials and conditions, what is the output and what is the tolerance around that output? What are the sustained and peak output rates? What is the average uptime? What training is required? What are the outcomes of the training (e.g., what do operators and mechanics need to do to run the facility?). These conditions will become part of the bid package and eventually part of the purchase order or

> Contracts without remedies are often without value.

contract. When preparing any specification, it helps to think about how well the contract will reflect it. The contract should answer these questions:

What are the performance specifications?

How will they be measured? What are the criteria and conditions?

What is the remedy when something is out of specification?

Contracts without remedies are often without value, except to the lawyers who will use the legal system to write what you forgot.

Specifications may also apply to intermediate steps, including, but not limited to, issues such as those shown in Figure 24–5.

F I G U R E 24–5

Issues That Must Be Covered

- Drawing submittal
- Certified drawings
- Shipment date
- Percent complete shipment
- Inspection
- Installation
- Startup
- Dates for full compliance to specification

Remember, each needs a definition of how performance will be measured and what the remedy will be if vendor performance is unsatisfactory. The consequences of a missed milestone date can often have large project consequences, even if the final ship date is met. For example, equipment that requires cavities or special mountings in a building might require certified drawings before the building drawings can/should be certified. A delay in equipment drawings could delay the whole building or the entire project. What, then, is the appropriate remedy? This can be determined through competitive bidding and negotiation, if it is in the bid package.

SUPPLIER QUALITY

There has been more written on this subject than perhaps any other subject addressed in this chapter. I will keep it short though, and deal only with a few principles. The first principle is that good projects have good suppliers. The second

> Good projects have good suppliers.

principle is that you need a system to define what is important to you and to do so in the most objective way possible. If this has been previously done by your corporation and you have preferred suppliers, selected suppliers, or partnerships, then you can proceed to the *supplier selection* section of this chapter. If not, you need to develop supplier evaluation mechanisms for at least equipment, engineering, and construction. Some of the evaluations will be for products (hard or soft), and some will be for services. These evaluations can be quite different.

In setting up evaluation mechanisms, you need to determine whether they will be made on the content of presentations (often future expected results) or on the evaluation of past performance. For example, will contractor safety be judged by promised safety programs or will it be judged by the contractor's experience modifier rate (EMR) to his Workers Compensation Insurance Premium?

For equipment, typical areas that can be evaluated are shown in Figure 24–6.

For the engineering activity, typical areas that can be evaluated include those shown in Figure 24–7.

F I G U R E 24–6

Equipment Evaluation Areas

- Quality
- Cost of use (price is a default)
- Delivery
- Service
- Business practices
- Ethics
- Technology/development
- Training

F I G U R E 24–7

Engineering Areas to Evaluate

- Process expertise
- Design expertise
- Drawing quality (errors per drawing)
- Custom design expertise
- Modules design capability
- Long-term operation and maintenance
- Alignment with owner
- Ethics
- Design safety
- Standards & procedures
- Timeliness

To evaluate contracting work, consider the list shown in Figure 24–8.

A uniform system of evaluation will result in at least three positive outcomes. First, the team will have a more consistent evaluation process. Second, unqualified suppliers will be eliminated. Finally, there will be a way to *objectively* evaluate "favorite suppliers" who are recommended by some party, including management.

F I G U R E 24–8

Contracting Evaluation Areas

- ◆ Safety (EMR, etc.)
- ◆ Quality control
- ◆ Ethics
- ◆ Planning/scheduling
- ◆ Billing accuracy, backup, and timeliness
- ◆ Financial stability
- ◆ Craftsman training
- ◆ Supervisors' skills
- ◆ Dispute resolution
- ◆ Relationship with subcontractors

REQUEST FOR PROPOSALS

When RFPs are issued, they should be complete and should only go to qualified suppliers. A qualified supplier is one that you would buy from if they provide the best response to the RFP. There is a lot of debate over this issue. In some instances suppliers are asked to bid on a job even though the company knows that they will never be awarded the contract, simply be-

> The effort of including stalking horses in your bid system is probably not worthwhile.

cause they aren't qualified. However, they are almost certain to bid lower than anyone else. That low bid is then held up to qualified suppliers as an incentive to bid lower. The bidder who initially gave the lowest bid is called a "stalking horse." Most leading companies have concluded that the wasted effort of including stalking horses is not worth the value of the time spent.

A request for proposal should include the items shown in Figure 24–9.

F I G U R E 24–9

Items to Include in RFPs

◆ Outline of total project   ◆ Installation services
◆ Scope of work for the RFP   ◆ Startup services
◆ Structural specifications   ◆ Payment schedule
◆ Life specifications   ◆ Recommended spares
◆ Performance specifications   ◆ Insurance coverage
◆ Measurement of specification   ◆ Evaluation criteria
◆ Remedies   ◆ Notification procedures
◆ Delivery of information   ◆ Names of key personnel
◆ Delivery of materials/services ◆ Confidentiality agreements
◆ Shipment methods

There will always be questions from bidders about RFPs. A list of these should be compiled, and the same answer given to all bidders. One method used to shorten this process is to invite all bidders to a single meeting. An advantage of this approach is that the number and quality of questions improves. One potential disadvantage is that all bidders are known to each other.

SUPPLIER SELECTION

A well-prepared RFP can make this process relatively straightforward. If the evaluation criteria have been stated objectively and weighted, each bid can be scored and totaled. If one uses a Kepner-Tregoe (1965) process (in which you list musts, wants, and nice-to-haves), the musts should be scored and totaled first. It is always a good idea to decide up front what range of totals will be considered equal. For example, if there are 10 factors of 10 points each, then one knows that an 87 is the same as an 88. Another method is to require that all musts need to be fully met, and anyone falling below 100 is a candidate for elimination. It is typical for the evaluation process to sort leaders from average responses and to identify clear candidates for elimination. Assuming there are several bidders that warrant further consideration, a ranking of the wants is in order. Experience shows that it is wise to keep more than one bidder before entering into the next process, which is negotiation. There are technical and commercial insights that can be obtained from the negotiation process. These can change the evaluation. Furthermore, changes can sometimes unseat the leading bidder. For example, their delivery can change due to a new order, or critical personnel can be assigned to other projects.

Negative things can happen during this process. Competitive bids can show that specifications were incorrect or missing. The delivery dates or estimated cost can be grossly in error. If the deviation is small, amended bids can be requested. If the deviation changes the scope, new RFPs may be needed. If the deviation changes project economics, the project may need to be changed or even canceled. Project managers or teams might be disappointed by a canceled project, but experienced project managers know this is a better outcome than having to manage a bad project.

NEGOTIATION

This is the point at which an owner's wants and musts have to be reconciled with the bidders' capabilities and desires. Everyone agrees that at this phase in the project, the owner has the advantage. Wise use of power will create a win-win situation. Unwise use of power is likely to create a win-lose situation or even a lose-lose situation. *The key questions should be resolved in favor of what's best for the project.* What's best is usually that all project wants are met by a

> Key questions should be resolved in favor of what's best for the project.

ൽ♦ൽ

After negotiations are complete, there should be no surprises for the owner or the successful bidder.

ൽ♦ൽ

strong supplier who is capable of dedicating the resources needed to make the project a success. Too many times, bidders accept conditions that cannot be met in order to secure an order. When this condition becomes apparent, the project is headed for trouble. The project mission and vision must include vendor success and eliminate "get something for nothing" thinking.

There are many approaches to negotiation. One successful approach is to break the negotiations into "technical" and "commercial" parts. The specifications should be negotiated first, because their resolution could change the price. If special materials or construction are needed, the price may increase. If an owner is willing to accept a standard offering, the price may decrease. Once all of the specification issues have been resolved, the commercial negotiations can begin. Here, all items that will appear in the purchase order must be discussed and agreed to, especially performance specifications, test conditions, and remedies. *After negotiations are complete, there should be no surprises for the owner or the successful bidder.*

The remedy deserves some special discussion because of the realities that occur when performance is not met. At this point, the project can be practically over. Usually, the budget has been spent. The same is true for the suppliers' budget. These forces can "seduce" both the owner's project team and the bidder to try a series of "low-cost" fixes that can take weeks, and usually months. When performance specs are missed, it is usually wise to invite upper levels of management on both sides to the solution meeting. Ideally, the time allowed to implement the remedy is addressed in the purchase order or contract. If the bidder is unwilling or unable to resolve the performance issue, then the owner can implement and charge back all or a percentage of the costs to the bidder. Some contracts have a liquidated-damages clause whereby the cost of the equipment or service is discounted until the owner achieves their original financial returns. Most bidders will insist on a limitation-of-liability clause. These conditions are all resolved through negotiation with the goal of creating a win-win situation. One form of a win-win is to negotiate penalty clauses for late delivery, poor performance, and so on. In return, there are incentive clauses for perfect delivery (early delivery can sometimes cause staging problems), good startup, above-average performance, or outstanding safety performance. The owner typically benefits from all of these, and sharing an unplanned benefit is easier than many would expect.

There are a number of negotiating processes that can be used, and most are satisfactory if the process is fair, ethical, and well understood by all stakeholders. Getting everyone at the same office on the same day is not in itself brutal. It may be very time efficient. Getting everyone there to "shop the low price" is at least unfair. Most experienced teams like to devote a half day to a day per major bidder and to separate close competitors by at least an evening. This is because there are usually many items to resolve, and it takes intense focus to get through the major issues.

THE PURCHASE ORDER/PURCHASE CONTRACT

There are numerous contract forms, and it takes an experienced project team to know what form to use and why. There are two general recommendations. First, the owner should have his contract forms reviewed and modified by expert outside legal counsel with experience in litigating contracts. This is a special skill that may require a slightly higher fee—once. However, it could save millions over time. Second, the owner should use his stationery and his contract as a starting point.

It is beyond the scope of this book to delve into contract law. It is not beyond the scope of this book to note that the owner has the responsibility and accountability that dictates he be good at contract negotiation and contract implementation. An experienced project manager will know the contracts better than the process or the equipment being purchased.

The major types of purchase contracts include those components listed in Figure 24–10. The elements to be addressed

F I G U R E 24–10

Components of Purchase Contracts

- ◆ Acceptance Certificate
- ◆ Affidavit and Release of Liens
- ◆ Construction Agreement, Cost Plus Fixed Fee
- ◆ Construction Agreement, Cost Plus Percentage Fee
- ◆ Construction Agreement, Lump Sum
- ◆ Contractor's Performance Incentive Fee
- ◆ Contractor's Safety Incentive Fee
- ◆ Corporation Consultation
- ◆ General Conditions, Cost Plus Fixed Fee
- ◆ General Conditions, Cost Plus Percentage Fee
- ◆ General Conditions, Lump Sum
- ◆ Individual Consultant
- ◆ Letter of Intent
- ◆ On-Site Work Addendum
- ◆ Purchase Order (Cost Reimbursable Construction)
- ◆ Purchase Order (Equipment Supplier)
- ◆ Purchase Order (Firm Price Construction)
- ◆ Renewable Construction Agreement
- ◆ Renewable Engineering Agreement
- ◆ Request for Contractor's Affidavit

include those listed in Part 5. Your most critical projects
should have your best contracts personnel, who can typically
be shared across a number of projects.

INFORMATION EXCHANGE

There are two forms of information exchange, one external
and one internal. External exchange of information requires
that the owner examine the project, the location of the project, and the types of information that will be exchanged. The
key questions are: What information is confidential? and
How confidential? On the one hand is a completely public
project, like building a park. On the other hand is a project
requiring high levels of security and in-depth security clear-
ance for all workers. In most projects there is considerable information that the owner wants to keep confidential. This
means that confidentiality agreements need to be signed with
each company receiving this information. For very sensitive
information, it is worth considering agreements for each person receiving the information. These agreements should state
how confidential information will be identified and marked.
Restrictions on copying the information need to be included
in the contract and on the markings. Verbal confidential information is usually confirmed in memo or noted in meeting
minutes. All official meeting administrators need to be aware
of the policies established. The owner needs to keep a log of
all confidential information distributed, and at the end of the
project may want to reclaim all of it. The owner's IT (information technology) or IS (information systems) person
should be consulted for the best way to handle confidential
information that may be transmitted electronically.

Internal document distribution is usually the larger job.
This is actually a communications function and should be approached in that fashion. The most common document control device is a spreadsheet with the documents listed in the
first column and potential recipients listed in subsequent col-

umns. Facility files and central files are critical recipients. Correspondence and meeting notes are critical documents.

Figure 24–11 shows a typical document distribution matrix. This matrix should be reviewed with all stakeholders up front and decisions agreed to by the project manager. Once this is done, each document can be coded as to its type (e.g., bill of material) and a process can be put in place for support personnel to make immediate distribution.

There should never be a bottleneck in communications, especially document distribution. E-mail facilitates distribution, but it is necessary to make sure that all recipients, and the server, have the capability to receive documents created by all kinds of software. This is particularly true for e-mail attachments. It is frustrating to receive files that cannot be opened.

Project review meetings are a critical communication mechanism. They are best when the meeting forum is open and critical stakeholders are present. See Chapter 25 on conducting project reviews. Typically, the project plan is the yardstick against which various groups track and report

F I G U R E 24–11

Document Distribution Matrix

Document Name	Project Secretary	Project Team*	Facility Engineer	Project Receiving	Accounts Payable	Project Files	Vendors*	Project Sponsor	Others (Specify)
Proj. Procedure	1	1	1	1	1	1	1	1	
Meeting Minutes	1	1	1	0	0	1	1	1	
Specifications & Bill of Materials	1	1	1	1	0	1	1	0	
Request for Proposals	1	1	1	0	0	1	NA	0	
Proposals	1	1	1	0	0	1	NA	0	
Progress Reports	1	1	1	0	0	1	1	1	
Audits	1	1	0	0	0	1	1	1	
Closeout	1	1	1	1	1	1	1	1	
Others (specify)									

Distribution of Documents (Sample, abbreviated form) — Project: — Date issued:

project status. These meetings should be scheduled in advance, and the agenda well planned. If the project manager does all the talking, she learns very little. The agenda should be structured so that the meeting is a status report and coordination meeting with problems identified and well defined but not necessarily solved in the meeting. Separate meetings can be established for problem solving. Status of safety, schedule, cost, and coordination are typical agenda items. Using earned value analysis to measure project status is a very useful approach. Minutes should be taken, issued promptly, and reflect action items with responsibility and timetables. Projects have a relatively short life, and action items take on particular urgency.

EXPEDITING

It is best to start with the premise that there is always something on the critical path, and that events could change the critical path. Therefore, expediting skills are needed. Once critical path items are known, it can be determined if expediting will be done by the owner, the supplier, or a third party. Early decisions and arrangements will allow this function the lead time it needs to be successful. It is sometimes necessary to book special trucks, trains, boats, or planes. It is sometimes expeditious to use a port of entry familiar to the expediter. It may also be necessary to obtain state permits to haul "oversized" loads. All of this takes time to plan and execute. The worst time to engage expediting service is after a critical date is missed.

DISPUTE RESOLUTION

Disputes can occur at many levels. This needs to be acknowledged up front, and procedures put in place so that disputes are identified and resolved in a professional manner. *In no event should a dispute become disruptive to the project.* Dispute resolution procedures should be included in every purchase order and in every contract.

There are a number of procedures that can be used, but two important principles should always be observed. First, the problem must be accurately stated and documented. Experience has shown that many disputes arise from an inaccurate or unclear description of the problem. Second, all parties should agree ahead of time on the dispute resolution process and agree to follow it.

> A dispute should never become disruptive to the project.

One process will be outlined here, but as previously stated, there are others. The first step is to establish a detailed definition of the problem, which all parties can support. The easy first step is frequently overlooked. The second step is to apply the principles of the purchase order or contract to the problem. This shows the importance of including quantifiable definitions of the three types of specifications in each purchase order or contract.

The third step is to negotiate a resolution of the problem. Use of established negotiating techniques can be of value at this step. The fourth step is to delegate the resolution to higher levels of management on each side. As you can see, it is helpful if the contract specifies the exact level of higher management by title or name. Typically, this will be someone who can approve a scope or funding change. The final step is to take the dispute to an "independent third party." Some choose arbitration. Others have noted that arbitration has a leveling or averaging impact and have specifically deleted this from all contracts. Their reasoning is that significant effort should be put into developing good contracts and selecting good suppliers, which results in few disputes. In the instance of an unresolved dispute, the legal system can be used to achieve an equitable resolution.

25 CHAPTER

Conducting Project Reviews

Throughout the life of a project, there are various reviews that should be conducted. The timing, manner, and follow-up of these reviews are important to the success of the project and subsequent ones.

There are three kinds of reviews that might be done on a project. These are listed in the following table:

Project Reviews and Their Nature	
Status	Looks at the status of cost, performance, schedule, and scope
Design	Examines a product, service, or software design to see if it meets requirements
Process	Examines project processes and asks if they can be improved

STATUS REVIEWS

The most frequent review is the status review. There are two levels of this review—cursory and comprehensive. A cursory review might be held weekly, whereas a comprehensive one might be held monthly. How often status reviews should be held is a judgment call, but my suggestion would be that for projects of less than a year's duration, a weekly cursory review is about right, with a monthly comprehensive review. For projects with a greater than one-year duration, monthly reviews are probably okay unless problems exist. When problems occur in a project, more frequent reviews are generally held until the problem is corrected. Care should be taken to avoid the trap of micromanaging—unless the team is in so much trouble that it is required.

I also do not consider as sufficient a review that goes like this:

"How is project googleplex going?"

"Okay."

"Great. How about project sillyputty?"

"It's okay."

The only way such a review can be valid is if "Okay" is backed up with some meaningful numerical data. This means that the project manager knows something about the actual level of cost, performance, time, and scope. In too many cases people tell you they are on target when they are nowhere close, so measures are necessary. This topic is covered in Chapter 21.

I do believe that reporting on projects should be on an exception basis. That is, I need to report on deviations that are greater than my variance thresholds and explain their potential impact and what is being done about them. A reporting form like the one in Figure 25–1 captures this. The form should be filled out *only* to report deviations. If no deviations exist, then a periodic report that says everything is okay, backed up by numerical data, is sufficient. You *do* need that report, since no information is uninformative.

F I G U R E 25–1

Progress Report Form

Project Progress Report	
Project:	Prepared by:
For the period from to	Date:
Accomplishments for this report period are:	
We are ☐ ahead, ☐ behind, ☐ on schedule	
List any changes to project objectives:	List any changes in our business climate that might affect your project:
What problems do we face that were originally unanticipated?	
What needs to be changed?	List anyone whose approval is needed for those changes:
List any additional *anticipated* problems:	Action steps which I plan to take:
Comments:	

CORRECTING PROBLEMS RATHER THAN PLACING BLAME

There are times when someone in a project team does something totally stupid or unprofessional. In such a case, that person deserves to be sanctioned. However, I am very opposed to the organization that operates in the blame-and-punishment mode all the time. If you are always looking for witches, you generally find them. If people know they are going to be trashed for every slip, then they will try to protect themselves by hiding problems, and this may mean that problems only reveal themselves when the situation is too serious to correct easily.

> Status reviews should always be conducted in a problem-solving mode.

Status reviews should always be conducted in a problem-solving mode. We want to know (1) what problems exist, (2) what is causing them, and (3) what must be done to solve them. Notice that the word "what" is used in each case. It is a good idea to delete the word "why" from your vocabulary. When you ask someone why a problem exists, you almost always arouse a bit of defensiveness. I personally think we become conditioned to be defensive when we hear the word "why," since our parents often asked why we did some unacceptable thing, then trashed us after we explained. So the sequence that we expect is:

1. Why did you do this forbidden thing?
2. I don't know. The devil made me do it.
3. That's not acceptable as an answer. Go to your room! You're grounded for 100 years!

So, since we don't want to be grounded for 100 years when we do something unacceptable in projects, we try to hide it, blame it on the guy in the next cubicle, or pretend we didn't notice it if someone finds out.

Once problems are identified, you should follow standard problem-solving procedure to deal with them. It is amazing to me how we often totally ignore this process. We need to get to the root cause of the problem rather than dealing with a symptom. Then we should generate alternative solutions. Next we should select a solution, try it, and revise it if it doesn't work. Often, what occurs is a lot of flailing around that only makes the situation worse. The most serious error is self-deception, in which we convince ourselves that the situation is not so bad. The ship is sinking, but since it is going down very slowly, there is no need for concern.

THE DESIGN REVIEW

Whether you are designing a new product, writing software, developing a new service, or planning to move a facility, the purpose of a design review is to ensure that the final "deliverable," or outcome of the project, is on track. Will it do what it is supposed to do? Are there performance issues that must be addressed? If it is an actual product being developed (I consider software a product), and it appears unlikely that it will meet the original specifications, do these need to be changed? If they are, will the customer still accept them? Design reviews are usually conducted at major milestones in a project.

To some degree, the design review is focused on the performance component of the cost, performance, time, and scope equation. If we do not perform the design work correctly, then the product will not do what it is supposed to do. That being the case, the project may be headed for serious trouble.

In the chapter on defining success and failure, we saw that one definition of failure is that the deliverable is not accepted by the customer. We can get through on time, within budget, and on scope, but if the product does not work correctly and the customer rejects it, then the project might be deemed a failure. The question is: How critical is the performance issue? If it is serious and we cannot achieve the required performance, should the project be canceled? Marvin Patterson, formerly vice president of product development at Hewlett-Packard, says that the most productive thing you can do is cancel a losing product development project *as early as possible* (Patterson, 1993). Cut your losses and get on with something else!

This is one area in which technical people can fool themselves. They are convinced that they can make it work, if just given enough time. Their egos won't let them admit that the product doesn't work, that they have no clue how to make it work, and that even if they are given forever, they still might not be able to make it work. So they plod on, ever hopeful of success. There is a difference between a positive mental attitude, wishful thinking, and a correct assessment of reality. It is certainly hard to tell sometimes. Success *might* be just around the corner.

This is where peer review is useful—if you can get peers to be honest with each other. Unfortunately, we find that people in technical professions tend to be reluctant to trash someone else's work. It may be a fear of reciprocation, or it may be an honest concern that solving problems is unpredictable, so they don't want to advise pulling the plug too soon. Whatever the case, peer review is the best feedback you can have. However, it's not always as objective as it should be, so sometimes nontechnical managers must make judgments to shut down a project over the protest of the technical people. You may be public enemy number one, but you will save the company a lot of money.

To ensure a proper evaluation of a design, ANSI N45.2.11 and ANSI/ASME NQA-1 have established design review criteria. These criteria are widely used and should be adopted for any program involving a design review. They are shown in Figure 25–2.

F I G U R E 25–2

Design Review Elements

DESIGN REVIEW ELEMENTS

1. Were the inputs correctly selected and incorporated into design?

2. Are assumptions necessary to perform the design activity adequately described and reasonable? Where necessary, are the assumptions identified for subsequent reverifications when the detailed design activities are completed?

3. Are the appropriate quality and quality assurance requirements specified?

4. Are the applicable codes, standards, and regulatory requirements—including issue and addenda—properly identified, and are their requirements for design met?

5. Have applicable construction and operating experience been considered?

6. Have the design interface requirements been satisfied?

7. Was an appropriate design method used?

8. Is the output reasonable compared to the inputs?

9. Are the specified parts, equipment, and processes suitable for the required application?

10. Are the specified materials compatible with each other and the design environmental conditions to which the material will be exposed?

11. Have adequate maintenance features and requirements been specified?

12. Are accessibility and other design provisions adequate for performance of needed maintenance and repair?

13. Has adequate accessibility been provided to perform the in-service inspection expected to be required during the plant life?

14. Has the design properly considered radiation exposure to the public and plant personnel?

15. Are the acceptance criteria incorporated in the design documents sufficient to allow verification that design requirements have been satisfactorily accomplished?

16. Have adequate preoperational and subsequent periodic test requirements been appropriately specified?

17. Are adequate handling, storage, cleaning, and shipping requirements specified?

18. Are adequate identification requirements specified?

19. Are requirements for record preparation review, acceptance, retention, etc., adequately specified?

Source: Excerpt from ANSI N45.2.11 and ANSI/ASME NQA-1. Reprinted by permission of American Society of Mechanical Engineers.

When products are being designed for manufacture, the review must include conditions of manufacturability and serviceability. The specifics of the manufacturing process should consider tooling, economics of special machinery and processes, and integration of the design with manufacturing to ensure overall optimization. As in the ANSI guidelines for serviceability and warranty in Figure 25–2, there are considerations such as ease-of-access, safety to operators and maintenance personnel, and protection from damage due to inadvertent use. To confirm proper scope and technical content, a scope description must be available against which comparisons can be made.

It should be noted that these conditions are for formal design reviews. Project managers are encouraged to practice management by walking around (MBWA) throughout the life of the project in order to have a feeling for whether the work is proceeding well in terms of design quality. It may be too late to easily and inexpensively correct minor problems if you wait until a formal design review to identify them.

PROCESS REVIEWS

Process reviews are focused on how we are doing what we are doing. Can the work process be improved in any way? What things are we doing that we want to keep on doing? Chapter 27 is devoted to process improvement, so in this chapter, I want to just deal with how the process review should be conducted.

A process is a way of doing something. Communication is a process. Leadership is a process. So are decision making, problem solving, meeting management, and planning. (For a more complete listing, see Chapter 27.) Process reviews should be held at major milestones in a project or every three months, whichever comes first. The reason for the

A process
is a way
of doing
something.

three-month rule is that this seems to be about the limit of people's memories. For very short projects, you might have a process review once a month.

The important thing to remember in process reviews is that you are trying to maintain what is being done well and improve those processes that need improvement. You are not out to get someone! So the process review should be conducted by asking two questions:

1. What are we doing well so far?
2. What would we like to improve?

Notice that I do not ask, "What are we doing wrong?" We may not be doing anything wrong, but we can almost always improve. I also do not like the method of writing a plus sign (+) on one flip chart page and a minus sign (–) on another to indicate "okay" and "needs improvement." A minus sign connotes things being done wrong, and when you suggest that things are being done wrong, people tend to get defensive. When that happens, you will never hear about things that should be improved.

As a matter of fact, one of the biggest barriers to doing process reviews is the aversion that people have to "airing their dirty laundry." This is especially true when you suggest that what we learn in one group should be shared with other teams so that they can take advantage of it. People don't want to do this. Yet learning is expensive, and an organization needs to take advantage of all learning.

I suggest that companies hold periodic reviews, perhaps quarterly, in which project managers share with each other in a public forum what they have learned. If organizations could adopt the approach used by the army to review themselves, they could improve tremendously. The army reviews actual military campaigns as well as practice drills, and their rule is that *after anything significant happens, we will take the time to ask what we can learn from it.*

Years ago I knew a fellow who was consulting with a glass company to help them improve their quality. One day he went into the plant and everyone was celebrating.

"What's going on?" he asked.

"We just had a great day," someone said.

"Tell me about it."

"Well, we just had an 85 percent yield," said the person.

"How did you do it?" asked the consultant.

"We don't know," was the response.

Clearly, if they don't know, they can't repeat it. And this happens all too often in organizations everywhere.

WHO SHOULD CONDUCT THE REVIEW?

Process reviews can be conducted by the project manager or an outside facilitator. There are advantages either way. If you, as project manager, have good group process skills, then you can conduct the review. One downside is that leadership is a process and should be open for improvement, and that means the group will have to give you feedback on your leadership style. Unless the group is used to doing this, they may be very hesitant. They don't know what the repercussions might be. If that is the case, an outside facilitator might get better information.

26

CHAPTER

Managing Quality
in Projects

As I have pointed out a number of times throughout this book, there are four variables that we always deal with in projects: cost, performance, time, and scope. Cost and time get most of the attention, scope is next, and performance (quality of work done) is dead last. In fact, when you put enough pressure on people to meet deadlines, stay on budget, and do all of the

> If you finish late, over budget, and below scope, and the thing still works, you will probably be forgiven.

work assigned to them, they invariably sacrifice quality. One problem with this is that we don't know about it until it is much too late to do anything about it.

A project manager at a steel mill told me once, "If you finish a project a little late, go over budget, and maybe don't quite have all the scope you originally promised, but the thing still works, you'll generally be forgiven. On the other hand, if all these things happen and it doesn't work on top of that, then you're in serious trouble." He makes a very good point.

It is now 17 years since the quality "movement" started in the United States, and I find people seem to be losing interest in quality. They have been part of so many program-of-the-month efforts to improve quality that they are a bit glazed over. Yet, if we lose sight of quality, we ultimately wind up in trouble.

WHAT IS QUALITY, ANYWAY?

After all these years of quality improvement, I still find people mistaking quality for sophistication. So it seems that we should revisit the definition of quality before going on. After all, if we don't have the same understanding of the word, much of the discussion won't make any sense.

> **Quality is meeting the needs of the customer.**

There are two common definitions of quality. One is that quality is conformance to specifications or requirements. The other is that quality is meeting the needs of the customer. Some people call this "fitness for use." Both definitions arrive at the same point, if you understand that the specifications or requirements must be developed in such a way that the customer's needs will be met if specs and/or requirements are met.

> **Only the customer can tell you what quality means.**

Another axiom of quality is that *only the customer can tell you what quality means to him or her.* Sometimes technical people want to shove their idea of quality down the customer's throat, but that is not the quality way. As we discussed in Chapter 14, QFD is one approach for determining those factors that must be met in order for the customer to be satisfied with a product or service.

Quality management is the managing of all functions and activities necessary to determine and achieve quality (fitness for use). Like functional managers, project managers must also manage for quality. Failing to do so can be costly.

In several places I have written that many experts estimate that as much as 30 percent of the cost to develop new products is rework. This is not surprising to those of us who have been associated with the quality movement since its early days in the 1980s. We knew back then that from 5 to 40 percent of factory effort to

> Rework is an inverse measure of quality!

produce products goes into scrap and rework. Rework is total waste. It is lost to the factory, since it cannot be reclaimed. Scrap is not quite totally wasted, because there is some salvage value to the waste product. The impact of this is that if you have 100 plants, all making the same products, and your scrap and rework total 30 percent, then this is equivalent of having 30 plants working full time to turn out nothing!

Hopefully, you won't find too many plants today with such high scrap and rework figures. If they have applied quality improvement methods to their manufacturing processes, they should have largely eliminated these problems. Trouble is, we haven't applied the things we learned in factories to knowledge work processes—at least not until recently.

Although Deming argued that we need to improve all processes, the awareness that this meant processes *outside* manufacturing seems to have been missed until it was provoked by Hammer and Champy's *Reengineering the Organization* (1993). This book made managers aware that the same improvements that have been made in manufacturing can be made in other areas of the organization. The focus is on *processes*—the way in which we get work done. In Chapter 27, I discuss improving those processes that specifically affect project management. However, within projects themselves, there are work processes that should be examined for improvement opportunities.

QUALITY COSTS

The term quality costs is actually misleading. What we are really concerned with is the cost of *poor quality,* or the cost of nonconformance to our requirements. For the purpose of brevity, however, I will use the term quality costs to mean the cost of poor quality.

Quality costs can be divided into three categories. These are easy to remember by using the acronym PAF—meaning *prevention, appraisal,* and *failure.* Prevention costs are normally considered to be quality assurance costs. These are the costs of any action taken to prevent or reduce defects and failures. Included would be the costs of planning and managing quality systems and the preventive elements of such systems.

Appraisal means inspection. These are the costs of determining the level of quality achieved. They include such factors as:

1. Inspection and testing.
2. Vendor control.
3. Checking documents.
4. Process validation.
5. Checking specifications.
6. Product sampling.

Failure costs are the costs of nonconformance. These are the result of doing things wrong, and include:

1. Repairs and rework.
2. Loss of customers.

F I G U R E 26-1

Distribution of Business Costs

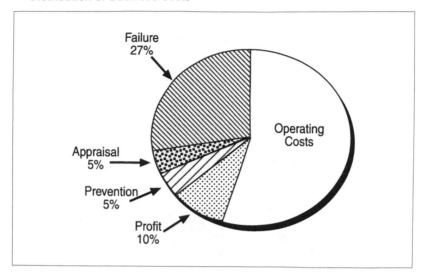

3. Warranty costs.
4. Increased insurance costs.
5. Investigating the causes of defects.

A typical distribution for these costs is shown in Figure 26–1. Note that appraisal and failure can exceed profits. Thus, any reduction in failure and appraisal costs can go directly to profits. This is discussed in the next section.

THE BENEFIT OF QUALITY IMPROVEMENT

Before the application of quality improvement methods, it is commonplace to find that the cost of appraisal and failure is 80 percent of total quality cost, while prevention is only 20 percent. By increasing prevention costs—that is, doing things that will prevent problems—you can reduce the cost

F I G U R E 26–2

Cost Benefit of Improved Quality

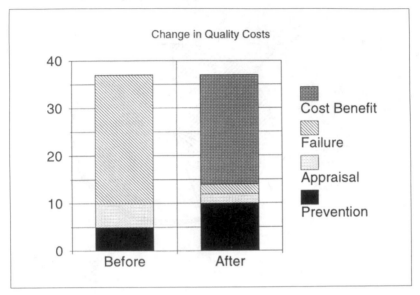

of appraisal and failure and gain a net cost benefit for the organization, which translates directly into a bottom line profit. This is shown in Figure 26–2. Notice that we have not totally eliminated inspection (appraisal). The long-term objective would be to eliminate inspection, but you may never completely get there.

QUALITY MANAGEMENT PRINCIPLES AND PRACTICES

There are three principles of quality management that must be applied in order to have an effective system:

   1. *Quality is everyone's business.* Every function in an organization must be performed in accordance with quality principles.

2. *Do it right the first time every time.* Phil Crosby, a former vice president of quality at ITT, was fond of saying that it always costs less to do it right the first time than to do it over. Rework is wasted effort and can be expensive, as has been mentioned before. It should be noted, however, that management must ensure that systems, equipment, and services used by employees to do their work are capable of sustaining the level of quality desired. If not, it is management's responsibility to replace these with the proper ones.

3. *Communicate and cooperate.* Everybody should know what to do, where they fit within the organization, and with whom they interface. In projects, this is achieved by proper planning, role definition, and coordination.

DEVELOPING A QUALITY SYSTEM FOR A PROJECT

Assuming that the organization has an overall quality system, there needs to be one specific to projects. If no overall system exists in the organization, then it will be next to impossible to achieve project quality of the desired level. Furthermore, a project quality system cannot stand alone and do the job.

A quality system is also known as a quality plan. Developing a quality plan for a project will depend on the total project work scope. Like the overall project plan, you should begin by defining your quality objectives. What is the system intended to achieve?

The quality plan should be part of the overall project documentation and should detail the specific quality practices, resources, and activities relevant to a particular product, service, contract, or project. The company's overall quality system will need some modification to suit each project.

These can be additions to or reductions of the company system. For example, if only design activities are involved, then the company's system dealing with design would be adapted for the project.

DETAILED PROCEDURES

Procedures should exist that, if followed, will ensure that work is done right the first time. Ideally, such procedures should be developed only by personnel familiar with the particular activities and functions. Each procedure should define the purpose and scope of the relevant activity and specify how it is to be properly performed. Sometimes the quality assurance department has to develop these procedures, though this is not the best approach, as mentioned above. Note that the project manager is ultimately responsible for the quality of the project on completion.

SECTION FIVE

OPTIMIZING PROJECT PERFORMANCE

27
CHAPTER

Improving Project Management Processes

There is a saying in psychology that says a lot about the need for performance improvement. It goes: If you always do what you've always done, you'll always get what you always got. The corollary to this is: If you have tried something repeatedly and have not gotten the desired result, try something different!

Dr. W. Edwards Deming used to say that there are two kinds of organizations—those that are getting better and those that are dying. If you're standing still, you're dying; you just don't know it yet. Your competition isn't standing still, so if you are, they will eventually pass you by. He used this point to argue for continuous improvement in organizations. The same can be applied to overall companies or groups within them. This includes project teams.

> If you always do what you've always done, you'll always get what you always got.

No sports team with any credibility would go an entire season without trying to improve. They don't practice just to maintain the status quo—they try to get better by watching game films, giving players feedback on past performance, coaching the players, trying new plays, and changing players and coaches if need be. In fact, the most dangerous place a team can be is successful, because they become complacent. They think they are on top and nobody can drag them down. The same is true of organizations. Judith Bardwick wrote a book entitled *Danger in the Comfort Zone* that echoes this idea.

Yet project teams seldom stop to ask if they can improve. In fact, this is a major cause of project failure. Team building is the forgotten side of project management. We get so focused on the task at hand that we totally forget about process issues. This is a concern for *what* must be done to the exclusion of concern for *how* it is being done. The flaw is that process issues will always affect task performance, to quote Marvin Weisbord.

> "Process issues will always affect task performance."
> —Marvin Weisbord

One pressure that is being felt by many project managers today is to get their jobs done faster and cheaper at the same time, while holding performance and scope constant. At first glance, this sounds contradictory, since there is usually an inverse relationship between reducing time in a project and the cost to do the work. That is, as we try to do the work faster, the costs tend to go up. This is shown in Figure 27–1.

However, this curve is drawn assuming that the processes of doing work remain unchanged and all we are doing is adding resources to the team. That being the case, you cannot simultaneously reduce time and costs both.

On the other hand, by changing the process by which work is done, you can reduce both at the same time. Note also that doing work correctly the first time will help achieve this result. Elsewhere I have written that the typical rework

F I G U R E 27–1

Time-Cost Tradeoff Curve for a Typical Project

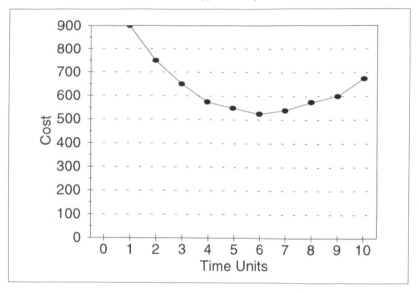

cost in a project ranges from 5 to 40 percent. Rework is totally wasted effort. As one chief engineer said, when the rework in a project is 30 percent, that is equivalent to having one person out of every three on the staff to just redo what the other two did wrong. If you reduce the rework, you get the job done faster and cheaper at the same time.

One of the contributors to rework is definitely a process issue. It is how well the project is defined and planned at the very beginning. The tendency here is to avoid the initial pain of planning. Unfortunately, you pay now or pay later, and it is almost always cheaper to pay now than later. As my colleague Bob Wysocki jokes, "You pain now or pain later." This is shown in Figure 27–2. Good project planning causes a lot of pain at the beginning, but the pain diminishes as the project progresses. With no planning or cursory planning, there is not much pain at the beginning, but it grows significantly as the project goes ahead.

F I G U R E 27–2

Pain Curve in Project Management

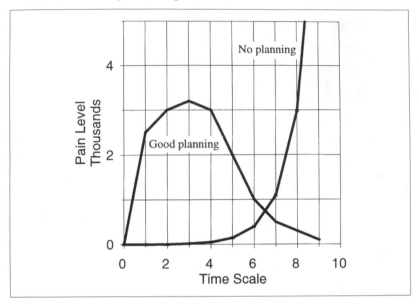

You might remember, from our discussion of systems issues, that one reason for this is that as rework goes up, more
overtime is required, which causes greater fatigue, which
leads to more errors that have to be corrected (reworked),
which means more overtime, and on and on. It is a vicious
spiral, getting progressively worse. This is indicated graphically by the exponential increase in pain.

IDENTIFYING PROCESSES

A process is a way of doing something. In Egyptian times, a
form of writing called hieroglyphics was invented. Each sym-
bol initially stood for a word, or maybe an idea. A similar system was invented by the Chinese. The problem is that you
need to remember about 1,800 of these symbols to have a good
working vocabulary. Eventually, alphabets were invented,

which permitted words to be built up from letters, so that with a knowledge of 26 to 30 characters, you could represent any word in the language. This also meant that the way you write those symbols changed. Hieroglyphics are often painted with a brush. Alphabetical characters can be easily written with stylus, pen, or brush. They can also be typed. Thus, the invention of the typewriter speeded up the process of putting words on paper. More recently, the advent of computers has taken us a step further. All of these steps were refinements of the process of conveying ideas to others through written means.

All process improvements tend to follow an S-curve, as shown in Figure 27–3. Initially, gains in process improvement are hard to come by. Then considerable progress is made. Finally, the gains become harder and harder to achieve. We sometimes say that we are *pushing the envelope* at either the beginning or end of the process improvement curve.

F I G U R E 27–3

Process Improvement Curves

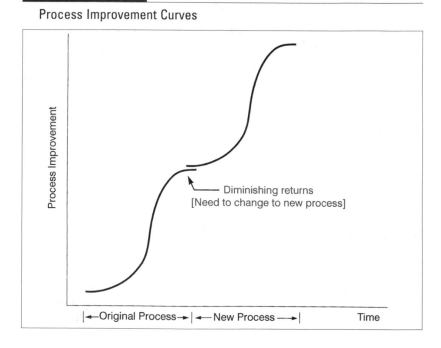

Notice that when the end of a process improvement cycle is reached and the gains become difficult to achieve, it is time to throw out the old process and invent an entirely new one. Unfortunately, some managers get hung up trying to improve a process that should be eliminated because it is at the end of its improvement cycle, but they don't realize this.

Interestingly, organizations that are just getting started with formal project management are down on the low side of the process improvement curve, and they experience significant startup difficulty. This sometimes causes them to throw out the process entirely, because they are experiencing too much initial pain. They don't realize that they will soon cross the peak if they stick with it, and will then be in for an easy ride down the right-hand slope of the pain curve (Figure 27–2).

> There is no point in trying to improve a process that should be replaced altogether.

Following is a list of some of the processes involved in getting projects done. None of these are meant to have to do with technical aspects of the work. They are all a part of the project management process only.

Some of the Processes of Project Management

Communicating	Decision Making	Leadership
Negotiating	Problem Solving	Creative Thinking
Scheduling	Planning	The Work Itself
Monitoring Status	Change Control	Meetings
Team Building	Conflict Resolution	Administrative

SOME PRINCIPLES OF PROCESS IMPROVEMENT

The first idea that I believe is useful to consider in process improvement is that if we have learned how to improve processes in one domain, we should be able to apply some of what was learned there to other processes. Part of the reason

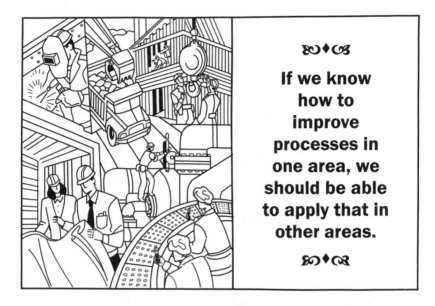

ະ∂♦ʊɜ

If we know how to improve processes in one area, we should be able to apply that in other areas.

ະ∂♦ʊɜ

for this is that processes must conform to some of the rules of system behavior, which we discussed in Chapter 13. In that chapter we found that systems that have similar structures can be expected to behave similarly, regardless of the content involved in the system process.

For that reason, since we have had so much experience with process improvement in manufacturing, we should be able to adopt some of the procedures used in that area and apply them to improving project management processes. In a previous section of this chapter, I mentioned the pressure to get projects completed quicker. There have been a number of books written in recent years on speeding up the product development process. These include *Accelerating Innovation* (Patterson, 1993), *Developing Products in Half the Time* (Smith & Reinertsen, 1995), and *Revolutionizing Product Development* (Wheelwright & Clark, 1992), to name just a few. As I have noted elsewhere, however, product development should not be confused with project management. Similar pressures to speed up projects are being felt in all kinds of projects, not just in product development.

One of the first points that must be made about improving a process is that it should be running smoothly already, or it is nearly impossible to tell if it has been improved. If you are familiar with statistical process control (SPC) methodology, we would say that the process should be in control before you begin changing it. The second point is that it requires good planning to improve a process, and this, in turn, requires that the process be well understood. We will discuss understanding processes in the next section.

Patterson lists a number of things that can be done to reduce manufacturing time, and it is instructive to examine these with respect to projects. I have adapted his list, as shown in Table 27–1 (Patterson, 1993, p. 101).

Improve process quality. Anything that you can do to reduce errors that lead to rework will improve overall process performance, especially speed. Improvements in planning generally reduce errors due to false starts. Time spent planning must be balanced, of course. It is not productive if the team goes into analysis paralysis because they are afraid to make any planning errors.

Implement concurrent processes. If we can do as many things as possible in parallel rather than in series, we can speed up project work. Care must be taken to balance risk with gains in speed. When interdependent tasks are per-

T A B L E   27–1

Actions That Reduce Manufacturing Cycle Time

- Improve process quality (in particular, minimize rework)
- Implement concurrent processes
- Add value as rapidly as possible at each step
- Improve quality and timeliness of incoming materials
- Eliminate work that adds no value
- Minimize changeover time (reduce setup time)
- Eliminate bottlenecks

formed concurrently, you definitely increase the risk that costs will be incurred because the work done in one step negates that done in the (normally subsequent) next step.

Add value as rapidly as possible at each process step. In manufacturing, raw materials have almost no value to customers. It is only after they have been formed, shaped, machined, stamped, or molded that they have value. In projects, the same idea applies. Every step in the project should increase the value of the final product that will be delivered to the customer. Related to this idea, perhaps as a corollary, is the point about *eliminating any step that adds no value.* Setup time, for example, is an operation that provides no value, but may have to be done if a single machine is used for multiple tasks. The longer the run of parts on that machine before a changeover is made, the smaller the setup time as a percentage of the total. The same is true of people. If we can reduce the interruptions and transitions that they experience, the more productive they become.

> Every step in a project should add value to the end "product," or it should be eliminated.

Elsewhere, I have discussed using design of experiments to eliminate the design-test-redesign iteration that creates an endless loop in projects. Wherever feasible, this approach is preferable to multiple iterations.

Another subject near and dear to the hearts of many of us is the wastefulness of meetings. For goodness sake, get a copy of *Mining Group Gold,* by Tom Kaiser (1995), and practice his model in running your meetings. It will improve your efficiency tremendously. (The model is also available on film from CRM Films. See the Resources chapter for ordering information.)

Improve quality and timeliness of incoming materials. A manufacturer who receives shoddy raw materials can hardly produce quality products. Considerable time and money were once spent on incoming inspection of materials. Selection of good vendors and partnership arrangements can greatly improve the quality of incoming goods and reduce later incurred cost of poor-quality manufactured product. In the same way, projects of any kind require good raw materials. When projects are done primarily by knowledge workers, this means *the right information at the right time*. If the information arrives too late, it will be of no benefit to the current job. If it arrives too early, it may not be recognized as relevant, though if an error is to be made, it should be made in the direction of too early as opposed to too late. A good reference librarian can be an immense help for this issue. What is needed is akin to a just-in-time (JIT) information system.

Streamline the flow of materials. In manufacturing, modern assembly lines are characterized by the well-planned flow of materials from beginning to end. Good project planning should result in the same smooth flow of information or work from one stage to another. For local project teams, this means that all members of the team have access to information on a timely basis through a local area network (LAN). For dispersed teams, a wide area network (WAN) is needed.

Eliminate bottlenecks. A bottleneck is a point in a process that restricts the flow of materials. In construction projects, bottlenecks are often caused by agencies that must approve building plans or perform environmental impact studies or archaeological surveys. You often can't eliminate these or speed them up, since you have no control over them. About all you can do is work around them.

Sometimes a single support group becomes a bottleneck because they are servicing so many teams that they lack capacity to do it well. Bottlenecks are resolved by identifying the root cause of the limited capacity and then investing in the resources needed to bring capacity up to the required level. Needless to say, the economy of keeping a support group "lean and mean" can be greatly offset by the loss of time in dependent teams. However, since project managers are not always able to influence the powers that be to deal with bottlenecks properly, the best defense is to have work that can be productively done while waiting for other work to clear the bottleneck.

OPERATIONAL DEFINITIONS OF PROBLEMS

I cannot stress strongly enough how important it is that problems be defined correctly so that we solve the right problem. It should be clear that such a definition must be one that everyone understands and agrees with. Unless everyone has the same understanding of a problem, there is no way to solve it. What is needed is an operational definition. An operational definition establishes a language that communicates the same meaning to everyone involved in solving the problem. Since our focus here is on improving processes, this language will specifically apply to the processes we are trying to improve. Words such as "defective," "unsafe," or "inadequate" have no meaning unless they are operationally defined.

> Unless everyone has the same understanding of a problem, it is almost impossible to solve it.

To illustrate how confusion can be caused by the absence of operational definitions, consider a label on a shirt that reads "75% cotton." What does this mean? Is it three-quarters cotton, on the average, throughout the shirt? Or is it three-quarters cotton applied to shirts over a month's production? Is it three-quarters by linear measure or by weight? If by weight, at what humidity? Does humidity affect the noncotton component the same as the cotton?

Another example: The team says communication is poor. What does this mean? Communication consists of transmitting and receiving. Is transmission the problem, or is it receiving? Is the person talking using precise language? Or are recipients not paying attention? Is the transmission being affected by noise, so that it is not received properly? What are the tangible effects of the communication? Misunderstandings, missed dates, work done incorrectly, or conflicts? Until we arrive at a shared understanding of what is meant by "poor communication," we can't possibly solve the problem.

A given operational definition is not necessarily right or wrong. It's importance lies in its acceptance by all parties involved in trying to deal with the process. As conditions change, the operational definition may change to meet new needs.

An operational definition consists of:

1. A criterion to be applied to an object or to a group.
2. A test of the object or of the group.
3. A decision as to whether the object or group did or did not meet the criterion.

The project team is told that they are expected to do their work on time and within budget, while maintaining performance as expected and doing the predefined amount (scope) of work. This statement is loaded with problems. What does on time and within budget mean? Can there be a tolerance? If so, how much? If not, we are expecting the impossible, because all processes vary. To expect people to get work done *exactly* on time is unrealistic. In the first place, where did the time frame come from? It was an estimate, so by definition, it is not exact.

Now, if we know that we can typically achieve schedule and budget tolerances of ±10 percent, then we can operationally define on time and within budget as being within this tolerance. By the same token, we must operationally define performance requirements. But if the person is writing software, say, how do you define performance requirements? Less than so many bugs in the entire program? It executes at a certain speed? It has no more than x lines of code? All of the above?

Here is an example of actually applying the conditions to arrive at an operational definition. A salesperson is told that her performance will be judged with respect to the percentage of change in this year's sales over last year's sales. What does this mean? Average percentage sales each month? Each week? For each product? Percentage between December 31, 2007 and December 31, 2008? How are we measuring sales? Is it gross, net, gross profit, net profit? You get the picture.

Step 1: Develop a criterion for percentage change in sales.

A percentage change in sales is the difference between 2008 sales (January 1, 2008 to December 31, 2008) and 2007 sales (January 1, 2007 to December 31, 2007):

Percentage change $(07 - 08) = (S08 - S07)/S07$

where:
  S08 = dollar sales volume for January 1–December 31, 2008
  S07 = dollar sales volume for January 1–December 31, 2007

S07 is measured in constant dollars.

Steps 2 and 3. Test the decision on percentage change in sales. This will be done by looking at 2007 and 2008 sales figures and performing the computations.

AN EXAMPLE OF IDENTIFYING A PROCESS PROBLEM

The team has missed the last two project milestones. The project manager is feeling the heat to make sure this does not happen again, as the project deadline is highly critical to the business and if milestones are slipping, it is likely that the end date will be missed. To help identify the possible cause or causes of this problem, you might want to use an Ishikawa diagram, which is shown in generic form in Figure 27–4. The model is also called a fishbone or cause-effect diagram. The problem you are trying to solve is noted in the box to the

The Generic Ishikawa Diagram

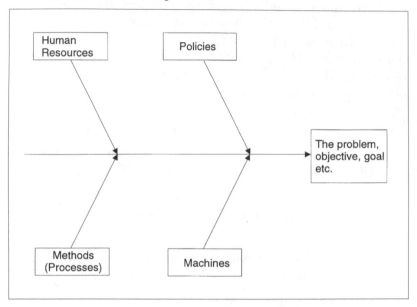

right and possible causes are listed on the "bones" of the diagram, grouped according to general categories. This list is usually generated through brainstorming.

Once the list has been created, you classify each variable with a C, N, or X, as follows:

      C (Constant):   These are variables that we intend to hold constant so that we can achieve the desired response, or possibly reduce extraneous variation in the response. For each of these variables, we need a standard operating procedure to tell us how the variable is being controlled.

N (Noise):   These are uncontrolled variables. They cause "noise" in the system. Although they do affect system response, they are too difficult or too expensive to hold constant.

X (Experimental):   If an experiment is to be run, these are the factors to be investigated. Not all cause-and-effect diagrams will contain *X* factors. However, a variable that is a *C* today could become an *X* tomorrow if we decide to investigate the effect experimentally (and vice versa).

In using the Ishikawa diagram or any other approach, you have to be careful not to fall into the trap of having people give you causes at too high a level. For example, you ask your group to tell you what problems they think are affecting project team performance, and you get a list like the following:

1. Lack of leadership.
2. Poor communication.
3. Unclear mission and objectives.
4. Inadequate workspace.
5. Lack of training.

The difficulty with this list is that people have concluded that lack of leadership is a cause, based on some lower-level cause. At this point, you don't know what the real problems are to which your team is attributing the causes. To understand the real problem, you now need to ask, "What *effect* is lack of leadership [or any of the others] having on our team?" The person says, "I think members of the team are demoralized just now."

She is attributing low morale to lack of leadership. But is that true? We would have to look more closely to determine if some aspect of the leader's behavior is causing morale problems. In all likelihood, there may be other factors in the situation that are causing the morale effect.

Once you have identified the root cause of a problem, the solution is often fairly obvious, although it is not always easy to implement. As examples, if your car is running rough and you find that a sparkplug is broken, then all you need to do is replace the plug and the problem is solved. If sales are down because you are in a recession, however, you can't necessarily solve the problem, even though you know its cause. I also might know that an employee is performing poorly because she has a really rotten attitude, but that knowledge won't necessarily help me solve the problem.

For our example of missed deadlines, here is the procedure you would follow:

1. The project manager calls a meeting to solve the problem of missed deadlines, and the Ishikawa diagram shown in Figure 27–5 is generated. As the diagram shows, there are not many causes under Policies and Machines, but there are several under each of the other two categories. The question is: What do you do with these guesses at possible causes?

2. The next step in the process is to allow people time to ponder the causes before evaluating them. Some questions to consider at this time are:
   ◆ Is this cause a variable or an attribute? A variable is one that has continuous measures, such as pounds, feet, and so on. An attribute is present or not present, such as a scratch, dent, or hole.
   ◆ Has the cause been operationally defined?
   ◆ Does this cause interact with other causes?

3. Once people have had time to think about the issue, the next step is to circle likely causes on the diagram. This will always be based on judgment

F I G U R E 27–5

The Generic Ishikawa Diagram

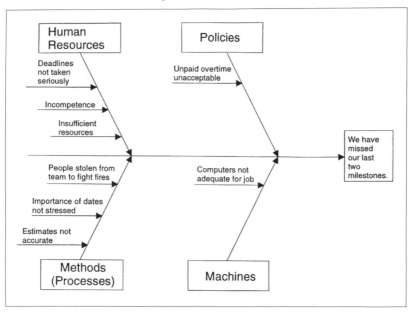

initially. Once this is done, you can rank them in order of most likely to least likely. Paired comparisons
is a good technique to use to rank the causes.

4. Finally, you need to verify the cause. You can do
this in a variety of ways. Begin by gathering data to
see if the most likely cause actually has a significant
impact on the problem. If not, then look at the next
most likely cause, and so on. You can also design
experiments to manipulate variables to see if they
have an effect, when they are amenable to such
treatment. A full treatment of such methods is outside the scope of this book. For more in-depth information, you might want to consult Gitlow et al.,
1989, or Schmidt et al., 1996.

28
CHAPTER

Improving Estimating Capability

In my seminars on project management, I have the class do an exercise. It goes like this. Suppose, I say, I give you a standard 52-card deck of playing cards that has been well shuffled. I ask you to sort those cards so that all of the diamonds, hearts, spades, and clubs are in numerical order. How long do you think it will take the typical person to sort the deck of cards?

Each person in the class writes down a number, and then I poll them to get the range. It generally varies from about 1 minute to as long as 10 minutes. Usually, the larger the group, the greater the variation. Ranges of 5 to 1 to as much as 20 to 1 have been obtained.

"Now suppose this group represents the Jim Lewis Card Sorting Company," I say. "I am the manager, and you are my troops. The reason we exist is that occasionally a truckload of playing cards overturns somewhere, and the cards get all shuffled up. They are mostly undamaged, so the company wants to recover them, but that means sorting them back into decks. I have just been asked to quote them on what we charge per deck to sort cards, and you have given me a 10 to 1 range on times. What should I quote?"

It is clear that if I quote 1 minute per deck, and this is too low, I will get the job but lose a lot of money. Conversely, 10 minutes is probably too high, so if I quote that amount of time, I probably won't get the job. What am I to do?

The problem is, we don't have any data on which to base our estimates. When I ask the class how they did their estimates, they say that they imagined how they would go about the process and estimated how long each step would take. Certainly, in the absence of data, all you can do is apply a mental model to the problem.

I also ask if they were to poll people back home for an estimate of work that they typically do, would they get similar ranges. Most agree they would. Then how are we to run a business with so much variation in estimates?

The answer is, we are going to have problems. Actually, the answer is that we already *do* have problems. One of the 10 major causes of project failure is that estimates are best guesses, made without consulting historical data. The reason for this is simple—most companies don't have good history on activity durations. So there is nothing to consult but memory, and you are in real trouble if you rely on memories!

As an example, I just finished writing a draft of the chapter entitled "Tracking Progress to Achieve Project Control." I started yesterday morning around 7 a.m. and finished this morning at 10 a.m. But that is *calendar time*. I know I stopped a number of times to answer the phone. I took several breaks. I got on the Internet and checked on the weather, searched for some information, and so on. In short, I don't know how many total *working hours* it took to do that chapter—and this is just for one day! Think how hard it would be to reconstruct if I went back in memory to one day last week.

HOW ACCURATE MUST AN ESTIMATE BE?

There certainly is no single answer to this question. Project jus-
tifications are often made using return on investment (ROI),
net present value (NPV), or breakeven (BE) analysis. Each organization has its own rules on what these figures must be to
justify doing a project. I once facilitated an end-of-project review for a large capital equipment project and saw that the initial ROI projection steadily declined throughout the life of the
project, so that by the end of the job, there was very little ROI
left. Had this been known at the outset, the project probably
would not have seen the light of day.

A LESSON FROM ROYAL DUTCH SHELL

At one time Royal Dutch Shell was having problems with the
forecasting accuracy of young geologists. Oil wells are drilled
based upon analysis of geological and seismic survey data.
Drilling a dry well is very expensive, and you naturally want
to minimize the number of these that you drill. The "hit rate"
for experienced geologists is not extremely good, but it was
far better than for the company's entry-level geologists.

    Finally, the company had an idea. They brought new ge-
ologists in for a training session. They began by giving them
data for wells that had already been drilled (without telling
them this) and asked them to make a forecast. The trainees
studied the data and made a recommendation. Then the
trainer told them what had actually happened. With this kind
of feedback, they were soon making predictions as good as
those of the senior geologists—and the company hadn't had
to drill another dry well! This illustrates a very important
point—no learning takes place without feedback.

    It also suggests that we can all improve the estimating
ability of our personnel if we conduct a similar program. I
find that in many companies people make estimates for how
long it will take them to do a job, but never track the actual

ஐ◆ଃ

To improve estimating capability, track the "actual" working time it took to do the task.

ஐ◆ଃ

time, so they have no way of knowing if they were right, and consequently, they never improve their estimates. What you get from most people in companies, when you ask how long some task will take, is calendar time. They are pretty sure they can get the job done in a few hours, but know that it will take all week to work it in, so they tell you they will have the work done by the end of the week. This is fine if calendar time is all that matters, but if you also want to know what the effort cost, you are out in the cold.

In order to improve estimating capability, you have to estimate a task duration, track the actual working time taken to do the task, and feed back that information to the person who is doing the work. In addition, the information should be recorded for future reference. Otherwise, six months from now, you may have forgotten how long it took.

The problem is, one sample is not enough. From statistics, we know that the average time it takes to perform a task cannot be determined by doing it only one time. Generally, at least 25 samples are required to know the task average duration and the standard deviation. So collecting enough data to build a reasonable database will take some time. Most organizations find that it takes several years to collect enough data to improve their estimates.

MOVING TARGETS

One concern in many projects is that technology is changing so fast that by the time you collect enough history to know how long tasks take to complete, the history is obsolete, because new technology has emerged. In other words, you are always shooting at moving targets.

In terms of the work breakdown structure, this argument is only true at high levels of the WBS. As you go further down in the WBS, you do reach a point where tasks become repetitive. A drafting supervisor can usually tell how long it will take to make a D-size drawing of a mechanical or electronic assembly, for example, because her department has done so many of them. A technician can tell how long it takes to run certain tests. Even a designer can tell how long it takes to design small circuits, even though the technology being employed is new.

So if we track at low enough levels in the WBS, we can build a database that has meaning. There is an important factor to consider here. The data on actual time spent working on the task must be accurate. This means that it should be recorded daily. The best approach is to record as you go (like an attorney), but most people find this hard to do. Failing this, workers should at least write down what they have done during the day to the nearest hour. At loaded labor rates of $50 to $100 an hour, costs add up very quickly.

FACTORS AFFECTING WORKING TIMES

A number of factors affect how long it actually takes a person to do work. These include learning curves, setup time, fatigue, and skill level. In the card-sorting example that I mentioned earlier, you could expect that a person would get faster at sorting cards the more times he does the task. This improvement in performance is called a learning curve. If you have such tasks in projects, you might want to consider performance improvement over time. A learning curve is shown in Figure 28–1.

Setup time in knowledge work is a function of how many times a task gets interrupted. Time management experts say that if a person doing knowledge work gets interrupted, it typically takes 15 to 20 minutes to get reoriented to his work. For that reason, several phone or personal interruptions in one hour can just about kill that time!

F I G U R E 28–1

Learning Curve

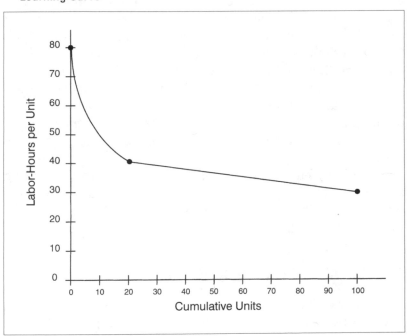

Other task interruptions arise from people working on too many projects at one time, constantly shifting gears. Moreover, the overhead of meetings takes its toll. When you work on several projects, you may easily spend an hour or more each week attending meetings for each project. This takes away time from getting project work done, and because meetings are often so badly managed, you lose in that additional way.

Fatigue is often not figured into knowledge projects. In construction projects, fatigue factors are understood much better (see Chapter 19). Estimates are sometimes made based on full-productivity performance of people, even though they are expected to work overtime routinely. In these cases, estimated times are seldom met.

The skill level of the person doing the work is also a factor. A more-skilled person should be faster than one of lesser skill. This is often covered by a multiplier: a number greater than one for a more-skilled person or a number less than one for a less-skilled person.

29

CHAPTER

Managing Innovation in Projects*

Whether you are in an organization that produces new products or does construction work, there is a need for innovation. Those organizations that offer the best array of innovative products and services have a competitive advantage over those that continue to offer the "same-old-same-old." In order for a team to innovate, the climate in which they operate must support innovation, and some climates do just the opposite.

Corporate America is largely risk-averse. We push managers to deliver short-term profits—monthly or quarterly—and many truly innovative efforts require long-term investments before a payoff is

> **Innovation:** The act of introducing something new.

achieved, and this may adversely affect short-term profitability. No doubt many innovative people in many organizations are restrained by a risk-averse climate.

---

* Some of the material in this chapter is also contained in my book *Team-Based Project Management* (2005).

THE INTELLECTUAL PROCESS

As I have shown in Chapter 27 on process improvement, there is no doubt that we need to improve project performance. The four objectives of a project are cost, performance, time, and scope, as was outlined in Chapter 11. Further, as was explained in that chapter, these are related as follows:

$$C = f(P, T, S)$$

meaning cost is a function of performance, time, and scope.

As I pointed out in Chapter 27, there is a tremendous pressure to reduce time. This is especially true in product development. Target reductions in time are as much as 50 percent. That is, get it done in half the time.

Further, the pressure is on to *simultaneously* reduce cost. At first glance, this seems contradictory, since reductions in time are often achieved by applying more resources, which raises costs. As I showed in Chapter 23, however, if we change the process by which the work is done, we can reduce both time and cost simultaneously. In product development, that process is largely intellectual, so this suggests something that seems strange at first glance—you have to improve the intellectual process, or you have to *think faster!*

> If you want to improve the intellectual process, you have to think faster.

Naturally, you might argue that thinking speed can't be improved, but in a sense, it can. Furthermore, thought processes can be aided by computers. This was done in designing the 777 airplane at Boeing. Using three-dimensional computer modeling, engineers could tell before a model was built that there was an interference between two components inside a wing. This greatly accelerated the design process (Sabbagh, 1996).

Now, before you dismiss the idea that the actual thought process can be improved, let me suggest that you study the literature on innovation or creative thinking. I have applied these techniques individually and in groups, with excellent results. In one case, a group of about seven scientists worked for two hours to generate ideas to solve some problems that concerned them, and they developed so many ideas that the team leader (chief scientist) said it would probably take another year to work through all of them. He was elated at the outcome.

It is important to note that I am not referring just to the old group brainstorming approach that has been around for a long time. Brainstorming is just one of a family of approaches for groups. There are also a number of techniques that can be applied by individuals. Creativity is not necessarily better with groups than with individuals. In fact, very few really new inventions have ever been developed by groups. Invariably, they are the product of one person thinking individually.

The conclusion to draw from all of this is that teams can benefit from training in the methods of innovation, since most individuals have not been exposed to these.

THE WORK ENVIRONMENT

Although it is outside the scope of this book to study in great detail, the work environment itself plays a part in making people more innovative. Some organizations have built special rooms in which groups can work to generate innovative ideas. These are usually brightly colored, may have walls with Lego\#170 panels, and usually have large white boards and a multitude of media, such as modeling clay, colored markers, and construction paper. Some innovation experts also say that a good way to start a group is to show cartoons for a few minutes, to get people laughing, because laughter is so strongly part of the creative mindset (Hall, 1995).

ADAPTERS AND INNOVATORS: DIFFERENCES IN COGNITIVE STYLE AND PERSONALITY

Michael J. Kirton has studied the creative-thinking process and determined that there are two aspects, one called the level of the intellectual process and the other called the *style* of problem solving. Level has to do with one's intelligence, experience, and so on. Style, however, is a single dimension, anchored on one end by innovators and on the other by adapters.

Adapters, when confronted with a problem, tend to turn to conventional rules, practices, and perceptions of the group to which they belong. This can be a working group, cultural group, or professional or occupational group. They then derive their ideas from the established procedures of this group. If there is no ready-made answer provided by a collection of conventional responses, the adapter will try to adapt or stretch a conventional response until it can be used

ᔆ◆ᘓ

The flaw in continuous improvement is that you eventually reach a point at which a process should no longer be improved, but should be eliminated.

ᔆ◆ᘓ

to solve the problem. Thus, much of the behavior of adapters is in the category of improving existing methods, or "doing better" what is already being done. This strategy, which tends to dominate management (Drucker, 1969), has been exemplified since 1980 by the continuous improvement process advocated by Dr. Deming. The flaw in continuous improvement is that you eventually reach a point at which a process should no longer be improved. It should be eliminated.

Innovation is the characteristic behavior of individuals who, when they have a problem, try to reorganize or restructure the problem and approach it in a new light. In doing so, they try to divorce themselves from preconceived notions about the nature of the problem and its solution. Their approach can be called "doing things differently," instead of "doing things better."

Relationships between Innovators and Adapters

Because of their different styles of problem solving, it can be expected that innovators and adapters might have conflicts in teams, and this is sometimes the case. Adapters tend to see innovators as abrasive, insensitive, and disruptive. They always want to change things, are always creating havoc. Innovators see adapters as stuffy and unenterprising. They are hung up on systems, rules, and norms of behavior that seem restrictive and ineffective to the innovators. So, when the extreme innovator meets the extreme adapter, sparks are likely to fly.

Organizational Climate and Innovation

As I have said earlier, organization climate affects the degree to which innovation is expressed. In general, organizations are inclined to encourage bureaucracy and adaptation in order to minimize risk. This is especially true of large organizations. Weber (1970) has written that the aims of bureaucratic organizations are precision, reliability, and efficiency. Such organizations exert fairly constant pressure on managers to be methodical, prudent (this often means risk-averse), and disciplined. They are also expected to maintain a high degree of conformity. Note that these are qualities that are generally ascribed to the adapter personality. For a strong adapter, the longer an institutional practice has existed, the more he takes it for granted. So when a problem arises, he does not consider changing the structure of the organization. Rather, he tries to find a solution within that structure.

The innovator, on the other hand, might challenge the existing structure and propose solutions that appear more risky and less sound to adapters. This makes the innovator seem less concerned with company needs and with the effect of his solutions on others.

This means, of course, that bureaucratic organizations tend to support adapters more than they do innovators, making incremental change the norm and thus making it hard to implement step-function or large-scale change. Innovators in such organizations often feel unappreciated and may very well leave, thus moving the organization further in the direction of adaptation and reducing its capacity for innovation. In a stable world, the stodgy bureaucracy can survive, but in a topsy-turvy, turbulent world, incremental change is often insufficient for survival. Yet the very person who might be able to save the stiff-necked bureaucracy is likely to be resisted and resented.

SOFTWARE FOR INNOVATION

There have been many techniques developed to help individuals and groups generate numerous ideas quickly. One of the best known is Synectics, developed and taught by the Synectics Corporation. Now software has been developed that is based on principles from Synectics. Called ThoughtPath™, it can be used by individuals or groups to solve problems.

In the problem-solving literature, we find that there are two kinds of problems—open-ended and close-ended. A close-ended problem has a single solution, whereas an open-ended one can be solved many different ways. As an example, a math problem is close-ended. So is a troubleshooting problem: Once you find what is broken, you can make a repair.

As you can imagine, most problems in this world are open-ended, yet most of our training is aimed at solving close-ended problems. The problem caused by this focus is that we want to frame all of our problems as close-ended and apply the tools of close-ended problem solving. Unfortunately, those tools are not very effective for solving open-ended problems.

ThoughtPath is used to solve primarily open-ended problems. These are also called creative problems, and they cover a wide range of applications in organizations, including the following:

- Strategic planning
- Product development
- Market positioning
- Process reengineering
- Total quality management
- Human resource planning
- Training course development
- Personal career planning

The program works by serving as a personal or small group facilitator and helps spur people on to new and creative ideas.

REFERENCES

Baker, Bruce; David Murphy; and Dalmar Fisher. "Factors Affecting Project Success." In David I. Cleland and William R. King (Eds.) *Project Management Handbook*, 2d ed. New York: Van Nostrand Reinhold, 1988.

Baker, Bud, and Raj Menon. "Politics and Project Performance: The Fourth Dimension of Project Management." *PM Network*, November 1995, pp. 16–21.

Beer, Stafford. *Brain of the Firm*, 2d ed. New York: Wiley, 1981.

Block, Peter. *The Empowered Manager*. San Francisco: Jossey-Bass, 1987.

Buzan, Tony. *The Mind Map Book*. New York: Dutton, 1993.

Cartwright, Dorwin, and Alvin Zander. *Group Dynamics*. New York: Harper and Row, 1968.

Cialdini, Robert B. *Influence: The Power of Persuasion*, rev. ed. New York: Quill, 1993.

Couillard, Jean. "The Role of Project Risk in Determining Project Management Approach." *Project Management Journal*, December 1995, pp. 3–15.

Dail, Hardy. Job Acceleration: What Does It Really Cost? *The Journal of the American Institute of Constructors, 10,* No. 1. 1986.

El-Najdawi, Mohammad, and Matthew Liberatore. "Matrix Management Effectiveness: An Update for Research and Engineering Organizations." *Project Management Journal, 28,* No. 1, March 1997, pp. 25–31.

Farson, Richard. *Management of the Absurd: Paradoxes in Leadership.* New York: Simon & Schuster, 1996.

Flaherty, James. *Coaching: Evoking Excellence in Others,* 2d ed. Oxford, England: Elsevier, 2005.

Fleming, Quentin, and Joel Koppelman. *Earned Value Project Management.* Upper Darby, PA: The Project Management Institute, 1996.

Fortune, Joyce, and Geoff Peters. *Learning from Failure: The Systems Approach.* Chichester, England: John Wiley & Sons, 1995.

French, J., and B. Raven. "The Bases of Social Power." In D. Cartwright (Ed.), *Studies in Social Power,* pp. 118–149. Ann Arbor, MI: University of Michigan, 1959.

Gitlow, Howard, et al. *Tools and Methods for the Improvement of Quality.* Burr Ridge, IL: Irwin, 1989.

Hammer, Michael, and James Champy. *Reengineering the Corporation.* New York: Harper, 1993.

Hammond, III, John S. "Better Decisions with Preference Theory." In *Harvard Business Review on Management.* New York: Harper & Row, 1975.

Harvard Business Review on Management. (No editor listed) New York: Harper & Row, 1975.

Janis, Irving, and Leon Mann. *Decision Making.* New York: The Free Press, 1977.

Juran, J. M., and Frank Gryna. *Quality Planning and Analysis.* New York: McGraw-Hill, 1980.

Kayser, Tom. *Mining Group Gold.* New York: McGraw-Hill, 1995.

Kelley, Robert, and Janet Caplan. "How Bell Labs Creates Star Performers." *Harvard Business Review,* July–August 1993, pp. 128–139.

Kepner, Charles, and Benjamin Tregoe. *The Rational Manager.* Princeton, NJ: Kepner-Tregoe, 1965.

Levine, Harvey. "Risk Management for Dummies: Managing Schedule, Cost and Technical Risk and Contingency." *PM Network,* October 1995, pp. 30–32.

Lewis, James. *Fundamentals of Project Management,* 3d ed. New York: AMACOM, 2006.

Lewis, James. *Project Planning, Scheduling, and Control* 4th ed. New York: McGraw-Hill, 2006.

Lewis, James. *The Project Manager's Desk Reference,* 3d ed. New York: McGraw-Hill, 2007.

Lewis, James. *Team-Based Project Management.* Beard Books, 2005.

Lock, Dennis (Ed.). *Gower Handbook of Project Management,* 2d ed. Hampshire, England: Gower, 1994.

Meredith, Jack, and Samuel Mantel, Jr. *Project Management: A Managerial Approach.* New York: Wiley, 1985.

Might, R. J., and W. A. Fisher. "The Role of Structural Factors in Determining Project Management Success." *IEEE Transactions on Engineering Management, EM-32,* No. 2, May 1993, pp. 71–77.

Mintzberg, Henry. *Mintzberg on Management.* New York: The Free Press, 1989.

Murphy, David; Bruce Baker; and Dalmar Fisher. *Determinants of Project Success*. Springfield, VA: National Technical Information Services, Accession No.: N-74-30392, September 15, 1974.

Patterson, Marvin. *Accelerating Innovation: Improving the Processes of Product Development*. New York: Van Nostrand Reinhold, 1993.

Pinto, Jeffrey K. "Power and Politics: Managerial Implications." *PM Network*, August 1996, pp. 36–39.

Pinto, Jeffrey K. *Power and Politics in Project Management*. Upper Darby, PA: Project Management Institute, 1996.

Saaty, Thomas L. *Decision Making for Leaders*. Pittsburgh: RWS Publications, 1995.

Schmidt, Stephen; Mark Kiemele, and Ronald Berdine. *Knowledge-Based Management*. Colorado Springs, CO: Air Academy Press, 1996.

Schultz, R. L.; Dennis Slevin, and Jeffrey Pinto. "Strategy and Tactics in a Process Model of Project Implementation." *Interfaces*, May–June 1987, pp. 34–46.

Schuyler, John R. "Decision Analysis in Projects: Summary and Recommendations." *PM Network*, October 1995, pp. 23–28.

Senge, Peter. *The Fifth Discipline*. New York: Doubleday Currency, 1990.

Senge, Peter, et al. *The Fifth Discipline Fieldbook*. New York: Doubleday Currency, 1994.

Smith, Preston, and Donald Reinertsen. *Developing Products in Half the Time*. New York: Van Nostrand Reinhold, 1995.

Thoms, Peg. "Creating a Shared Vision with a Project Team." *PM Network*, January 1997, pp. 33–35.

Tuckman, Bruce W. "Development Sequence in Small Groups." *Psychological Bulletin,* 1965.

Watzlawick, Paul; Janet Beavin, and Don Jackson. *Pragmatics of Human Communication.* New York: Norton, 1967.

Watzlawick, Paul; John Weakland, and Richard Fisch. *Change: Principles of Problem Formulation and Problem Resolution.* New York: Norton, 1974.

Weisbord, Marvin, and Sandra Janoff. *Future Search.* San Francisco: Berrett-Koehler, 1995.

Wheelwright, Steven, and Kim Clark. *Revolutionizing Product Development.* New York: Free Press, 1992.

Wheatley, Margaret. *Leadership and the New Science.* San Francisco: Berrett-Koehler, 1994.

GLOSSARY

Activity The work or effort needed to achieve a result. It consumes time and usually consumes resources.

Activity Description A statement specifying what must be done to achieve a desired result.

Activity-on-Arrow A network diagram showing sequence of activities, in which each activity is represented by an arrow, with a circle representing a node or event at each end.

Activity-on-Node A network diagram showing sequence of activities, in which each activity is represented by a box or circle (that is, a *node*), and these are interconnected with arrows to show precedence of work.

Authority The legitimate power given to a person in an organization to use resources to reach an objective and to exercise discipline.

Backward Pass Calculations made working backward through a network from the latest event to the beginning event to calculate event late times. A forward pass calculation determines early times.

Change Order A document which authorizes a change in some aspect of a project.

Control The practice of monitoring progress against a plan so that corrective steps can be taken when a deviation from plan occurs.

CPM   An acronym for critical path method. A network diagramming method which shows the longest series of activities in a project, thereby determining the earliest completion for the project.

Crashing   An attempt to reduce activity or total project duration, usually by adding resources.

Critical Path   The longest sequential path of activities which are absolutely essential for completion of the project. It will also have no slack, or float.

Dependency   The next task or group of tasks cannot begin until preceding work has been completed, thus the word "dependent," or dependency.

Deviation   Any variation from planned performance. The deviation can be in terms of schedule, cost, performance, or scope of work. Deviation analysis is the heart of exercising project control.

Dummy Activity   A zero-duration element in a network showing a logic linkage. A dummy does not consume time or resources, but simply indicates precedence.

Duration   The time it takes to complete an activity.

Earliest Finish   The earliest time that an activity can be completed.

Earliest Start   The earliest time that an activity can be started.

Estimate   A forecast or guess about how long an activity will take, how many resources might be required, or how much it will cost.

Event   A point in time. An event is binary. It is either achieved or not, whereas an activity can be partially complete. An event can be the start or finish of an activity.

Feedback   Information derived from observation of project activities, which is used to analyze the status of the job and take corrective action if necessary.

Float   A measure of how much an activity can be delayed before it begins to impact the project finish date.

Forward Pass Method   The method used to calculate the earliest start time for each activity in a network diagram.

Free Float   The amount of time that an activity can be delayed without affecting succeeding activities.

Gantt Chart   A bar chart which indicates the time required to complete each activity in a project. It is named for Henry L. Gantt, who first developed a complete notational system for displaying progress with bar charts.

Hammock Activity   A single activity which actually represents a group of activities. It "hangs" between two events and is used to report progress on the composite which it represents.

Histogram   A vertical bar chart showing (usually) resource allocation levels over time in a project.

Inexcusable Delays   Project delays that are attributable to negligence on the part of the contractor, which lead in many cases to penalty payments.

Latest Finish   The latest time that an activity can be finished without extending the end date for a project.

Latest Start   The latest time that an activity can start without extending the end date for a project.

Learning Curve   The time it takes humans to learn an activity well enough to achieve optimum performance can be displayed by curves, which must be factored into estimates of activity durations in order to achieve planned completion dates.

Leveling   An attempt to smooth the use of resources, whether people, materials, or equipment, to avoid large peaks and valleys in their usage.

Life Cycle   The phases which a project goes through from concept through completion. The nature of the project changes during each phase.

Matrix Organization   A method of drawing people from functional departments within an organization for assignment to a project team, but without removing them from their physical location. The project manager in such a structure is said to have *dotted-line* authority over team members.

Milestone   An event of special importance, usually representing the completion of a major phase of project work. Reviews are often scheduled at milestones.

Most Likely Time   The most realistic time estimate for completing an activity under normal conditions.

Negative Float or Slack   A condition in a network in which the *earliest time* for an event is actually later than its *latest time*. This happens when the project has a constrained end date which is earlier than can be achieved, or when an activity uses up its float and is still delayed.

Node   A point in a network connected to other points by one or more arrows. In activity-on-arrow notation, the node contains at least one event. In activity-on-node notation, the node represents an activity, and the arrows show the sequence in which they must be performed.

PERT   An acronym which stands for program evaluation and review technique. PERT makes use of network diagrams as does CPM, but in addition applies statistics to activities to try and estimate the probabilities of completion of project work.

Pessimistic Time   Roughly speaking, this is the *worst-case* time to complete an activity. The term has a more precise meaning, which is defined in the PERT literature.

Phase   A major component or segment of a project.

Precedence Diagram   An activity-on-node diagram.

Queue   Waiting time.

Resource Allocation   The assignment of people, equipment, facilities, or materials to a project. Unless adequate resources are provided, project work cannot be completed on schedule, thus resource allocation is a significant component of project scheduling.

Resource Pool   A group of people who can generally do the same work; therefore, they can be chosen randomly for assignment to a project.

Risk   The possibility that something can go wrong and interfere with the completion of project work.

Scope   The magnitude of work which must be done to complete a project.

Slack   Same as float. The amount of time a task can be delayed before it impacts the finish time for a project.

Subproject   A small project within a larger one.

Statement of Work   A description of work to be performed.

Time Now   The current calendar date from which a network analysis, report, or update is being made.

Time Standard   The time allowed for the completion of a task.

Variance   Any deviation of project work from what was planned. Variance can be around costs, time, performance, or project scope.

Work Breakdown Structure   A method of subdividing work into smaller and smaller increments to permit accurate estimates of durations, resource requirements, and costs.

INDEX

ABOUT THE AUTHOR

James P. Lewis, Ph.D. is an experienced project manager who now teaches seminars on the subject throughout the United States, England, and the Far East. His solid, no-nonsense approach is largely the result of the 15 years he spent in industry, working as an electrical engineer engaged in the design and development of communication equipment. He held various positions, including Project Manager, Product Engineering Manager, and Chief Engineer, for Aerotron, Inc. and ITT Telecommunications, both of Raleigh, NC. He also was a Quality Manager for ITT Telecom, managing a department of 63 quality engineers, line inspectors, and test technicians.

While he was an engineering manager, he began working on a doctorate in organizational psychology, because of his conviction that a manager can only succeed by developing good interpersonal skills.

Since 1980, Dr. Lewis has trained over 30,000 supervisors and managers in Argentina, Canada, England, Germany, India, Indonesia, Malaysia, Mexico, Singapore, Sweden, Thailand, and the United States. He has written articles for *Training and Development Journal, Apparel Industry Magazine,* and *Transportation and Distribution Magazine,* and is the author of *Project Planning, Scheduling and Control, Fourth Edition, Working Together: The 12 Principles Employed by Boeing Commercial Aircraft to Manage Projects, Teams, and the Organization, Project Leadership,* and *The Project Manager's Survival Guide.* He is coauthor, with Louis Wong, of *Accelerated*

Project Management, published by McGraw-Hill, and *Fundamentals of Project Management, Third Edition,* published by the American Management Association; and *Team-Based Project Management,* published by Beard Books. He is coauthor, with Bob Wysocki, of *The World-Class Project Manager,* published by Perseus in 2001. The first edition of *Project Planning, Scheduling and Control* has been published in a Spanish edition, and the AMACOM book *Fundamentals of Project Management* has been published in Portuguese and Latvian. Several of his books have also been published in Chinese, and *Project Leadership* has been translated into Spanish and Russian.

He has a B.S. in Electrical Engineering and a Ph.D. in Psychology, both from NC State University in Raleigh. He is a member of the Project Management Institute. He is also a certified Herrmann Brain Dominance Instrument practitioner.

He is president of The Lewis Institute, Inc., a training and consulting company specializing in project management, which he founded in 1981.

Jim lives in Vinton, Virginia, in the Blue Ridge Mountains.